P9-BZP-941

HTML & Web Artistry 2

more than code

Natalie Zee | Susan Harris

New Riders

201 West 103rd Street, Indianapolis, IN 46290

HTML & Web Artistry 2: More Than Code

Copyright © 2003 by Natalie Zee and Susan Harris

All rights reserved. No part of this book shall be reproduced, stored in a retrieval system, or transmitted by any means—electronic, mechanical, photocopying, recording, or otherwise—without written permission from the publisher. No patent liability is assumed with respect to the use of the information contained herein. Although every precaution has been taken in the preparation of this book, the publisher and author(s) assume no responsibility for errors or omissions. Neither is any liability assumed for damages resulting from the use of the information contained herein.

International Standard Book Number: 0-7357-1029-5

Library of Congress Catalog Card Number: 00103707

Printed in the United States of America

First Printing: August 2002

06   05   04   03   02   7   6   5   4   3   2   1

Interpretation of the printing code: The rightmost double-digit number is the year of the book's printing; the rightmost single-digit number is the number of the book's printing. For example, the printing code 02-1 shows that the first printing of the book occurred in 2002.

Trademarks

All terms mentioned in this book that are known to be trademarks or service marks have been appropriately capitalized. New Riders Publishing cannot attest to the accuracy of this information. Use of a term in this book should not be regarded as affecting the validity of any trademark or service mark.

Warning and Disclaimer

Every effort has been made to make this book as complete and as accurate as possible, but no warranty of fitness is implied. The information provided is on an "as is" basis. The authors and the publisher shall have neither liability nor responsibility to any person or entity with respect to any loss or damages arising from the information contained in this book or from the use of the CD or programs accompanying it.

PUBLISHER
David Dwyer

ASSOCIATE PUBLISHER
Stephanie Wall

EXECUTIVE EDITOR
Steve Weiss

PRODUCTION MANAGER
Gina Kanouse

MANAGING EDITOR
Sarah Kearns

ACQUISITIONS EDITOR
Theresa Gheen

PROJECT EDITOR
Michael Thurston

COPY EDITOR
Daryl Kessler

TECHNICAL EDITOR
Osman Kahn

PRODUCT MARKETING MANAGER
Kathy Malmloff

PUBLICITY MANAGER
Susan Nixon

MANUFACTURING COORDINATOR
Jim Conway

COVER DESIGNERS
Natalie Zee
Susan Harris

INTERIOR DESIGNERS
Natalie Zee
Susan Harris

COMPOSITOR
Kim Scott

INDEXER
Chris Morris

Contents at a Glance

Table of Contents

Dedication

Natalie Zee

For all the interactive designers who continue to have a passion about the Internet.

Susan Harris

To my mom and dad.

About the Authors

Natalie Zee is an award-winning interactive designer and writer based in San Francisco. She has amassed years of experience building leading-edge interactive projects for such top clients as Mattel, Levi's, 3Com, Visa, Apple, and Macromedia. Her work has been featured in such publications as *I.D. Magazine*, *Communication Arts*, and showcased in other web design books. She started her career as a web designer at Macromedia, where she was an integral part of the initial launch of Shockwave in 1995 and the development and growth of Macromedia.com. Following Macromedia, Natalie worked at frog design and MarchFIRST (starting back with CKS and then USWeb/CKS).

Natalie is a regular contributor to books and articles on the subject of web design, rich media, and broadband. Her writings are based on the theme that designers can empower themselves by understanding more about technology. She is the co-author of two best-selling web design books—*HTML Artistry: More than Code* (New Riders) and *HTML Web Magic* (Hayden). Her essay, "The Design Technologist," is part of Steven Heller's book *The Education of an E-Designer* (Allworth Press). As a specialist on broadband, she co-authored *The Last Mile: Broadband and the Next Internet Revolution* (McGraw-Hill), a book that explains how the changing nature of the Internet will affect our lives and business. She is a regular speaker at web conferences around the country and enjoys teaching sessions on web design. Natalie holds a degree in Mass Communications and Technology from the University of California at Berkeley. She is currently the Creative Director of Rich Media at SBI and Company (www.sbiandcompany.com) in San Francisco.

Photograph: Jack Huynh Orange Photography, www.orangephotography.com

Susan Harris has been specializing in multimedia since 1995. She studied design and later taught at the California College of Arts and Crafts (CCAC) in San Francisco. Susan began her career at Macromedia in San Francisco, where she worked on the Macromedia web site and in the first generation of Flash. After working for various designers and then freelance, Susan founded Fluent Studios (originally known as Slow Clouds Design).

Fluent Studios is a full-service design agency specializing in interactive, motion, print, identity, and Internet design. Fluent Studio's clients range from non-profit organizations to large corporations. Their clients include Autodesk, KQED, MarchFIRST, Macromedia, Sumitomo, Red Advertising, and PBS. A full client list and portfolio can be viewed at `www.fluentstudios.com`.

Susan's work has been published in *How Magazine*, *ID Magazine*, and *Communicatin Arts*. Susan continues to teach interactive design at various programs in the Bay Area. She is currently the Creative Director at Fluent Studios in San Francisco.

About the Technical Editor

Osman Khan is Creative Director of Elliance, a full-service eBusiness development firm. His current work involves reexamining interactions with these systems, especially in the realm of workspace applications, e-commerce applications/sites, and email broadcasts. His interests include using new media technologies for artistic expressions. More information about Osman can be found at `www.elliance.com`, `ilab.elliance.com`, and `www.circusabsurd.com`.

Acknowledgments

Natalie Zee

My deepest thanks and gratitude to the many designers, developers, and dear friends who have helped contribute to this book. I am deeply humbled by the talent that has been assembled here and appreciate your time. My thanks extend out to my New Riders family who has taken such good care of me over the years. Sincere gratitude to my executive editor Steve Weiss and editor Theresa Gheen—I thank you both for your patience, kindness, and compassion in a year full of historic events. Also thanks to Katherine Murray, Jennifer Eberhardt, Kathy Malmloff, and Chris Nelson.

Thanks to my parents, friends, and co-workers for their continued support as I worked on this book. To my co-author and dear friend Susan Harris, thanks for making work seem like so much fun.

Finally, a huge thanks to all the faithful readers of the first *HTML Artistry* who have sent us some great emails over the last few years and have patiently waited for this second edition. You have been my inspiration.

Susan Harris

I would like to thank the people who inspire and support me. To my family: Mom, Dad, Dave, and Krista. To Uncle Al, thanks for all the legal help— your web site is coming! To all my dear friends, near and far.

Thank you to Theresa and Steve at New Riders. You have been understanding and beyond accommodating in this crazy year. Thanks for sticking with us!

Thanks to all the people who have been a part of Fluent Studios and Slow Clouds Design. Your contributions have made Fluent Studios what it is today.

To all my clients, thank you for challenging us with interesting work and thank you for having faith in a small company.

And, last but far from least, to my favorite design geek, HTML teacher, great friend, and co-author Natalie Zee. Nat, it is an honor to work with you and a joy to be your friend. Thanks for all the support, faith, and fun times!

A Message from New Riders

As the reader of this book, you are our most important critic and commentator. We value your opinion and want to know what we're doing right, what we could do better, in what areas you'd like to see us publish, and any other words of wisdom you're willing to pass our way.

As Executive Editor at New Riders, I welcome your comments. You can fax, email, or write me directly to let me know what you did or didn't like about this book—as well as what we can do to make our books better. When you write, please be sure to include this book's title, ISBN, and author, as well as your name and phone or fax number. I will carefully review your comments and share them with the authors and editors who worked on the book.

Please note that I cannot help you with technical problems related to the topic of this book, and that due to the high volume of email I receive, I might not be able to reply to every message. Thanks.

Fax: 317-581-4663
Email: steve.weiss@newriders.com
Mail: Steve Weiss
            Executive Editor
            New Riders Publishing
            201 West 103rd Street
            Indianapolis, IN 46290 USA

Visit Our Web Site: www.newriders.com

On our web site, you'll find information about our other books, the authors we partner with, book updates and file downloads, promotions, discussion boards for online interaction with other users and with technology experts, and a calendar of trade shows and other professional events with which we'll be involved. We hope to see you around.

Email Us from Our Web Site

Go to www.newriders.com and click on the Contact Us link if you

- Have comments or questions about this book.
- Want to report errors that you have found in this book.
- Have a book proposal or are interested in writing for New Riders.
- Would like us to send you one of our author kits.
- Are an expert in a computer topic or technology and are interested in being a reviewer or technical editor.
- Want to find a distributor for our titles in your area.
- Are an educator/instructor who wants to preview New Riders books for classroom use. In the body/comments area, include your name, school, department, address, phone number, office days/hours, text currently in use, and enrollment in your department, along with your request for either desk/examination copies or additional information.

Introduction

Why Read This Book

HTML and Web Artistry 2 is for people who want to learn about the web and how to design for it from a designer's perspective. It's been a few years since the first *HTML Artistry* was published and we are excited and proud to bring you a new, updated version filled with new techniques, case studies, and more.

This book teaches you to think about your design decisions before diving into production. You'll learn to overcome technical burdens that in the past may have forced you to compromise your design. We'll teach you techniques for making interactive experiences more exciting and give you all the code to really make it work. We believe that good web design begins with a strong HTML foundation. We'll teach you the ins and outs of hand coding HTML. If you already know HTML and want to learn how to add DHTML, JavaScript, Flash, and other Multimedia to your pages, this book is for you, too.

HTML and Web Artistry 2 is your guide to better web design. This book discusses, explains, and encourages a cross-disciplinary approach to web site development. First, we focus on design and basic programming skills. We discuss color, layout, typography, and web technology. We provide case studies and explicit directions that will give you a complete technical understanding for how to bring your designs to life. Second, we share insight and inspiration from numerous professional designers from multiple disciplines. We encourage looking away from the web to observe what design is and how it affects our culture.

Overview

This book is divided into two parts. The first part deals with classic HTML and fundamental design principals. We cover HTML layout, principals of interactive design (user interface and navigation), typography, and color theory. The second part introduces you to the concepts and techniques behind creating more complex interactivity. We show you how to incorporate DHTML, JavaScript, Flash, video, and sound into your HTML pages. We teach you how to use Macromedia Dreamweaver and Flash to add exciting interactive features and stunning animation to your pages. Because each chapter builds on previous chapters, we encourage you to go through the book in a chronological order.

Each chapter provides the following:

- Full HTML code and examples
- Tips on how to conceptualize your design as it relates to your content
- Step-by-step techniques that show you how to add interesting features to your pages
- Case studies that spotlight beautifully designed web sites
- Insight from inspirational design models

The companion web site to this book, `www.htmlartistry.com`, is filled with examples from the book, updates, and links to design and technical resources on the web. We encourage your feedback on the web site. We hope you'll use this book as a springboard for creating beautiful multimedia and as a source of inspiration as you move forward in the world of design.

Inspirational Design Models

Design is everywhere we look. It's the buildings you pass on your way to work, the ticket you use to take the bus, the cell phone you hold in you hand. Our biggest inspiration is the world around us.

Between the chapters in this book, we have included Inspirational Design Models—profiles of designers, developers, artists, and studios that we feel are shaping our interactive and digital future.

Through interactive video, print, 3D, gaming, and product design, these creative individuals have all figured out how to build careers with their passions while at the same time balancing their work life with play. These people have inspired us with their vision, work, and sense of humor. We hope they will do the same for you.

Part One
Web Design Essentials

User Interface
& Navigation

Designing Interactive User Experiences

CHAPTER 1

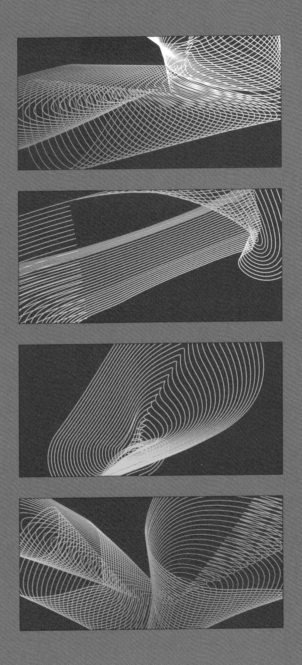

Having a great home page and beautiful graphics is just not enough to ensure a great web site. If visitors to your site cannot find what they need or don't know where to go, you can be sure that they probably won't come back. One of the most important (and hardest) aspects of designing a great web site is the stuff that goes on behind the scenes, the things you need to plan carefully before you begin working on your design. Some of the most important components of web design are things like user interface, site flow, navigation, and content. The way your site looks and feels to users, the ease with which they'll learn how to get around, and the graphics and text you choose as content all play major parts in how users interact with and experience your web site.

Web designers today are tasked with designing "interactive experiences" for visitors, which involves much more than designing a simple web page. Creating a great web experience means planning carefully and building your site so that it works in harmony with your visual design concepts.

So, how do you walk that fine line between your design vision and your client's wish for links to everything on one page? How can you make sure you are addressing and making the right decisions when it seems like there are always a bevy of new technological advancements and choices?

Relax. We are here to help. This chapter will provide the structure you need to begin building the right foundation for a great site. In this chapter, you will see some great examples of designing the right user interface, creating intuitive navigation, and gathering and organizing your content for a web site. We'll not only refresh your memory with some fundamentals, we'll show you how to do it with HTML, JavaScript, and more.

Planning Your Site

The planning stage for a web site is one of the most important ones. Depending on the complexity of the web site you are designing, your ideas, sketches, and documentation will be the starting ground when you start work on the actual look and feel design of the site.

As you start to establish a plan for your site, keep these three key points in mind:

- **Goals and Objectives.** Establish clear goals and objectives for the site.
- **Audience.** Determine the main audience of the site.
- **Technology.** Understand the technological limitations you are working with.

For example, suppose you are building a promotional web site for your fictional design studio, a* design. The goals of your site include promoting the work you do as well as finding ways to recruit new employees. From that understanding, you can assume that your audience will be a mix of new and existing clients, as well as new recruits. Knowing that, you can begin to speculate on the type of access to technology the audience has. Will they be primarily surfing on T1 lines or 56K modems? Will they be more likely to be using PCs or Macs?

To put this in a context of planning with a site for a new client, suppose that you have been hired by an independent music label to help promote its current artists and provide resources that attract new independent artists. In your initial meeting with the client, you'd focus on finding the answers to those three key elements: goals, audience, and technology. You might ask questions like these:

- What do you want to accomplish with the site?
- Is there a story you want the site to tell?
- Who will use the site?
- What do you want users to do while they're there?
- How comfortable is your audience with technology? What type of hardware and software are they likely to use?

To start the brainstorming process, first gather all the content and potential categories or "buckets" for the site. By researching all the content, you'll be able to figure out how to organize everything efficiently. And if your client company has done market research that will help you identify and understand their customers, use it to get a clearer picture of who the site visitors are

likely to be. In some cases, you may want to create user scenarios to help make the planning stages more effective. You can come up with a handful of characters (for example, David, the corporate CEO or Stacy, the recent design school graduate) to have a sort of real-world reference to help you figure out ways in which these users will interact with the site and what methods you will need to organize and present the information.

Web sites such as the content-rich Art and Culture site (www.artandculture.com) have an extensive user interface and navigation scheme that runs deep into varying categories and subcategories (see Figure 1.1). Careful planning to detail allows different items to be cross-referenced through secondary pages, such as those shown in the fashion design section (Figures 1.2 and 1.3). The expandable and collapsible navigation allows for users to get to different sections easily and quickly. All of this would not have been possible without clear and concise planning.

Mapping the Site Architecture

After you have gathered all your content and done your preliminary planning, you can start mapping out your site with a site architecture map. The site architecture map is your blueprint for the site and it will help you throughout the design process. You can use any tool to create your map, but we use Adobe Illustrator to help create nicely organized boxes for our buckets.

1.1

1.2

1.3

figure 1.1

Art and Culture's home page.

figure 1.2

Art and Culture's Fashion Design
Category, featuring Isaac Mizrahi.

figure 1.3

Isaac Mizrahi's page on the Art and
Culture web site cross-references
Todd Oldham.

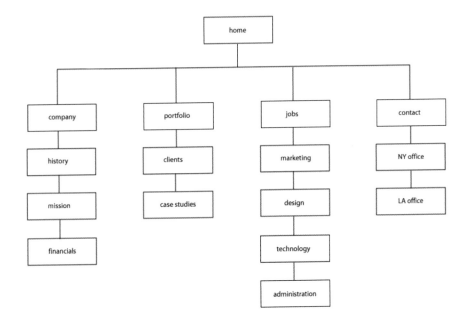

figure 1.4
Simple site architecture map.

Figure 1.4 shows a simple basic site map that encompasses four main buckets for the site a* design. The buckets are "company," "portfolio," "jobs," and "contact." By creating a map, you are able to get an overarching view of what the various subpages are within the buckets. You can use your map to help you figure out ways to consolidate and organize areas that are too big or ones that don't seem to have enough content.

Similarly, these maps also play an integral part in client projects. Can you imagine an architect building a house without showing the client the blueprint? Of course not. The site map is a great way for you and your client to sit down and get an overview of the site to make sure that the site is on its way to reaching its goals. What should

you focus on when creating a site map? Here are a few ideas for starters:

- **Visualize your outcome.** Make sure the map shows your client in the clearest possible way a straight navigation to the site. If the paths look difficult or convoluted, you'll lose the interest (and maybe the enthusiasm) of a client not at home with web design.

- **Forget the bells and whistles for now.** Because your first goal of a site map is to communicate the site strategy clearly to a client (or to your co-workers), don't get too fancy in the initial design. Save your best creative energies for the visual design mockups and opt for simple and straightforward in your maps.

- **Be clear with start and end points**. Be sure to highlight the start and end points on the map in some way so your client will immediately have a context for the structure. If the navigation strategy isn't obvious, your client may wander off into "Where does this go?" land and not pay attention to your talk-through of the site.

- **Show where the site can easily expand or contract.** Some clients get stuck in the details and want to see everything in black and white before you begin. Prepare for flexibility in your site map by showing where the site can easily be expanded or contracted as needed.

- **Keep it as simple as the design allows.** Some site maps will require multiple layers in a navigation strategy, whereas others will be simple, surface structures that

don't need the complexities of larger sites. When you have a choice, show the functionality in a streamlined and simple way. Initially you're mapping the concept; later on, when design is really underway, you'll be able to take the client through the richer experience.

Working on the Barbie.com redesign project, the user interface designers at the San Francisco office of SBI and Company did an extensive and colorful site map for Mattel so that the client was able to understand which new areas of the site were going to be added (see Figure 1.5). You can see that the complexity of the structure links beyond Barbie.com to other existing sister web sites. Planning like this ensures that the sites can be developed cooperatively and exist together with enough room to grow and expand over time.

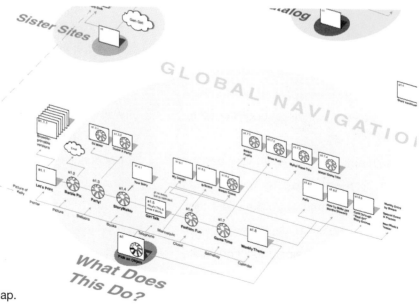

figure 1.5

Barbie.com site map.

Planning the User Interface

Now that you have your site architecture, you need to think about how users will interact with your screens of content. Consistency and clarity are two important rules: You want your visitors to see the same elements—or at least find the same look and feel—from page to page, and to be able to understand at a glance how to get around in your site. Creating a logical and inviting page design will help visitors learn how to navigate easily. Creating a good structure on the page level will ensure that users will know where everything is. The technology you design for and with also has an impact on the user interface you create.

Technology grows at a rapid pace, and we have found that the old standard 640×480 screen width and height dimensions just don't make sense anymore. As 17"+ monitors become the standard now with all shipping PCs and Macintosh computers, most designers are now designing for an 800×600 resolution. But that doesn't mean you should open up Photoshop right now and create a new document with 800 width and 600 height. There are other issues to think about when designing for this screen size.

First off, don't forget that the browser itself takes up real estate on the screen. The top tool buttons, URL address bar, and bottom status bar are there to help users as they navigate on the web. Take these things into consideration and make sure that you are allotting for the default browser settings in your design. You might not like icons on your tool bar buttons, but that doesn't mean the visitors to your site will feel the same way.

So we thought we'd make it easy for you. Figures 1.6 and 1.7 give you two templates to use when you design for the web. You can see that the actual size you should be designing for on a Mac and on a PC is really 717×390. Keeping the main pages under 390 ensures that the content can be seen within one screen and users won't have to scroll.

At the same time, keep in mind that there are users out there on higher resolutions, as well. Although the numbers for 1024×768 are low, they are growing. Unless your target audience is users set at this high resolution, it isn't a good idea to just go ahead and design big. A good practice is to consider ways in which your 800×600 design can scale to look good in 1024×768. Think of clever ways table cells can scale or larger background images can appear so that audiences at all resolutions will see a well thought-out design.

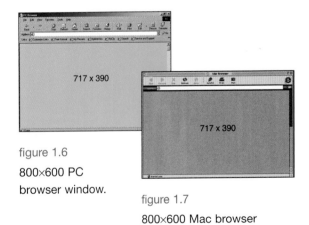

figure 1.6
800×600 PC browser window.

figure 1.7
800×600 Mac browser window.

Note:

Of course, issues in user interface get complicated when you get into more complex sites, especially e-commerce. Research and usability issues are the key to ensuring that most users have a good experience on your site.

Another thing to think about as you design the user interface is the use of sound. Will your site open with background music? Will you make audio clips a part of your general design? Consider carefully the goals of your site, the expectations of your audience, and the technical capabilities of the hardware and software your visitors will be likely to use. To find out more about adding sound to your site, see Chapter 8, "Multimedia: Moving Forward with Video and Sound."

Creating Good Navigational Elements

Navigation is not just a laundry list of links or cute buttons that decorate web pages. Navigation should be thought of as the journey or path you want your users to take when they visit your site. Users need a sense of place—where they are—and direction—where to go from here. Books of fiction have an intuitive navigation because you know that you have to read them from beginning to end.

With a web site, navigation is different. Think of your web site as a compact file cabinet. You have to organize your papers into categorical files and place them in a way so that you can quickly find specific topics. The key is in organization, presentation, and naming formats. Some sites lose grasp of this and create either a massive index of links or cute names to areas of their site that make no sense. This makes the user feel either overwhelmed or confused as to where to go.

To begin, there are some fundamental things to think about as you start to design navigation for your site. Here are just a few of them:

- **Organization/Presentation.** Include a clean, clear direction and structure; limit the number of links.
- **Naming Convention.** Use intuitive names for areas on your site.
- **Hierarchy.** Place the important information first or on top.

In the sections that follow, we'll look more closely at each of these items and see how they relate to your site design.

Organizing Your Links

One of the keys to designing navigation is organization. By organizing your site well, you can focus on the areas you want to promote on your site. Cluttered pages with millions of links only confuse your users and leave you with a big mess! Instead, choose to have a limited number of links from the beginning and have more links within each subsection. The best-designed sites offer only a handful of links off of the main home page. In turn, the rest of the links lie within specific category pages. This allows you to better control the direction of where you want your users to go.

Figures 1.8 and 1.9 illustrate how clean navigation and a limited number of links help steer a direction for your users. Having nested subcategory links, like the car model names used in this example, allows users to better navigate and find where they want to go without having to list everything on the screen at once.

Naming Your Links

If you have an area on your site for feedback, call it "feedback." Just say what you mean and users can easily find where they want to go. This becomes especially important when you consider that the web is also an international communications medium, and visitors from other countries may not understand cute terms for areas of a site. Pick a simple word or two your audience will understand that clearly describe the area of your site—no need to get too verbose.

The BCBG web site (www.bcbg.com) uses simple words to describe areas on its site so users won't be confused (see Figure 1.10). The layout of the home page is nice and clean, letting users focus on the main image from the current collection and the links to other pages on the site.

figure 1.8

Audi USA home page.

figure 1.9

Audi USA expanding sub-navigation.

figure 1.10

BCBG web site has a clean home page.

Graphics Versus Text Links

Going deeper into site design issues, we need to take a look at the type of links you will use on your site. HTML text links work well with graphic links, enabling you to quickly edit and update your links rather than having to go through the tedious task of redoing all your graphics. You've seen them used smartly all over sites such as Communication Arts (`www.commarts.com`).

It can be easy to update text links rather than having to make new graphics each time you add a section to your site but having only text can be a bit of a drag for your web visitors. You can combine both the use of a graphical navigation bar with an alternative text link for a more balanced look. Most sites now have text footers on their pages with links to the top areas of their sites as a measure of consistency so that users will always be able to see main navigation in case images have trouble loading. The Communication Arts web site has a text footer bar (see Figure 1.15) as well as a pop-up site map window that allows users to find things quickly (Figure 1.16).

figure 1.15

Communication Arts HTML text footer.

figure 1.16

Communication Arts pop-up site map navigation.

> **Tip:**
> Don't forget the difference between absolute and relative links. *Absolute* links indicate the full server address like this: `http://www.website.com/info/main.html`, whereas relative links are references to files on your site like this: info/main.html. Because relative links maintain their relationship to the site, you can move site files from one place to another without losing the link. If you use absolute links, however, moving site files means you need to update and/or repair any links that are broken in the move.
>
> Text footers provide the user optimum methods from which to navigate around your site. Whether people are more comfortable with text links or graphics, you'll know that they can get around no matter which method of navigation they prefer. Also, in instances when users have images turned off, they will always have an alternative to move around the site.

Using Client-Side Image Maps

When creating navigation graphics, an easy way to link up graphics to URLs is by creating an image map. An image map connects the coordinates you specify in a certain image and enables you to correspond matching URLs to that area. The most popular image maps today are client-side image maps.

Client-side image maps have both the coordinates and their respective location recorded right on the HTML page. This saves valuable surfing time because users don't have to wait for the server to retrieve the URL; it's all on the page. Another plus is that the bottom browser status bar displays the actual location you'll be going to instead of numbered coordinates. Combine that with the text status rollovers that are discussed later in this chapter and you can create an effective combination of graphic navigation and textual browser status messages.

On the other hand, you may want to use server-side image maps. Server-side image maps have the coordinates of the graphic and their corresponding URL recorded on a text file somewhere on the web server. By referencing that .map file in the HTML, the browser calls upon that file to find out where to go. This is why when you roll over server-side image maps, the graphic coordinates show up instead of URL paths in the status bar. This process can slow things down on your site, which is why client-side image maps are much faster and hence more popular.

Creating an image map nowadays is really simple. With tools such as Adobe ImageReady or Macromedia Fireworks, you can set up image coordinates and their URLs in a snap.

For this technique, we will be using Adobe ImageReady because its seamless integration with Adobe Photoshop makes it easy to flip back and forth between tools so that you can continue to edit your graphics and map the areas as well.

We are making a text navigation for a page and want the colorful text images to be linked to the areas of the a* design site (see Figure 1.17). With your graphic open in Photoshop, click the bottom button in the tool bar as shown to switch your image from Photoshop to ImageReady.

As you can see, each graphic text occupies its own layer, but to create a rectangular boxed area to link a URL, we must create a transparent boxed layer for each layer of text. Each layer thus represents a separate URL link. As shown in Figure 1.18, create a new layer called company link to be the URL for the corporate text. Draw a box around the text and fill it in with any color. Your box can be either above or below your text layer. Because the box will be transparent, it won't be visible when the final GIF is outputted. To make it transparent, click on the Effects button in the Layers toolbox. Choose Color Fill, and set Opacity to 0% (see Figure 1.19). You have now created a transparent box for the company link.

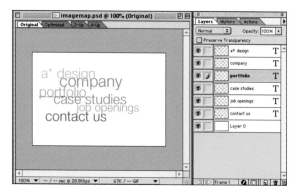

figure 1.17

Graphic in Photoshop that will become an image map.

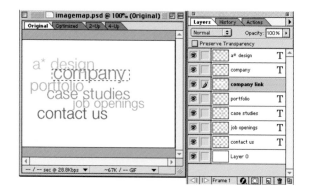

figure 1.18

Creating a new layer for the company URL link.

figure 1.19

Making the URL box transparent.

Double-click the layer company link and a dialog box will appear (see Figure 1.20). Check the box Use Layer as Image Map and enter in the URL where you want the company area of the graphic to go to. Repeat the above steps for the rest of the text layers. When you are finished, set your optimization values in the Optimize toolbox and choose Save Optimized As. When you do so, make sure the HTML box is checked so that ImageReady will generate not only the graphic but the image map HTML as well.

To make sure the preferences are set correctly, click the HTML Options button. When the HTML Options dialog box appears (see Figure 1.21), make sure Client-Side is selected from the Image Maps pull-down menu. You can choose to use either ImageReady HTML code or Adobe GoLive code as a preference. Client-side image maps are usually already set as the default setting to the application.

Drag the HTML output into a browser window and you'll see the image map in action (see Figure 1.22). When you roll over the text, you'll see that the URL info appears in the browser's bottom status bar. When you upload the file and image to its correct directory on the server, it will take you to the right links when you click on each text area of the graphic.

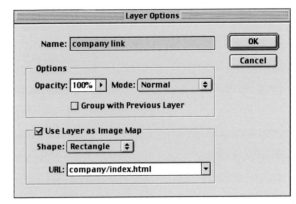

figure 1.20

Layer Options dialog box.

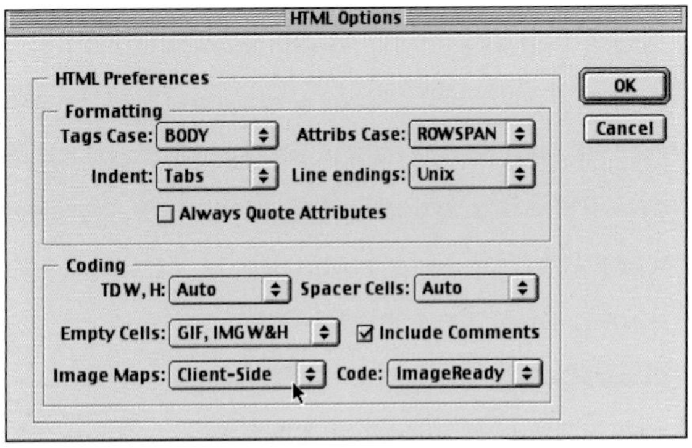

figure 1.21

HTML export settings.

figure 1.22

Final image map.

Customized Status Bar Rollover Messages

Most people rely on the bottom status bar to let them know where the link will take them. Why not take it a step further and tell them where they are going rather than show the URL? With simple JavaScript added to your HTML, you can show customized messages when users roll over a link or a graphic.

Figure 1.23 shows a simple graphic that takes users into the site when they click the bottom-right square. Usually when you click on a graphic, the URL is displayed in the status bar, as illustrated in client-side image maps. In this case, the message "Welcome to a* design" is displayed rather than the linked URL (see Figure 1.24).

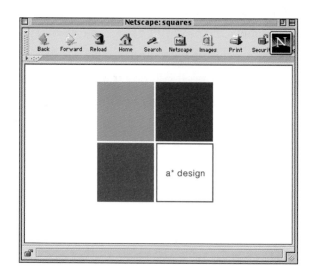

1.23

figure 1.23

A simple graphic button.

figure 1.24

Status bar rollover message, "Welcome to a* design."

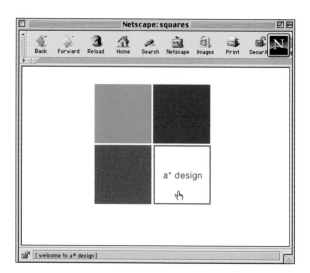

1.24

Targeting New Browser Windows

You will often have links that go outside your site and although you want your visitors to go off and explore, you also want them to find their way back. Your best option is to target a new browser window each time you have a link off of your site. The new browser window opens with the new link while the other browser window stays in the back. Some sites use the target new browser function too generously, frustrating users with an array of open browser windows. Make sure that if you do open a new window, it makes sense and doesn't lose users between different browser windows.

To target a new browser window for any given link, all you have to do is add the target property to that link using one of the following examples as a guide:

```
<a href="http://www.avantmedia.com"
target="window">
```

```
<a target="window"
href="http://www.avantmedia.com">
```

It doesn't matter where you put the target attribute, as long as it's in the `<A HREF>` tag somehow. You must also make sure the target is set to "window" so that a new browser window will open. Figure 1.25 gives you an example of a new browser window that is opened when the user clicks a link.

Note:

See Chapter 5, "Personalization," for more on JavaScript pop-up windows that allow you to customize the browser.

Implementing Virtual Headers and Footers

For managing large web sites, an easy way to keep your navigation updated is to use virtual headers and footers. These are the standard interface elements that appear on most pages, such as ad banners, header graphics, text link navigation, and so on. Making virtual headers and footers means that instead of having the full HTML code on all the pages, you have it on just one. That way, all you have to do is update one

figure 1.25

Targeting new browser windows.

file for the rest of the site. It doesn't even have to be a header or footer. If you need information duplicated in multiple areas, having to update just one text file makes it fast and easy. Most virtual headers and footers involve CGI scripts because they are server-side includes. But if you want to avoid the complications that come with CGI scripting, JavaScript can now be used to create virtual files for your site. Figure 1.26 shows an example of a virtual footer that you can create on a single page and display throughout your site.

First, you need to create an external JavaScript file to live on your site.

```
//JavaScript File for virtual footer
//Update this document only to change
footer on site
```

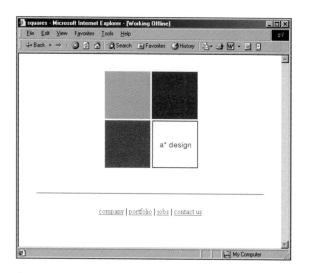

figure 1.26
Virtual footer.

```
function printVirtualFooter(){
document.write("<hr
width="500"><br>");
document.write("<a
href="company/index.html">company</a>
|");
document.write("<a
href="portfolio/index.html">portfolio
</a> |");
document.write("<a
href="jobs/index.html">jobs</a> |");
document.write("<a
href="contact.html">contact us</a>
|");
}
```

> Note:
> Each `document.write` must be on its own separate line. Don't word wrap the code because that will mess it up.

Save this file as footer.js. You can name the file whatever you want, but it must have the .js (JavaScript) suffix. Now when you need to update the content of your footer, you just have to modify your .js document. You can add as many lines as you want, and updating is a breeze.

For your HTML pages, you need to use <SCRIPT> to reference the .js file at the top of any HTML document in which the footer should appear, like this:

```
<HTML>
<HEAD>
<SCRIPT LANGUAGE="JavaScript"
SRC="footer.js">
</SCRIPT>
</HEAD>
```

Then for the exact area in which you want the footer to appear, add this code:

```
<SCRIPT LANGUAGE="JavaScript">
        printVirtualFooter();
</SCRIPT>
```

The final result, as seen in Figure 1.26, is a virtual footer that can be made once and used throughout your site.

To create a virtual anything, just follow the same previous steps for the virtual footer. If you use multiple virtual files, make sure that you go through the code and change the names for each of the commands, such as printVirtualHeader or printVirtualText.

Summary

We hope that this chapter has helped you understand the importance of planning and organizing your web site. Content buckets, site architecture, user interface, and navigation all have important roles in web design because with

good structure your site will be usable and can be flexible and grow. Make sure that you establish clear goals and objectives for your site and that you are targeting the right audience. Also, understand the technological limitations you may be bound to.

These techniques, HTML, and JavaScript code can help enhance the navigational structure of your site by letting users always know where they are and helping them get to where they need to be more quickly. From basic HTML text links or graphic client-side image maps, there are many different options for presenting navigation on your site. For a more in-depth look at JavaScript rollovers and DHTML, refer to Part II, "DHTML and Web Interactivity: Make It Move."

URLS In This Chapter

- **Art and Culture**
  www.artandculture.com
- **BCBG**   www.bcbg.com
- **Communication Arts**
  www.commarts.com
- **Audi**   www.audiusa.com

Inspirational Design Model

Annette Loudon
Niftycorp

"I tend to be pretty passionate about most

sites I work on, and I always follow the same

process. Maybe I'm uptight, but the idea of

proceeding in some sort of haphazard way

just freaks me out."

figure 1

niftycorp.com

portfolio

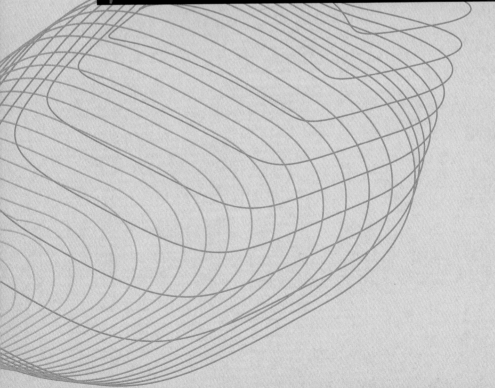

"Clever girl" sounds like something designer Annette Loudon would say, but never about herself. Yet, this Australian native is one of the most clever people you'll ever meet. She spent five years at Construct, one of the first web design studios in San Francisco, which she also helped found.

Fast forward to the present and Annette is hard at work on her own gig with Niftycorp (www.niftycorp.com). She has spent most of 2001 traveling in and around Senegal, Africa as part of the *joko project* (www.jokoclub.org), a non-profit initiative to build Internet access centers, a cultural content web site, and an online community for Senegalese people. The web site component aims to entice people online with local music, news, and community features that will allow expatriates to communicate with their families.

A designer, a cat lover, an adventurer, an inspiration—Annette's the ultimate model of the gal that can do it all.

What inspires you?
I just never know where to start with specifics on questions of inspiration. I feel like I'm relentlessly bombarded by inspiration.

I'm inspired by the possibilities the networked environment offers. I'm inspired by the idea that this crazy mess of wires and code still leaves so much room for poetry.

I think a lot of people were drawn to the net by tales of a new frontier, exciting new ways to communicate and be creative. And perhaps by the time many of them arrived, it was harder to

figure 2
Localmusic.com

figure 3
Innovations Interiors

find those things through all the spam and banner ads. But for me the net has always been, and continues to be an amazing thing. (Of course, if you caught me after battling some moronic browser incompatibility, you'd be sure to hear a whole different story.)

I'm also continually inspired by clever people and the clever things that they make. Anything intelligent, poetic, personal, beautifully crafted (or any combination thereof). But it makes me dizzy to list that stuff.

What's your dream project?

I've actually just started my dream project. Myself and a bunch of clever designers will be making web music videos for indie bands that we like. When we're done we'll put them all up, and include links to places you can buy the CDs online.

I'm hoping we can complement efforts of sites like insound.com and epitonic.com, and help to create a new model for music promotion and distribution. I just love the idea of a music industry that actually supports the musicians. I know, it's a crazy concept!

I'm ridiculously excited about the project. I've always wanted to do this kind of work, and it turns out I'm not the only one. And when I look at the lineup of designers and bands, and who's paired with who...well, like I said, I'm pretty excited about this project.

figure 4
niftycorp.com

figure 5

Goth Bounce—Shockwave multi-user game

You really sound passionate about music and this project in particular. Since this is more or less a project of passion for you, what is your criteria for design versus those of client projects? How do you know when you are finished?

The only real difference between this and a client project is that I have to be the client and designer. So I'll start by dreaming and brainstorming, and come up with a clear picture of what I think my ideal site would be like—almost trying to forget what I know about technical realities. Then I'll get in designer mode and hash out the practicalities—which technologies to use, site structure, interface, and so on. I'll probably

indulge in a more organic process for developing look and feel, but other than that it's business as usual.

That's the way I make sites. I tend to be pretty passionate about most sites I work on, and I always follow the same process. Maybe I'm uptight, but the idea of proceeding in some sort of haphazard way just freaks me out. I can't imagine doing a good job that way.

How do you think Broadband will change the way in which the digital medium will be thought of and designed for?

I imagine it'll be the same as usual. People will try to transfer inappropriate paradigms from old media for a while. Then they'll realize that just doesn't make sense. And some clever people will start really thinking about it and start to come up with design strategies that really make sense in these new contexts.

I keep trying to think of something positive to say about Broadband and Wireless, but right now they feel more like marketing concepts than real mediums to me. I just see a lot of money being put into generating demand for new gadgets and technologies, investors looking for a way to make some more money. I'm sure I'll get involved at some point, but at the moment it's not my scene.

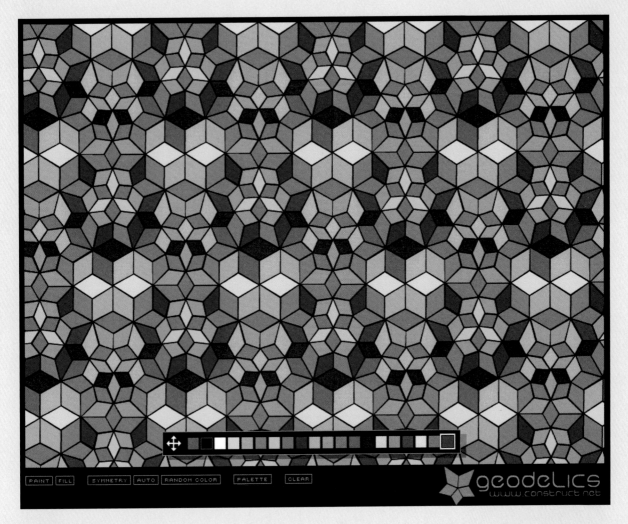

figure 6

geodelics

Who are your design heroes?

John Maeda (www.maedastudio.com) is quite clever. I love the way he thinks about and plays with technology. And unlike a lot of artists who have conceptual and/or technical tendencies, the end product itself is generally gorgeous.

I'm constantly in awe of work by Tree Axis (www.tree-axis.com) and The Chopping Block (www.choppingblock.com). Both those shops have a great mix of tech and design, and there's often a sense of playfulness in their work.

And as far as graphic design goes, I'm a sucker for a wide range of stuff including J. Otto, Designers Republic, and almost anything Dutch or Japanese.

Do you have any advice that you would like to share with all the aspiring designers out there?

There's nothing worse than socks that get swallowed by your shoes, or ill-fitting underwear. So if you stock up on good-quality socks and undies, you'll always be ready to tackle your projects without irritating distractions.

If you could be a superhero, who would you be and why?

The Incredible Hulk, 'cause I think if I got huge and green every time I was mad, I'd always get my own way.

What are three things in the world you can't live without?

Music, friends (including my cat, Ally), and Milo (Australian chocolate milk drink that I often drink instead of eating real food).

Please name a bad habit you have.

Getting overly excited (usually about something geeky) and babbling about it in an unintelligible fashion.

Annette Loudon URLs:
- **Niftycorp**   www.niftycorp.com
- **neumu**
  www.neumu.net/twinklepop
- **Innovations Interiors**
  www.innovationsinteriors.com

On the video store:

I seem to have some sort of problem with pattern recognition. So many mundane tasks that are mindless for most people can utterly baffle me. Looking for a video one night, my friend walked right up to a particular shelf in the new releases section, looked, then said it was too bad it wasn't in. I thought it was odd that he only looked on the one shelf and said so. I mean it could be anywhere, right? He seemed very confused for a second, then said "You know it's in alphabetical, order right?"

figure 7

mothman

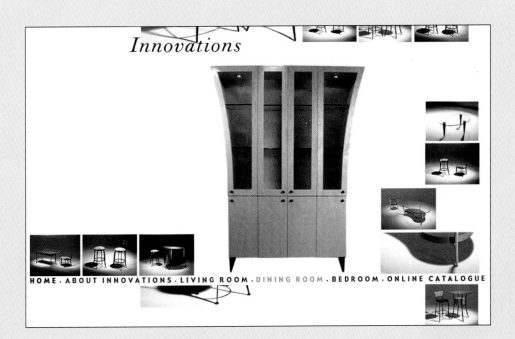

figure 8

innovations.com

Layouts

Creating Compelling Layouts
with Tables and Frames

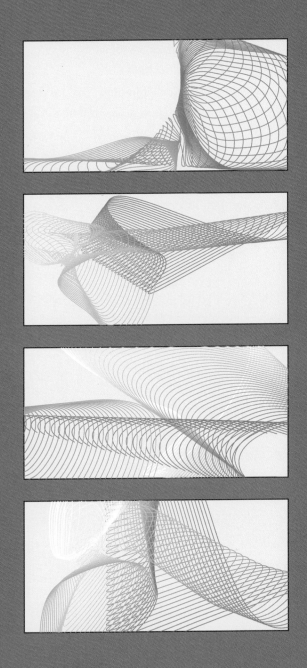

The production process for creating your layout for your web site can be one of the most challenging aspects of web design. As we learned from the last chapter, it's important to plan and organize your site and have your navigational and site structure done before you start building. With so many different options to choose from, it's important that you focus your search on the best production process to meet the demands of your web site. Whether you go with tables, frames, or a mix of the two, we'll help you find the best choices for your needs.

What's the difference between tables and frames? How can you align text next to images? In this chapter, we'll go over everything you need to get your layout intact. We believe that tables and frames are the basic foundations to building a site—having a comprehensive grasp of tables and frames will make you a better web designer. We'll cover plenty of techniques on how to maximize your tables with graphics, colored backgrounds, and nested tables. Next, you'll move on to frames to discover some different frameset options, border control, and targeting frames. There is no simple formula, but this chapter shows you the many options that are before you and explores how you can maximize your site with the best layout to fit your needs.

Tables: The Foundation for Layout

HTML tables were originally created for data, not for creating layout as it is widely used today (see Figure 2.1). Because designers found limitations in HTML, they began to use tables to better align images and text. The technique soon found its way to aligning and formatting a whole page. Sure, working with HTML tables can be messy, but if you learn and grasp the basics, you'll be able to hand code everything. It's a powerful attribute for designers to be able to go into their code and tweak it in order to make their designs look good.

figure 2.1

The Shockwave.com site uses tables to lay out the content.

These are a few things you can do with tables:

- You can cut up a large image and slice the pieces into tables to help ease loading time.
- Colored background table cells can help add color or enhance your graphics without adding more weight to your page.
- You can set the width to percentage values or exact pixel widths in order to control text wrapping in your layout.
- Use tables to justify your text alignment with images—have text flush to the right to align next to your image.
- You can use tables to place items side by side, breaking up the vertical format of the page.

Of course, tables can also get complicated and confusing with various table rows `<TR>` and table data `<TD>` cells, many of them nested within each other so that your code can become a crazy mess of tags everywhere. We'll go over some techniques on using tables for layout as well as learn a few tips so that you can organize your table data better.

Start Simple with One Table

We want to help make you a pro and, like any pro, in order to get there, you'll need to start out with a basic exercise or a refresher course. Just remember with any project to start small and grasp onto some of the simple concepts and build from there.

Start out by outlining the HTML code for just one table (nothing fancy here) so that you can get a better idea in this chapter how to build upon it and create an effective layout.

```
<TABLE>
<TR>
<TD>This is box #1</TD>
<TD>This is box #2</TD>
</TR>
</TABLE>
```

> Tip:
> It's a good idea to set border = 1 when you are developing a table so that you can see the table structure clearly as you work. When you're finished creating the table, set border = 0.

This simple one-row (`<TR>`, table row), two-data cell (`<TD>`, table data) table shows how easy tables can be (see Figure 2.2) Okay, you found us out—we did add a 2-pixel border to the table in the graphic, but that's so that you could see it all better. Pretty much the code listed above is the foundation and framework from which you'll always be working with as you add enhancements and properties to make your content look good. Replace the generic data cell text with some graphics and text to better illustrate how to start a layout. It's not very exciting, nor very pretty, but this simple table is all you need in order to start pouring in your content.

figure 2.2

The basic table.

figure 2.3

Aligning text with images in a table.

Tip:

Always make sure you use the closing `</TD>` and `</TR>` tags even though most browsers display tables fine without them. This just ensures that users with older browser versions won't have any complications. And it's a good rule of thumb to close tags that you've made open. And most importantly, remember the closing `</TABLE>` tag. Without it, Netscape users will see only a blank screen where your table should be.

In the example that follows, you can see how the graphic and text in the data cell can create some good alignment with the graphics and text. But there are a few problems with the table. With the browser resizing, the text stretches out to the ends of the browser (see Figure 2.3).

```
<TABLE>
<TR>
<TD><img src="images/windows.jpg"
width="200" height="293"
alt="Windows"></TD>
<TD>
Lorem ipsum dolor sit amet,
consectetaur adipisicing elit, sed do
eiusmod tempor incididunt ut labore et
dolore magna aliqua. Ut enim ad minim
veniam, quis nostrud exercitation
ullamco laboris nisi ut aliquip ex ea
commodo consequat. Duis aute irure
dolor in reprehenderit in voluptate
velit esse cillum dolore eu fugiat
nulla pariatur. Excepteur sint
occaecat cupidatat non proident, sunt
in culpa qui officia deserunt mollit
anim id est laborum.
</TD>
</TR>
</TABLE>
```

Always make sure when you have graphics in tables that the closing `</TD>` is flushed right up against the `<IMG SRC>` tag. Sometimes having a space or line break between them causes the browser to read it wrong and the table cell won't fit snug around the graphic. Also, if your image is a link, you have a messy remnant underline next to your image.

In addition to solving the problem of stretched text, the following example aligns the text vertically so that its top edge aligns with the top of the graphic. Here's the code for the improvement:

```
<TABLE WIDTH="500">
<TR>
<TD valign="top"><img
src="images/flowers.jpg" width="300"
height="248" alt="Flowers"></TD>
<TD valign="top">
<font face="arial, helvetica, *">
Lorem ipsum dolor sit amet,
consectetaur adipisicing elit, sed do
eiusmod tempor incididunt ut labore et
dolore magna aliqua. Ut enim ad minim
veniam, quis nostrud exercitation
ullamco laboris nisi ut aliquip ex ea
commodo consequat. Duis aute irure
dolor in reprehenderit in voluptate
velit esse cillum dolore eu fugiat
nulla pariatur. Excepteur sint
occaecat cupidatat non proident, sunt
in culpa qui officia deserunt mollit
anim id est laborum.
</TD>
</TR>
</TABLE>
```

Figure 2.4 shows a fixed-width table in which the text is aligned vertically at the top of the graphic by using the `VALIGN` property. (All the table properties are listed for you in Appendix A, "HTML Reference List," in the back of the book.) You also can set the widths of `<TD>` cells and `VALIGN` your graphic or text with the top, middle, or bottom of the selected cell (the default is middle).

figure 2.4
Controlling alignment and table width.

figure 2.5

Controlling distance and space with `cellpadding` and `cellspacing`.

figure 2.6

Colored table cells.

`Cellpadding` and `cellspacing` properties also give you some control as you use tables for layout. *Cellpadding* is the space in pixels between the items in the `<TD>` cell and the table borders. *Cellspacing* is the thickness of the table borders. These properties are used in the following code. The effects are illustrated in Figure 2.5.

```
<TABLE WIDTH="500" CELLPADDING="10"
CELLSPACING="5" BORDER="2">
```

As you can see, by modifying the `cellpadding` and `cellspacing` values, you can gain better formatting control over your table layout.

Colored Tables

Using HTML hexadecimal code for colors, you can add more color splash without the weight of GIFs or JPGs. Coloring tables can be a great way to separate information, blend your graphics to a different background, and create different shapes. You can also create very quick-loading navigation bars using colored tables. Color the whole table or individual table data cells by using the `bgcolor` attribute and the color's hexadecimal number in your code.

Figure 2.6 shows a sampling of table data cells in different colors to illustrate how the colors work. You can also color an entire table by using the same `bgcolor` attribute in each of the `<TD>` tags, like this:

```
<TABLE Border="2">
<TR>
<TD bgcolor="#993300" width="100">
<br><br><br><br><br></TD>
<TD bgcolor="#CC6633" width="100">
<br><br><br><br><br></TD>
</TR>
<TR>
<TD bgcolor="#FF9933" width="100">
<br><br><br><br><br></TD>
<TD bgcolor="#FF9966" width="100">
<br><br><br><br><br></TD>
</TR>
</TABLE>
```

For more complex action, use colored tables within your layout to separate text and graphics. Figure 2.7 shows a colored table that takes on different colors and shapes to create an almost graphical screen.

Nested Tables

To create a compelling layout, you might find the need to have multiple tables within one larger one to gain better control. One problem with nested tables is that the larger they are, the longer they take to load. Your page won't show up until the final closing `</TABLE>` tag is read by

figure 2.7

Color tables and images can work together to create more space.

the browser. Therefore, it's better to break tables into sections if you can. Make the first table small so that it can load quickly. This way, the user will always have something to see while the rest of the page loads. Here's an example of code for a nested table:

```
<TABLE Border="2" BGCOLOR="#336633">
<TR>
<TD>this is data cell #1</TD>
<TD>
        <TABLE Border="2"
        bgcolor="#FFCC33">
```

```
<TR>
<TD>this is the nested table
cell #1</TD>
<TD>this is the nested table
cell #2</TD>
</TR>
</TABLE>
</TD>
</TR>
</TABLE>
```

As you can see, you can nest a complete table within the original table by inserting another table between `<TD>` and `</TD>` tags. Figure 2.8 shows the nested table.

Tip:
To keep organized within your nested tables, you can use comments such as `<! -- main section is here -->` to help keep track. Also, you can indent your code to better read where the nested tables lie.

Tables and Graphics

Designers are finding a workaround when displaying big images. By cutting them up and putting them in tables, it gives the illusion that the image is loading faster than if it were one single, huge graphic. Also, you can section off areas in your graphics to either animate them or create individual lines.

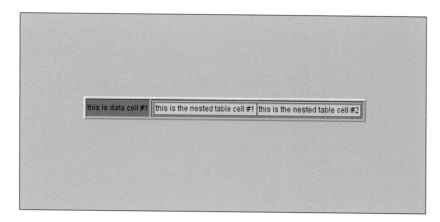

figure 2.8
A nested table.

The Target web site (`www.target.com`), shown in Figure 2.9, not only uses a table to create a grid for the navigation and content, but also cleverly uses smaller cut-up images overlaid atop a larger image in order to create a rich, colorful page.

> ## Note:
>
> When using images, it's a good idea to always define the width and height properties of the graphic. This enables the browser to read the file dimensions and reserve that space for your graphic. Your graphics will load faster as a result.

By breaking up your graphics, you not only can create the illusion of a faster download, but can also creatively use it to your advantage. You can animate certain parts of an image and try different loading techniques such as 1-bit graphics for `<IMG LOW SRC>`. You might also create interesting rollover effects. The possibilities are endless.

One downside to dividing graphics is that even though the image seems to load faster when broken up into many parts, the actual total file size may end up being larger than what you started with. If overall file size is an issue (and not simply load times), keep an eye on the weight of the individual graphics you create.

figure 2.9

Target.com uses a combination of cut-up graphics overlaid atop each other within a table layout.

Case Study

Smithsonian's National Museum of American History's Star-Spangled Banner

americanhistory.si.edu/ssb

This web site serves as a comprehensive online resource about the Star-Spangled Banner, the famous flag that inspired the words to the National Anthem. Intended as an educational site, it is part of Smithsonian's National Museum of American History's Star-Spangled Banner conservation laboratory and exhibition (see Figure 2.10).

"One goal for the site was to bring the Star-Spangled Banner alive in an interactive environment, encouraging learning and exploration of American history," describes David Lai, CEO of Hello Design.

The site needed to serve as a comprehensive educational resource for teachers and students alike. The project is also designed to signify the importance of the Banner as a national treasure, emphasize the significance of its preservation for future generations, and instill a sense of pride and patriotism in America and its history. Another challenge in building the site was the information architecture. It needed to allow users to choose the depth of knowledge they would like on a given subject, but at the same time show as much detail as possible on each historical artifact.

The major objective for this site was to generate active user participation while providing an interface with intuitive navigation to accommodate a great amount of information. The illusion of the outlined boxes with corresponding images on the flag was created with a well-thought out grid and complex table layout (see Figure 2.11).

"It was important to portray the Star-Spangled Banner as a living part of history, not a flat, static piece of fabric. To do so, we took full advantage of the interactivity of the web to get users involved in the story of the Banner," says Lai.

2.10

The flag on the home page got users to start interacting from the onset. By rolling the mouse over the flag, users are given insights about the Star-Spangled Banner and introductions to various sections of the site (see Figures 2.12 through 2.14). Clicking on a rollover image leads the user directly into that section.

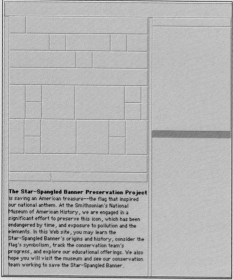

The Star-Spangled Banner Preservation Project is saving an American treasure—the flag that inspired our national anthem. At the Smithsonian's National Museum of American History, we are engaged in a significant effort to preserve this icon, which has been endangered by time, and exposure to pollution and the elements. In this Web site, you may learn the Star-Spangled Banner's origins and history, consider the flag's symbolism, track the conservation team's progress, and explore our educational offerings. We also hope you will visit the museum and see our conservation team working to save the Star-Spangled Banner.

2.11

The Star-Spangled Banner Preservation Project is saving an American treasure—the flag that inspired our national anthem. At the Smithsonian's National Museum of American History, we are engaged in a significant effort to preserve this icon, which has been endangered by time, and exposure to pollution and the elements. In this Web site, you may learn the Star-Spangled Banner's origins and history, consider the flag's symbolism, track the conservation team's progress, and explore our educational offerings. We also hope you will visit the museum and see our conservation team working to save the Star-Spangled Banner.

2.12

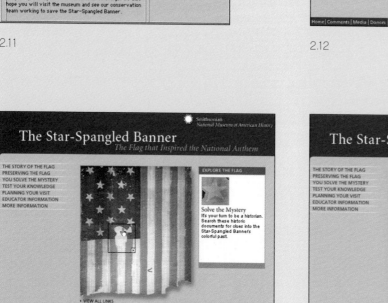

2.13

2.14

Frames

When frames first arrived on the web design scene years ago, there were a lot of mixed feelings among designers. Frames were confusing to design, the browser support was horrible, and cross-linking got confusing. With each new edition of the browsers, frames today have become an increasingly effective solution for layout. Navigation can be inserted in a frame rather than be reloaded each time you switch pages. Borderless frames provide a slick, seamless look between frame panels and eliminate the nasty default gray browser border. Frames can help you organize and lay out things in ways that avoid the pesky refresh (see Figure 2.15).

figure 2.15

The Blank + Cables site (`www.blankandcables` `.com`) uses frames to separate the navigation from the content.

Frames 101

To make some simple frame layouts, technically just remember that according to the layout and look you want, each frame is an individual HTML page. These individual pages work together much like a puzzle to form an overall look that is your layout, or frameset. Deciding upon which frameset look you want can be a difficult task because there are a wide variety of possibilities. This section focuses on some of the basics to help you maximize your frames as you work.

Things you can do with frames include these:

- You can refresh sections of your content without refreshing a whole web page.
- You can set the width to percentage values or exact pixel widths in order to control area on your page.
- Set borders on or off, and make the scroll bar viewable or hide it.
- Keep your navigation on your site at all times.

The `<FRAME>` tag simply enables you to reference your HTML file, name the specific frame, and define some of the other attributes, such as scrolling or resizing.

```
<FRAME SRC="mysite.html" NAME="main"
SCROLLING="auto | none" NORESIZE>
```

Each `<FRAME>` tag is referenced within the `<FRAMESET></FRAMESET>` tag. This tag defines the layout, such as the number of rows and columns used and frame border specifications.

```
<FRAMESET ROWS="rowheight, %, *"
COLS="colwidth, %, *">
```

The following are Frame attributes:

- `NAME="namehere"` Frame name
- `SRC="url"` Frame reference, location of HTML page for frame
- `MARGINWIDTH="number"`
- `MARGINHEIGHT="number"`
- `SCROLLING="yes | no | auto"` Controls frame scroll bar
- `NORESIZE` Frame is not resizable by user
- `FRAMEBORDER="no"` Borderless frame

Figures 2.16 through 2.18 show some simple and popular two-frame layouts and their corresponding `FRAMESET` code.

Figure 2.16 has a left side bar that can be used for navigation. The width of the side bar is determined in the `FRAMESET` column attribute. The browser reads the code in order from left to right, so by setting the first column number as 110, that means that 110 pixels over from the left of the browser, frame red.html will display. The wild card sign (*) means that the second frame's (black.html) viewable area is determined by the browser. You can control whether or not a scroll bar is visible with the `SCROLLING` attribute. Setting it to `auto` means that a scroll bar's visibility is determined by the browser. Should the user need to scroll, one will be there.

The `FRAMESET` code for Figure 2.16 follows:

```
<FRAMESET COLS="110, *">
<FRAME SRC="red.html" NAME="side"
SCROLLING="auto">
<FRAME SRC="black.html" NAME="main"
SCROLLING="auto">
</FRAMESET>
```

Tip:

Sometimes, those scroll bars do get in the way of design. But always make sure that before you say "no" to scroll bars that you test and make sure on all monitor resolutions that one isn't necessary. Otherwise, you'll have frustrated users who want to continue on an HTML page but can't because a scroll bar isn't present.

For Figure 2.17, the top frame becomes the navigation bar. This is a great layout because you can have a larger main frame by having the navigation at the top. Now instead of reading columns, we define the number of rows for this layout. The top row is 80 pixels high and the rest defaults to the browser.

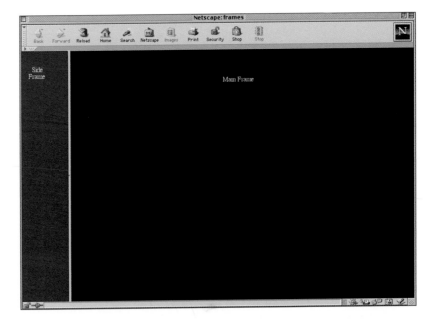

figure 2.16

Two panel frames layout, main area with side frame.

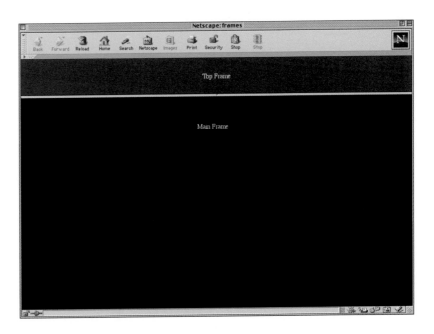

figure 2.17

Two panel frames layout, main area with top frame.

Case Study: Frames

Neutrogena Careers

www.neutrogena.com/careers

Neutrogena's Human Resources department decided to strengthen its online recruitment efforts by building a database-driven resumé collection and review tool (see Figure 2.18). The Careers site needed to reflect not only the Neutrogena brand but also the open and entrepreneurial company culture. Most importantly, the Careers site needed to communicate to potential employees why Neutrogena is a great place to work.

2.18

2.19

To emphasize Neutrogena's focus on its people, Southern California-based design firm Hello Design started by asking the question, "Why is Neutrogena a great place to work?" and found the answer in its people.

"We noted that Neutrogena employees exhibited a great sense of pride in the company and in their work," says David Lai, CEO of Hello Design.

The Neutrogena Careers site is comprised of four separate frames: one for the QuickTime video window, one for the navigation, one for the profile information, and one for the content area. The separation into these four frames allows each frame to serve its own function: The content area is the only scrolling frame so that it could accommodate the necessary amount of information. The profile information area is a separate frame so that the employee information does not scroll with the content (see Figure 2.19).

2.20

2.21

"We used rollovers for the employee information so that when rolling over each employee's image, the corresponding profile information would appear," Lai explains. "The profiles not only bring out the uniqueness of each feature employee, but they also help to introduce the employee to the user as well as prompt them to click on the image to start playing their interview."

To make Neutrogena's people the focus of the site, images of the employees were placed with the navigation elements (see Figure 2.20). Clicking on the image begins the QuickTime movie of the profile interview. To keep the QuickTime movies always available, they were placed in a separate frame so that the movies could play uninterrupted while the user navigates throughout the site. With the QuickTime videos embedded into the interface, users can navigate freely throughout the site, looking for job openings or company benefits while a video is playing (see Figure 2.21).

Here's the `FRAMESET` code for Figure 2.21:

```
<FRAMESET ROWS="80, *">
<FRAME SRC="red.html" NAME="top"
SCROLLING="no">
<FRAME SRC="black.html" NAME="main"
SCROLLING="auto">
</FRAMESET>
```

Figure 2.22 is just the inverse frame look of the previous one. It's a good look for creating a kiosk-like interface for the web. Because the navigation is at the bottom, the main frame contains limited scrolling information or a good color contrast so that it is not difficult to read from top to bottom toward the bottom navigation bar.

The `FRAMESET` code for Figure 2.22 follows:

```
<FRAMESET ROWS="*, 80">
<FRAME SRC="black.html" NAME="main"
SCROLLING="auto">
<FRAME SRC="red.html" NAME="top"
SCROLLING="no">
</FRAMESET>
```

With the varying options for framesets, you can coordinate your navigation and your content by the reliability of the fact that your navigation will always be present for your audience to use. What's even better is that you can lose the frame borders and create a seamless frame look.

```
<FRAMESET FRAMEBORDER="no" BORDER="0"
FRAMESPACING="0" ROWS="*, 80">
<FRAME SRC="black.html" NAME="main"
MARGINWIDTH="0" MARGINHEIGHT="0"
SCROLLING="auto">
<FRAME SRC="red.html" NAME="top"
MARGINWIDTH="0" MARGINHEIGHT="0"
SCROLLING="auto">
</FRAMESET>
```

By combining the border elements and `MARGINWDITH` and `MARGINHEIGHT`, you tighten up the layout and create a great seamless web page layout. The `FRAMESPACING` or `BORDER` attribute works much like `CELLSPACING` in tables. This controls the space between each frame, hence each HTML page. By setting it to zero, the pages sit closer together and you lose the borders. `MARGINWIDTH` and `MARGINHEIGHT` for each `<FRAME>` tag do double duty with the `FRAMESPACING` or `BORDER` attribute and specify the top and bottom margins of each frame/HTML page. By setting them also to zero, they erase any visible space.

> ## Note:
> The `FRAMESPACING` attribute only works in Internet Explorer. The `BORDER` tag works for both Netscape and Internet Explorer.

It's also important that each `FRAME` tag be named with the `NAME` attribute. Even if your layout isn't that complex, it's a good rule of thumb to make

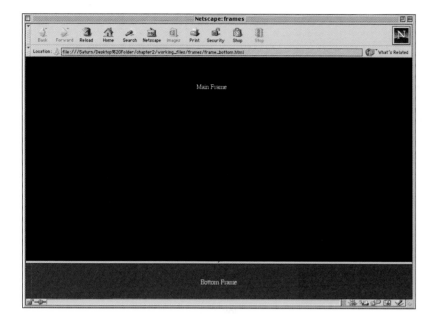

figure 2.22

Two panel frames layout, main area with bottom frame.

sure that the grid is organized. Depending on what function each frame is playing within your layout, the name should be one that is obvious for you to work with. For example, your main content frame can be named "main" and your navigation frame can be named "nav". That way when you are working on targeting frames and links to specific frames, you'll know that every-thing is going in the right place.

Tip:

Just in case users are visiting your site with browsers that don't support frames, you can use the <NOFRAMES></NOFRAMES> tag in your frame index page. Add the desired content between the tags and users who can't see frames will see something.

Nesting Frames

For more advanced framesets, just as there are nested tables, there are nested frames. Nested frames can help you organize your information better but can also keep things loading faster. As long as you can keep track of specific targeting, you'll have no problems keeping track of the individual frames. An example of nesting frames is shown in Figure 2.23.

Here are the frame targeting attributes:

- TARGET="_self" (Default) Link loads in the frame from which it was clicked.
- TARGET="_parent" Link clears any previous framesets and loads in the full browser window.
- TARGET="_window" or "_blank" Link opens in a new browser window.

- TARGET="_top" Like parent, link clears framesets and loads in the full browser window.
- TARGET="name of frame" Like parent, link clears framesets and loads in the full browser window.

```
<FRAMESET COLS="85,*">
    <FRAME SRC="side.html"
    NAME="navbar" SCROLLING="no">
    <FRAMESET ROWS="80,*,80">
        <FRAME SRC="top.html"
        NAME="banner"
        SCROLLING="no">
        <FRAME SRC="middle.html"
        NAME="main"
        SCROLLING="auto">
        <FRAME SRC="bottom.html"
        NAME="footer"
        SCROLLING="no" NORESIZE>
    </FRAMESET>
</FRAMESET>
```

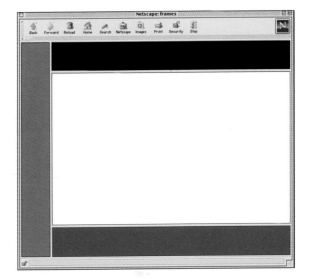

figure 2.23
More complex nested framesets.

Summary

Keeping the needs of your audience in mind as you create your web page layout is important. Whether you decide to use tables or frames, thinking of your web page as a whole will help you design a more effective site. With so many available options, it's best to try a few techniques and see if they can work on your site. Tables are still probably the most widely use HTML for laying out content. Whether it's colored tables, graphics that are pieced together for dif- ferent animation techniques, or more complex nested tables for a full-page layout, tables are a staple in web design. As for frames, they have become much easier to use, and creatively you can better utilize and organize the overall space of your browser window. The most important thing to keep track of is targeting the right links in frames. Nonetheless, both tables and frames can work together to help you build a great layout.

URLS In This Chapter

- **Shockwave** www.shockwave.com
- **Target** www.target.com
- **Star-Spangled Banner, Smithsonian** americanhistory.si.edu/ssb
- **blank and cables** www.blankandcables.com
- **Neutrogena** www.neutrogena.com/careers

Inspirational Design Model

Daniel Jenett
Jenett.com

"Everything I do in America is filtered through

my knowledge of a different culture and lan-

guage. The way I experience my surround-

ings is still very visual because there are

many things in every day that surprise me."

figure 1

jenett.com opening animation

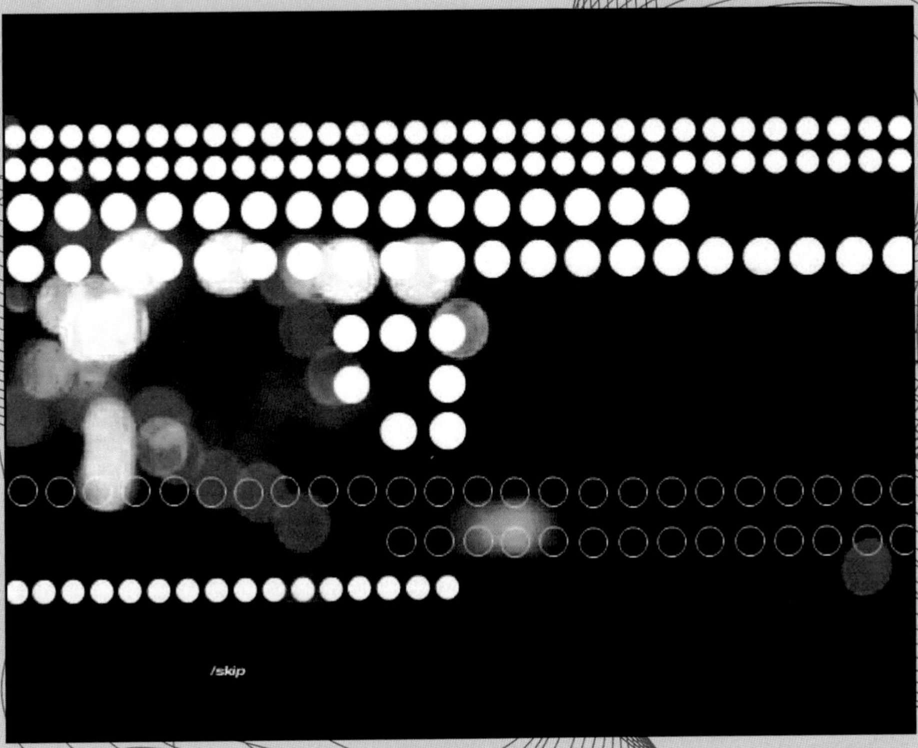

/skip

If there's one thing about designer Daniel Jenett that most people might not get from the forward-thinking work that he does is that he *loves* coffee. There was a time, before he relocated back to his native Germany, that he worked in San Francisco at frog design. Daniel could be relied upon at least twice a day to make the trek with me across the street to get coffee at Café Centro in South Park. It was from those coffee moments that we formed a friendship based on our love for coffee, as well as discovering our mutual passion for interactive design, and its potential with Broadband.

With various design stints with Razorfish in New York and later Los Angeles, Daniel decided to move back to Hamburg, Germany to start his own design studio with his brother, Florian. Focused on making his Broadband dream a reality, Daniel's plan of a creative environment is something we can all aspire to—a place for free exploration, true creativity, and plenty of coffee.

What inspires you?

Similar basic ideas are the source of inspiration in all my free projects and in much client work I am involved with. The main difference for me is that I can state something with my own work that can exist without (logical) explanations, and I can follow ideas uninhibited. The bigger the clients are, or the more tangible their interests are, the harder it is to break ground. With that

said, I am also enjoying being in a fixed framework with the companies I am working for, and having the freedom to focus on the art aspect of the work more than the business side.

I also learn tremendously from all the people I am working with—Meta, frog, and Razorfish are places with many like-minded creatives. I sincerely enjoy the plurality of opinions and approaches that I have seen in the last 2–3 years.

figure 2

jenett.com homepage

How do you explore your creativity in projects?

My own web site started off as a very classical designer's approach; it was basically my portfolio in a different medium. You know I am a trained communication designer, so after having left my first company I felt I needed to present my work to potential clients, and so on. It was very intuitional the way I designed it. Basically it laid out the way I always work on my free projects. I always try to make statements with or through my work on a visual communication level by following rather abstract concepts.

I practically do not use anybody else's material; I use my own copy, my own photography, and so on. That way I have control about even the smallest aspect of the product; there is no hidden meaning in there that I was not aware of.

The portfolio section of my web site, for example, uses a lot of images in the background that are tinted in deep red, to resemble photographic processes as you can find in the darkroom, because I based the whole layout on a black and white negative-stripe from the days when I was developing films and prints myself. So there is a context that connects the different levels of the site, and it is a communication design way of expressing something rather than an information-driven way of working.

My contribution to the Remedi Project is a comparison of different media formats: static, active, and interactive. All three circulate around the idea of typography that is not generated in Adobe Photoshop but actually shot on the street. Of course I would not tell all the thinking that went into it, so the message comes across in a subtle way, or not at all.

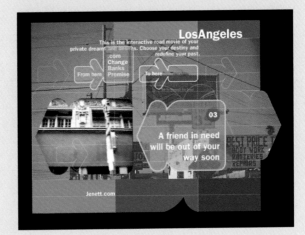

figures 3 and 4
Born Magazine / Los Angeles

A more recent project that I did for *Born* magazine is a knock-off of one of my own projects. It uses and re-uses elements that I established in a piece for the Italian school Fabrica earlier this year. The hidden statement here is that it is actually the content that matters and not the form itself.

You've worked in the design industry for a while, having been at places like Meta Design, frog design, and now at Razorfish. But, you also have a distinct personal design style when you do your own work. How do you separate your work work from your personal work? Do you have a different process?

My creative process really isn't a process. I have to think with all my senses for quite some time, seeing, drawing, talking, running around until I have one (or more) things in the project that I'd love to follow. These are usually pretty minor aspects or attributes, just enough to make myself interested. Next I have to sit down and actually design. In the old understanding of the word, design in itself means a process of trial and error. So I do iterations for myself that I compare (with my sense of how things have to be) and recombine or reject or approve until I am satisfied. Sometimes I also need feedback to see somebody else's reaction to what I am doing. If I agree with the person I am showing my work to, I am happy; otherwise, I try to not completely reject his opinion.

figure 5

Montreux, Suisse
Project

Of course I am talking about projects that I do for myself rather than for a client; usually I compare professional projects with the brand attributes and everything else I can know about the desired digital product.

In general I try to bring as much of my personal work as possible into my daytime projects, and I have benefited from this approach in many ways. The clients as well, I hope! On a design level I am doing something very similar to Joshua Davis; I am reusing ideas and schemes of my private work in client projects and vice versa. Maybe there isn't really that much of a difference after all.

Please talk more about the project you did for Fabrica. What was the goal? How did you come up with your concept?

Oh ja, Fabrica. I was trying to do a couple of things in this project. First I wanted to show how digital video can be used and integrated into a web design project, and second I wanted to follow a specific idea of mine: I believe that images are very influential for what we do and how we evaluate things. The point here is that I am haunted by images that I received by watching TV when I was a kid. By that time there were a lot of American soaps and series on German TV—God knows why, Kojak and Streets of San Francisco. So I have to travel to all the places that I have already seen on TV when I was small and easy to influence. Maybe a little weak for a

concept, but definitely it is a project about New York including all the classic tourist places, seen through the eyes of my PC100.

The project also has a follow-up. When I was doing a contribution for *Born* magazine (www.bornmag.com), I was using the same structure and layout to emphasize the importance of content. By just changing some aspects and not the complete structure, the small differences are actually emphasized, the differences between New York and Los Angeles. Also the projects of course reflect stations of my worldwide design travel.

In my more personal projects, I almost always do the complete job myself, including photography, illustration, and of course programming and design. This way I have a tighter control of all connotations within the material, and it also helps creating a voice.

Your passion for Broadband has been ongoing for the last few years. How do you think Broadband will change the way in which the digital medium will be thought of and designed for?

Oh, that is a tricky question. My quick answer would be that once the bandwidth is no longer a restriction, neither for up- or downstream, the whole world will again change dramatically. There will no longer be a digital medium, everything will be digital, and by that it will become ubiquitous. How long the way will be that gets us there and how many twisted bends it will take nobody can really predict, as much as how many brilliant ideas will lose against more populistic approaches.

From a design perspective, a renaissance of communication design (instead of information design) will certainly shape the picture within the next years. The big question about what design really is will become more obvious when we realize that there is no big difference between the tools used to make broadcast design identities and banner animations.

Out of my head, I will watch the following areas: digital film-making, storytelling and life action, animation, motion graphics, kinetic information (design), moving identity, and of course screen type. All these will be in high demand to design non-linear communication spaces, places, and projects.

Now what does that mean for designers? I guess they will at some point in time have to decide if they want to become film directors or focus on screen graphic design.

Personally the biggest question for me in design is not really affected by the changes of our environment. Only my means of expression become richer and easier to use.

figure 6
Fabrica / New York

Who are your design heroes?
Not necessarily in this order: Paul Rand, Dan Friedman, Lutz, Basquiat, Andy Warhol, Goya (and now the list extends endlessly...). A few more: Cindy Sherman, Gauguin, and Vivienne Westwood.

figure 7
Gas Book Project

Do you have any advice that you would like to share with all the aspiring designers out there?

Take earplugs, forget everything you ever thought and heard about what you have in front of you, and *just see*! Eyes are so much smarter than your mouth. You can see if it is good all by yourself.

If you could be a superhero, who would you be and why?

There are really two superheroes that I am like: the Incredible Hulk and the Green Lantern. I would probably be the Incredible Hulk. Little talking, badly dressed, not really good or bad as far as I remember, a bit aggressive—not that I am aggressive.

The Green Lantern I like because the character is so much based on the weird logo. I do also sympathize with Batman as drawn by Frank Miller— I think it's called "The Return of Batman."

In general, superheroes have a very simple life and that is definitely different with me, so the dark ones are more appealing to me. And also I really don't remember the last time I read a comic.

What are three things in the world you can't live without?

I do have a long-lasting love affair with coffee… In order of importance: Friends and family are the top priority, although it might not look like that to them.

On a day-by-day basis I must admit that I am a total email junkie, and besides coffee I really crave good food...and then: "Everybody loves the sunshine." I am a much better person in a nice car with good music turned on, driving from Montreux to Lausanne on the coastal route in Switzerland.

Okay—three tangible things: cell phone, banana yogurt, and warm water.

Please name a bad habit you have.
I am always too early for meetings and appointments.

Daniel Jenett URL:

- **Daniel Jenett**   `www.jenett.com`

On being the "Foreigner":
Okay, here it comes: I am actually German. Everything I do in America is filtered through my knowledge of a different culture and language. Of course I understand a lot about the U.S. and the common habits, but I can still get excited about packaging and architecture and cars here like any other tourist. The way I experience my surroundings is still very visual because there are many things in every day that surprise me (because they are different from Europe).

I know that sounds a bit childish, but basically what I want to say is that the pleasure of seeing for me is essential in my life and in my work. I want to communicate the things that matter to me.

On lost worlds:
The first things I remember drawing were actually maps of some kind of dream-country. Complete with streets and rivers, lakes, and very important bridges and canals. I must have been between five and seven. Then and now I can get lost in working with visuals; there is a certain thought-lessness that I feel is very liberating (that sounds horrible but it's the truth!). I just like to create very much.

figures 8 and 9

Remedi Project / Typography

Type Effects

Enhancing Your Interface with Stunning Typography

CHAPTER 3

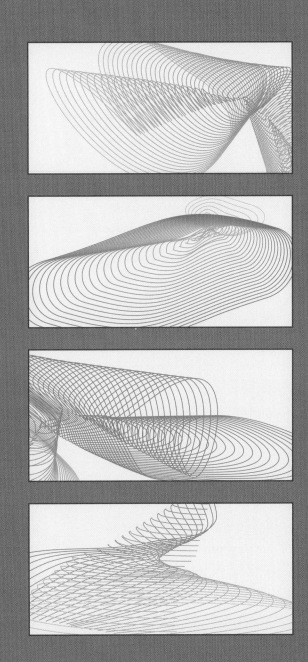

Typography is an integral part of web design. Type is much more than simply paragraphs, sentences, and blocks of text. It can be used to graphically add emotion to your design. It can create a context or feeling for the subject matter. When typography is appropriately used, it adds a new level of meaning to the words that are being typed.

This chapter introduces you to some of the basic ways you can use type effectively in your design. We will introduce you to the language and terminology associated with typography, as well as teach you some simple tricks to use in your HTML. What you will learn in this chapter is a springboard for unlimited possibilities in future designs. Think of type not only as a means to deliver copy, but also as a way to illustrate the words that are being delivered.

Type and the Web

The fundamental basis of design is typography and the ability to use type in both a communicative and beautiful manner. With the web, there have been many problems in trying to achieve the caliber of design predicated by print and motion graphics. HTML type served a clear purpose in the beginning because it was used more for communicating rather than being beautiful. With the rise of the web, there was a clear indication that the aesthetics of type needed to be there also.

A Brief Type History

Setting type was not always as easy as the press of a key. Originally, all type had to be set by hand. Craftspeople painstakingly placed tiny metal letters into lines with precision tools. Typesetting was an art form that only those with a steady hand and a lot of patience could endure. Most of the vernacular surrounding typography dates back to traditional typesetting. Some common typographical terms include these:

- **Typeface:** The name of the style of type you are using (such as Times, Helvetica, or Courier). The "face" part of the word originally referred to the flat part of the metal letter that impressed upon the paper. Today we commonly interchange the word typeface with font.
- **Size:** Letters are measured in points; the text you are reading now is set in 10-point type.
- **Weight:** The thickness of the letters you use, such as bold, black, heavy, demibold, and so on.
- **Style:** A variation of the typeface being used, such as Italic, Condensed, or Wide.
- **Leading:** The amount of space between each line of text.
- **Kerning:** The amount of space between each letter.

To gain a better grasp of typography, there are few great web sites that can introduce you to the intricacies and history of the evolution of type. TypoGRAPHIC, a site created by Razorfish, contains valuable information on the history of type, a full glossary, and recommended readings (see Figures 3.1–3.5). Another useful site is Counterspace (see Figures 3.6–3.7). The site uses beautiful typography in Flash to describe the history, anatomy, classification, and anything else you want to know about type.

Now that typography is making it onto the web, we can take advantage of the great possibilities that effective text design offers.

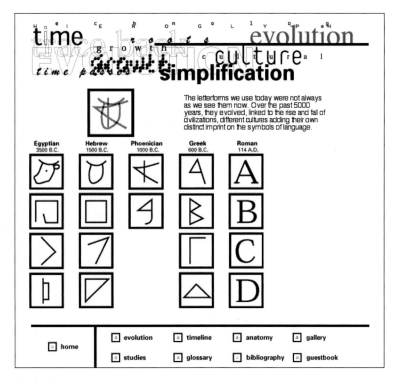

figure 3.1

The typoGraphic web site visually illustrates the details of type.

3.2

3.3

3.4

3.5

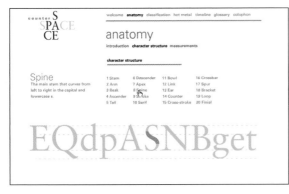

3.6

3.7

figures 3.2–3.5

Screens from the gallery of the typoGRAPHIC web site.

figures 3.6 and 3.7

Counterspace uses Flash to interactively teach about type.

Font Attributes: The Basics

The basics of HTML typography is to understand all the attributes so that you can later mix them together for a look that can be cool, classic, elegant, or whatever you want. Font sizes, colors, HTML, and system typefaces all come into play when dealing with type for the web. You can build upon these basics to create the special effects later in this chapter.

Here are the common tags used for HTML fonts:

- Font coloring `<FONT COLOR>`
- Font naming `<FONT FACE>`
- Font sizing `<FONT SIZE>`

Note:

When choosing colors for your text and links, make sure that the colors don't clash in a way that would be hard for the user to read. Legibility is also a part of the overall design aesthetic. It's also a good idea to keep your HTML text in the web-safe palette. This way, you can be confident that no one sees broken, fuzzy text. You can read more about the web-safe palette in Chapter 4, "The Power of Color."

Thinking of creative ways to use HTML text can be difficult, but it can be done. Just look at the p2output site (see Figures 3.8–3.10). The majority of this site uses images for text, but the designers did some really creative HTML work in the press section. Using the different font attribute tags, the site combines HTML text in different sizes in a subtle gray color that complements the link text. The mixture and combination with the background image work well to create a seamless integration.

There is a limited range of font sizes as dictated by HTML; they usually go from size 1 to 6, with 1 being the smallest and 6 being the largest. The standard base font is a size 3. The code for specifying fonts is quite simple:

```
<font size="1">font size=1</font>
<font size="2">font size=2</font>
<font size="3">font size=3</font>
<font size="4">font size=4</font>
<font size="5">font size=5</font>
<font size="6">font size=6</font>
```

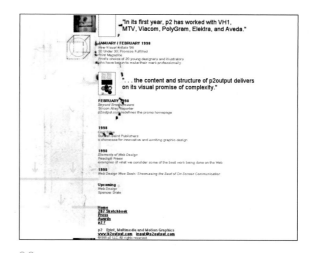

3.8

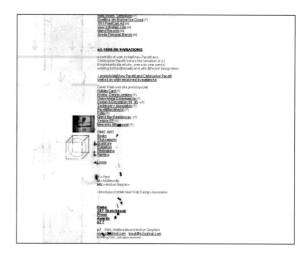

3.9

figures 3.8–3.10
P2output combines simple background patterns and a few images with HTML text to create a useful hierarchy and compelling composition. The rough background texture combined with HTML type creates an interesting depth in the composition.

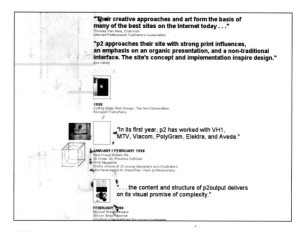

3.10

You can create a really interesting composition by interchanging type sizes (see Figure 3.11).

Take also into consideration that you don't need to specify font size=3 because this is the default browser size font. But if it isn't used for too much text, this font can be a good choice in case the user has changed font size preferences in his or her browser.

Another way to specify font sizes is to use + or -. For instance, you can use the line of code `<font size="+2">`, which is the same as `<font size="5">`. Why? Because the base font size is 3, using the + or − formula, you are adding or subtracting from the base font size. Therefore, 3+2=5, so you have a font size of 5. It's a personal preference which technique you use. `<font size="-2">font size= -2</font>` is actually the same as the following: `<font size="1">font size=1</font>`.

HTML Default Fonts Versus Computer System Fonts

Tired of the default font Times New Roman? Most designers are. That's why you often see pages displayed with HTML type such as teletype, code, or preformatted text. Teletype (`<tt></tt>`), code (`<code></code>`), and preformatted text (`<pre></pre>`) look very much the same, using Courier as the display text (see Figure 3.12). Depending on the monitor and platform, code is supposed to appear as a fixed-

figure 3.11
The only specifications used in this composition are type size and color.

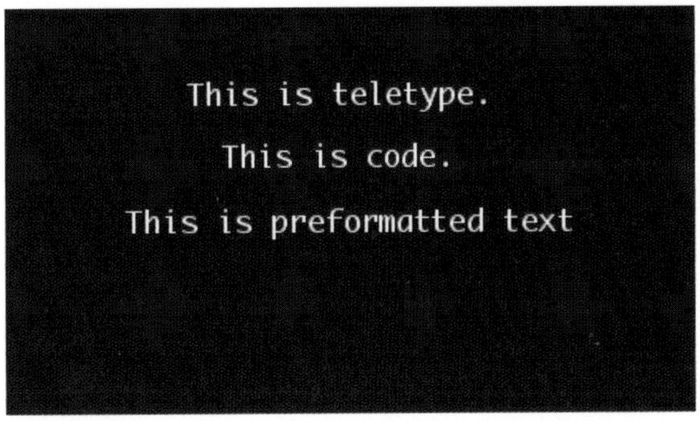

figure 3.12
Preformatted text.

width font and teletype is supposed to create a keyboard typeface. Preformatted text can be an alternative usage for layout because it aligns the items within the `<pre>` tags in the exact same place on the web page as it appears on the HTML document.

Unfortunately, the default Times New Roman type can often be hard to read. It is best to test your pages in a few different typefaces before committing your site to the default. Verdana and Arial are both easy to read and look clean for large bodies of text. Experiment with the different sizes and faces and choose a typeface that is both appropriate for the design and easy to read.

Most designers, however, have found that for even more type options they choose to specify system typefaces with the `<font face>` tag to have a customized look. Because there are a few base fonts that come with every Macintosh and Windows machine, you won't have to worry about whether or not these fonts are installed on a user's machine.

The Carlson Non-Flash site uses the combination of Verdana, Arial, and Helvetica to ensure that users on all platforms see virtually the same thing (see Figure 3.13).

```
<font face="Verdana, Arial, Helvetica,
sans-serif; *">
```

The wildcard * indicates that if none of the fonts reside on the system, the default browser font will appear. The default font will appear regardless of the * sign anyway. The system displays the font based on the order specified. The first typeface detected by the system will be the one displayed.

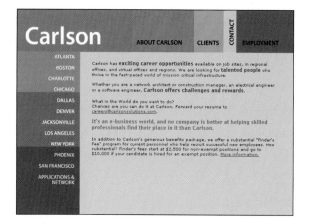

figure 3.13

Designers specified the serif typefaces so everyone sees the same thing.

Mac Type Versus PC Type

You've seen the differences in the system fonts on the Mac and PC, but as a designer, I'm sure you're also aware of the many other differences between these two platforms.

For instance, there are visible font-size differences on Macs and PCs. Fonts on PCs tend to be larger. This size difference can be frustrating because sometimes it can affect the design. From text in tables to text in frames, you have to keep the slight differences in mind as you design.

Special Type Effects

You can enhance the design of your site with a few quick and simple HTML type effects. Special looks such as drop caps and creative text alignment can give some style to your site without leaving you bandwidth heavy.

Another great effect is the text color change rollover that gives some simple link color changing to your HTML links. If you find yourself out of ideas for HTML type, this section suggests some techniques to help you achieve the effects you want.

Drop Caps

Creating a drop cap look is a simple combination of `<font size>` and `<font color>`. To create this look that is often used in books and magazines, see Figure 3.14. The paragraph begins with the letter O. Similar to classic book design, the first letter of the chapter is large and the rest of the copy is in the normal text size.

Here's what the code looks like:

```
<font size="6"
color="#FFFF66">o</font>nce upon
a time
```

But what about when you want more size options? This is when simple style sheet commands such as inline HTML styles come into play. Without coding a whole document in style sheets, you can insert styles directly within your HTML.

Within your HTML, instead of `<font size>`, use `<font style>` and the accompanying font-size attribute and pick a font size you like.

```
<font style="font-size: 40pt"
color="FFFF66">O</font>nce upon a time
```

The final result (see Figure 3.15) is a font displayed in 40 points. Quite a difference from a simple `<font size=6>`.

figure 3.14
Drop caps create a classic effect.

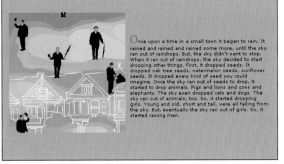

figure 3.15
The drop cap appears smaller in this example.

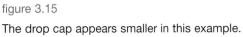

Text Color Change Rollovers

Another fun text treatment is creating simple rollovers that change the link color of the HTML text. It's more of a special effect than navigational necessity and can be a simple way to call attention to your links (see Figure 3.16).

You can change the color by adding `<a href="" onmouseover="javascript:this.style. color='colorname'">` to set the color for the rollover state. You can do the same for the `<onmouseout>` command if you want, but leaving it blank defaults to the HTML link color that you specified in the `<body>` of your HTML.

The code here shows that the color changes to yellow when the mouse is rolled over the link. You can use color names or the equivalent hex codes to name colors:

```
<A HREF="PAGE.HTML"
ONMOUSEOVER="javascript:this.style.
color='YELLOW'"ONMOUSEOUT="javascript:
this.style.color=''">LINK HERE</A>
```

For Netscape, the JavaScript is a bit different and takes a little more effort. The JavaScript needs to live in the HEAD of your HTML document. Each link has to be named a layer; here "text" is specified as a layer. The first part indicates the rollover state of the link color (yellow) and the second part indicates the static color (brown):

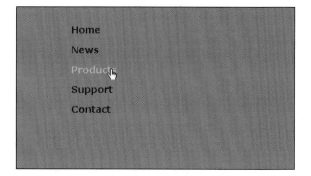

figure 3.16
The word "Products" is highlighted when rolled over.

```
<HEAD>
<SCRIPT LANGUAGE="JAVASCRIPT1.2">
function changeTo(){
document.layers["Text"].document.write(
"<FONT COLOR=BLUE>
<A HREF=HTTP://WWW.URLHERE.COM>
LINK HERE</A></FONT>");
document.layers["Text"].document.close(
);
}
function changeFrom(){
document.layers["Text"].document.write(
"<FONT COLOR=RED>LINK HERE</FONT>");
document.layers["Text"].document.close(
);
}
function link(){
{
</SCRIPT>
```

Then in the body of your HTML document, you need to specify the link with the `<LAYER>` tag:

```
<LAYER NAME="Text"
ONMOUSEOVER=changeTo();
ONMOUSEOUT=changeFrom();
ONMOUSEDOWN=Link()><FONT
COLOR="RED">LINK HERE</FONT>
</LAYER>
```

You get the same results as Internet Explorer, but make sure when you have more links you organize and separate the code well.

Text Alignment

With some creative text alignment, you can allow your text to jump out and blend within your pages in creative ways. Use tables or `<PRE>` tags to get the effect you want.

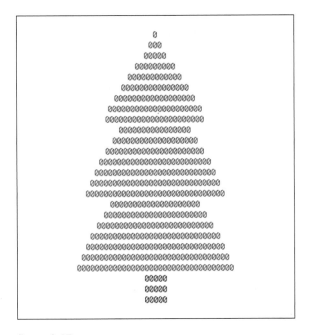

figure 3.17

You can make simple illustrations with code by specifying text alignment.

Here's the code for a simple text alignment shown in Figure 3.17:

```
<CENTER>
<PRE><FONT COLOR="#006600">
0
000
00000
000000000
000000000000
000000000000000
00000000000000000
0000000000000000000
00000000000000000000000
00000000000000000000000
0000000000000000
00000000000000000000
00000000000000000000000
000000000000000000000000
0000000000000000000000000000
0000000000000000000000000000000
0000000000000000000000000000000000
0000000000000000000000000000000000000000
0000000000000000000
00000000000000000000000
00000000000000000000000000
0000000000000000000000000000000
0000000000000000000000000000000
000000000000000000000000000000000
0000000000000000000000000000000000000000
00000000000000000000000000000000000000000
<font color="#333300">00000
00000
00000</font>
</font></PRE>
</CENTER>
```

By using the `<PRE></PRE>` tags, you can format your pages based on how you format the text within the tags. That means any line breaks, spaces, and so on will appear! It's not meant for general formatting of HTML pages, but you can use them for special creative instances. Test your artistic coding skills by creating simple illustrations of plants or animals with code.

Anti-Aliasing Type

So you're in Photoshop and you see the Anti-Alias pull-down menu in the Type box. What does this mean? By simply selecting a level of Anti-Aliasing (None, Crisp, Strong, or Smooth) your text will appear more blended (see Figure 3.18). Anti-aliasing removes all the jaggies—those pixels that line around the edge of the graphic text—and blends them to the background.

For example, in Figure 3.19 the bottom graphic is anti-aliased to a green background and the top is not. Notice the difference that anti-aliasing can make. At a 500% zoom, you can see that when text is aliased, the pixels of the text to the background are defined by harsh lines that are in turn blended in the aliased version on the bottom.

Is it a good idea to always anti-alias your graphics? At times, when you're working with transparent graphics, you can get better results by leaving your text aliased. This is particularly true when you work with patterned backgrounds or when you intentionally create pixel-like text for the sake of design.

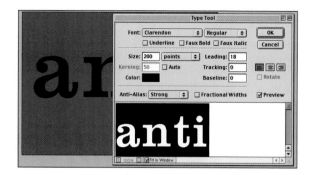

figure 3.18

In Photoshop, you can select a level of Anti-Aliasing in the type window.

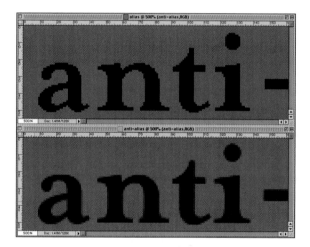

figure 3.19

A close-up view of text.

Using Vector Graphics Tools to Achieve Maximum Type

You might be wondering when you should use HTML text and when you should use graphics. The answer is simple. Use HTML text for the main body of text and for things that need to be updated quickly and easily. Use graphics for times when you want to use special text effects, blend text and images, or use color combinations for enhancement to pages through graphic headers, buttons, and navigation.

Most designers use Photoshop when creating their graphics for the web. What some designers don't know is that vector graphics tools such as Macromedia FreeHand or Adobe Illustrator can give you more precise text leading, kerning, and more.

FreeHand has the most text power, although Illustrator and Photoshop are made by the same company and work seamlessly together. We aren't going to be biased here, so whichever tool you use, here are some techniques on how to create some type that will look good on the web.

Laying Out Your Type

For best text results, you can lay out all your type in FreeHand or Illustrator and save it as an EPS file. This ensures that you can keep all the kerning and leading information that doesn't work well in Photoshop. The result is that you'll have more control over your text, and smaller point sizes will be more legible.

First, create all your type in FreeHand or Illustrator (see Figure 3.20). For words that are going to lie on the same line, make sure you have them aligned all together on one line in Illustrator or FreeHand so that they anti-alias the same.

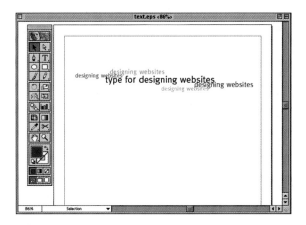

figure 3.20

Text laid out in Illustrator.

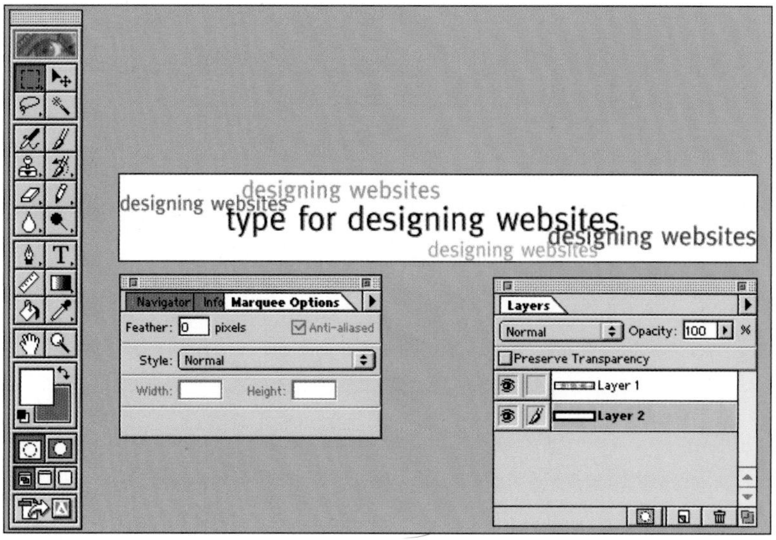

figure 3.21

Importing the EPS file into Photoshop.

Then as you import the file into Photoshop (see Figure 3.21), you can cut and paste each word as you need it in your graphic. Notice that even the small 10-point type looks nice and legible.

Curved Text

Another interesting text effect allows you to create curved text, such as that curved around the buttons in the Barbie site.

First draw an outlined circle with the arc you want your type to lay on. Next, click on the Type tool and hold, and select the third option of the text tool (see Figure 3.22). (You should have the circle selected while you do this.)

Choose the typeface, color, and size you want. Now, select on the circle outline where you want to begin typing. Type your word (see Figure 3.23).

Finally, export the document as a Photoshop EPS and import the text in Photoshop you want included with your graphic (see Figure 3.24).

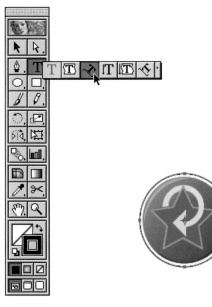

3.22

3.23

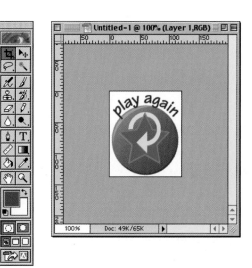

figures 3.22–3.24

It's easy to wrap test around a
shape in Illustrator.

3.24

Experimental Type

One of the best ways to learn type tricks is by experimenting. Sometimes the best designs happen from a computer "mistake." If you approach a project knowing it is an experiment, you will be more free with your design decisions. Things will happen that you never could have planned, and you can use what you learn in client projects.

Fuse 98 is an entire site dedicated to experimental type projects on the web (see Figures 3.25–3.28). Look at all the different ways type is used to add emotion and interest to the compositions. Although three years in web time can seem like eons, the site still has cutting-edge examples of innovative use of typography on the web.

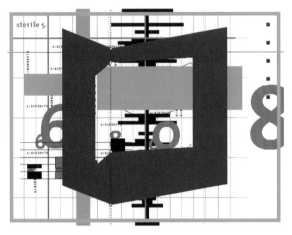

3.25

3.26

3.27

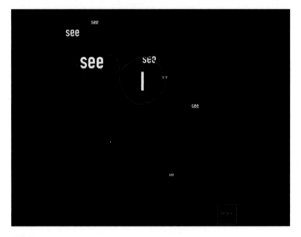

3.28

figures 3.25–3.28

Experimental use of typography
online in the Fuse Lab.

Summary

The possibilities for innovation in the world of Internet typography are unlimited and, with medium still so young, there are millions of designs yet to be created.

No matter what text treatment you choose to use, don't think you are limited by the options provided by HTML. With combinations of font color, size, and face, and working in combination with images, you can successfully achieve some different techniques that definitely enhance your web pages.

URLs In This Chapter

- **Typographic** `typographic.rsub.com`
- **Counterspace**
  HTTP://counterspace.motivo.com/
  `www.studiomotiv.com/counterspace/`
- **p2output** `www.p2output.com`
- **fuse98** `www.fuse98.com`
- **Carlson Solutions**

  `www.carlsonsolutions.com`

Inspirational Design Model

Jimmy Chen
Typographic

"...without my own playground, I wouldn't

have been able to do interesting things to

clients' sites."

figure 1

typographic.com

Like the hidden tunnelway into John Malkovich's head in the movie *Being John Malkovich*, who wouldn't pay a ticket to see what the world looks like through the eyes of designer Jimmy Chen? After all, with his slick visionary site, Typographic (`www.typographic.com`), SoCal-based Jimmy Chen has painted himself a world in which intricate, nebulous formations of letters and words smolder and flicker across the screen, inviting us into his creative stream of consciousness.

A self-proclaimed TV addict, Jimmy is also the guy you wanna hang out with. He could even be dubbed the "Hemmingway" of the web design world—not for prose, but for the number of creative references he can make to "having a drink." You can't have a conversation with Jimmy without references to drinking, TV, or music—his favorite things. He's the kind of friend that you email at 2 a.m. and get a response two minutes later. (He's a hard worker.) His emails are in turn filled with a multitude of short rants that would make even Dennis Miller proud. Jimmy Chen is the all-around guy with a casual lifestyle and carefree attitude. It almost makes you wonder, "Hmm…if I just watch TV all day and drink beer, could I build a great web site?"

What inspires you?
Competition. Typically, it would be the television. So many nice things happen in there. Other things, such as emotional problems, can also influence me. Anger is another good thing to have.

How did you come up with the concept for Typographic.com?
I would say same as above. Every time I do a version of it, I try to do something different. I don't want to be recycling crap all of the time like other designers. I am just trying to prove something to myself…to see if I can do it. Not up to other designers. At the beginning, most of the concepts came from personal experiences. Now it's more and more about the animation itself. Maybe it's bad sometimes, doing it for the sake of it. But at least it's a motivation. It's different all of the time. I may change my mind some time down the road and do something completely different.

What's your dream project?
Luckily I experienced that a few times. All of them involve clients who are really open to ideas. And most of them involve pushing myself both creatively and technically.

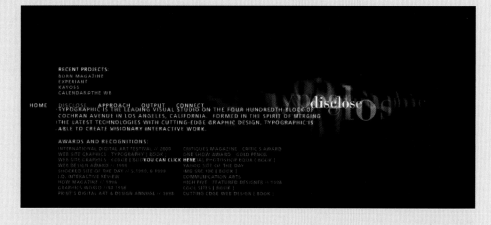

figures 2 and 3
typographic.com

Which projects have you felt that way about and why?

There were a few. Some are now either offline or updated by some other people. One of my favorite ones is Getty Center's Gateway site (`www.getty.edu`). Now there's some wacky drawing sitting there. How sad. That was done about two years ago. It's going to be redesigned soon.

I worked with Getty a couple of times before, and they were pretty receptive to my ideas and designs. After the lady that I worked with was promoted to a higher position, I was fortunate enough to do it to their Gateway site. It was cool because I had to be creative while being intelligent about usability. Coding the site was pretty fun. It wasn't as much as the project before this one, which was 400 or so pages.

Warner/Chappell Music (www.warnerchappell
.com), Inc was a fun one earlier in my Internet
years. I went wacko over the design. Didn't really think about anything else besides the design.
But I really liked working on it. Although the
design took more than a year to do.

I guess I would have to say Typographic, too.
Because without my own playground, I wouldn't
have been able to do interesting things to
clients' sites.

**What's your creative process when you are
working on a project? How do you factor in
the technology?**

Sometimes I don't even have a process when I
work on a project. Most of the time, the process
would go like this: Open up Photoshop, stare at
a blank canvas for an hour or so, and then start
putting text or texture until I see something
potentially useful.

Usually before the project starts, I think about
what sort of technology I would like to use for a
particular project. Whether there's design technology or server technology, I like to iron that out
before I start.

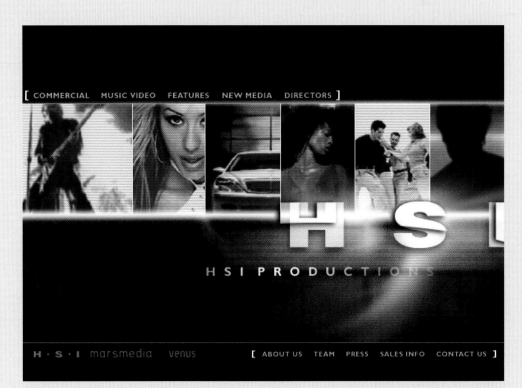

figure 4
HSI Productions

How do you think Broadband will change the way in which the digital medium will be thought of and designed for?

I think the message that we are going to communicate will be a lot more verbose. Personally, I think the change that I will experience will be gradual. I've been sort of pushing the limits of tolerable downloading time for a site...I am just afraid one day I will be making a 10MB splash page simply because people have the bandwidth.

All I know is that when that technology becomes available for everyday people, the experience will heighten.

You do some amazing things with type. How did you develop a passion for motion graphics and type?

Not all that amazing...but I try. This type thing started when I was in school reading books/ magazine from Carson, Keedy, Brody, Deck, Makela, etc. I was fascinated by type. During my first job as a designer, I used type as graphical images because there was no access to photographs. I was lazy, so I used type. It was a corporate company, so I got to use lousy font icons and stuff. During that time, I got my first font catalog from T-26. And then I started designing typefaces for fun. I've always doodled letters, so I decided to design all 256 freaking characters. Licensed two typefaces to T-26... now that

figure 5
Summer @ the WB

I think about it, it was kind of ugly. I did about six or seven different ones, but after those two, I didn't want to do them anymore. It just took too much time.

The motion part didn't come in until later... I guess during the initial Remedi Project (www.theremediproject.com) launch. I did some flat graphics, then I saw John Hill's QT movies and thought to myself how lame my part was; I had to do something about it. Then I tried to put my images in motion. Ever since then, I just wanted to do as much as I can to give type a life. Most of the time, I have no idea what I am doing. As a matter of fact, I don't know what I am doing now.

Did I even answer the question? Essentially, I like pretty pictures.

Who are your design heros?
Too many to name. I don't want to be unfair and name some and forget others.

Do you have any advice that you would like to share with all the aspiring designers out there?
Be cool, stay in school.

Use a lot of drop shadows.

Listen to other designers.

If you could be a superhero, who would you be and why?
Yikes, Mister Fantastic is the first one that comes to mind. I am sure there are other ones that I'd rather be, but this one is probably my first choice. Man, he can stretch like a crazy mofo. Um, since I am one of the laziest people on earth, I would love to be able to sit on my couch and stretch my hands/head and or whatever so I can "not move" and still be able to do something. Don't really care if he is smart or anything like that...just the flexibility which can increase my productivity through laziness.

What are three things in the world you can't live without?
Other than water, food, and air?

The Geek in me: emails, multiple computers/ monitors, and all-in-one remote control. The Alcoholic: Sierra Nevada, Sierra Nevada, and Sierra Nevada. The Geeky Alcoholic: waterproof keyboard (with a computer attached to it), Pink Dot (including Internet), and pink flowers. The LA driver: my right middle finger, my left middle finger, and my horn. General things: music, TV, and food.

So to sum it up, my three things are: multiple-waterproof-computers-and-are-networked-that-will-allow-me-to-email-and-order-every-thing-including-Sierra-Nevada-from-Pink-Dot, shoot-my-middle-fingers-at-idiots-on-the-freeway/streets-and, when-I-go-home-I-am-able-to-listen-to-my-music-and-watch-tv-con-trolled-by-that-all-in-one-remote-control-while-eating-food-ordered-online...and maybe take a freakin' math class to find out what the hell "three" means.

figure 6

Scenes from typographic.com

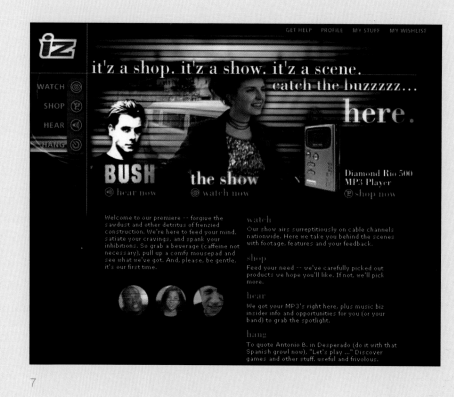

7

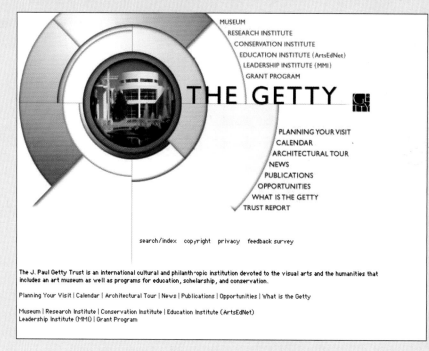

figure 7

The iz site

figure 8

The Getty Center

8

Please name a bad habit you have.

Being me. I am a walking bad habit. Name it, I've got it. Refer to the two previous answers.

Jimmy Chen URLs:

- **Typographic** `www.typographic.com`
- **The Getty Center** `www.getty.edu`
- **HSI Productions**
  `www.hsiproductions.com`
- **Warner/Chappell**
  `www.warnerchappell.com`

On architecture:

My dad was an architect. He was the one who taught me how to draw straight lines and cars. I wanted to be an architect; studied it for a while. I gave it up because of the California recession and it will take me forever to finish (due to the insane amount of internship hours).

On GPAs:

I failed out of University of South Carolina from biology major, going into pre-med. Ick! I shouldn't even be saying that. First semester 1.5 GPA, second semester 0.5. Drank too much and didn't go to class.

On LA freeways:

Easily irritated; one day I will either get beat up or shot while driving.

The Power
of Color

Color Palettes, Theory, & More

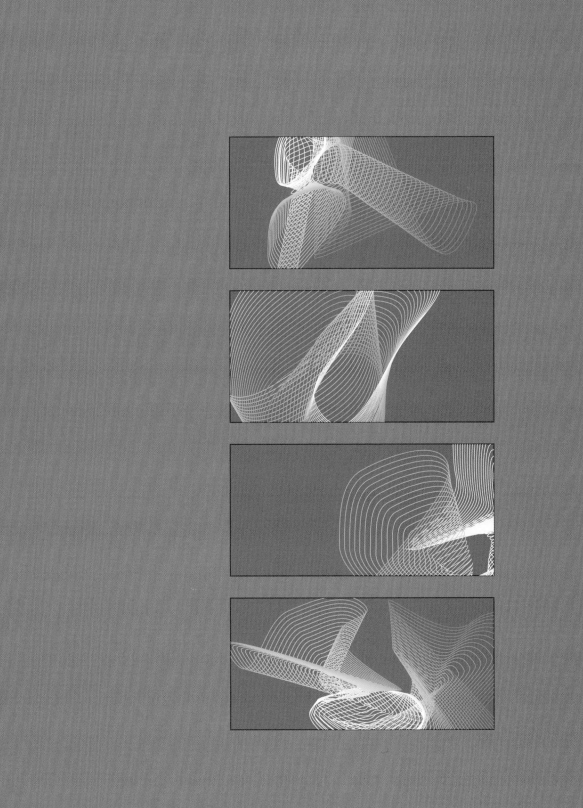

Color is one of the most important and most fundamental elements of design. Color creates the mood of your design, thereby defining the experience for your audience.

However, and at times unfortunately, we as web designers are somewhat limited by our medium. Where print designers can choose from a plethora of paper, inks, bindings, and print processes, the web designer must assume that his work is being experienced by a viewer looking at a monitor. Because web design in a sense is a virtual art, we can't use a softly embossed paper to create the feeling of elegance for a wedding invitation or design a book cover made from handmade paper to create a feeling of intimacy with the subject matter. Instead, we use color and composition with color to evoke the feeling and emotions associated with our work.

In this chapter, you will learn some fundamental ideas about color. We will discuss the different ways to look at color, and how color can be used to express emotion. You will learn how to integrate color into your design on both practical and philosophical levels. The main goal is to learn how to use color conceptually and organizationally to push the concepts of your design.

Understanding Color

Just as no two people are alike, no two individuals experience color in precisely the same way. Color triggers both physical and emotional responses based on one's experiences and personality. Every person has a unique reaction to seeing a color or combination of colors.

What Do You *Really* See?

As unbelievable as it may sound, some people see as many as one million colors. Most of us can see tens of thousands, and some (unfortunate) people can only see a few. Different shades of the same color create depth and enable us to see form in objects and contours on surfaces. For example, boundaries of space are indicated with color variation on maps (see Figure 4.1).

The many shades of green on the map show water depth. If you only saw one, or just a few shades of green, you would never be able to distinguish information. The map would look like a blur, and though you might see slight variations in tone, you would never see the detail required to understand the information. If the cartographer had used other, unrelated shades of color instead of variations of the same color, the information would not read as water. Instead, you would have an entirely different experience with the image. Too many colors would most likely provide too much unrelated information and would thereby defeat the map's purpose.

The colors you see are entirely dependent on light (see Figure 4.2). Take a moment and look around you for a plant or tree. What colors do you see in the leaves? You probably see green somewhere. Notice how the green varies

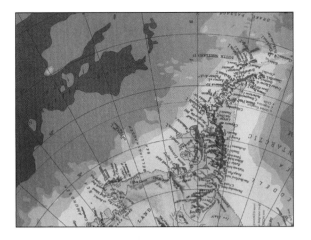

4.1

4.2

figure 4.1

Different shades of the same green enable you to distinguish water depth.

figure 4.2

Light enables you to see the vibrant colors of the lanterns. Photo by Mark Linnemann.

depending on where the light hits the leaf. The shade is entirely different under the bend of the leaf where the light is not as intense. Notice how the greens vary as you focus on different areas of the plant. Now imagine what you would see if you turn out the lights. You probably wouldn't even see green any more. You would still see the shape of the plant. However, if you tried to distinguish the plant's colors, you would probably see different shades of deep, dark blues and greens, almost black. It's still the same plant, but your perception of the color has changed entirely.

More than Meets the Eyes

The power of color lies far beyond the eyes. Association with memory is what makes us feel emotion in relation to what we see.

An infant and an adult have completely different associations with colors. For example, an infant may respond to a red, white, and blue striped poster in a purely formal way, but an adult would make the association of these colors with the American flag and respond to it from a political view.

The example goes much deeper than obvious cultural connections. Every individual has unique associations that come from experiences in life. A particular shade of blue combined with a certain yellow may jog the memory of a shirt your mother wore when you were young. These types

4.3

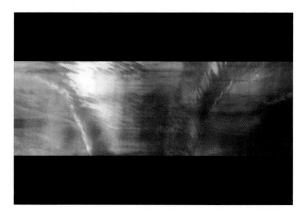

4.4

of associations are the most powerful of all because they can bring in other senses like the scent of the perfume she was wearing and the memory of that time in your life.

What Difference Does Color Make?

Knowing that every person has a unique experience with color and that color need not be categorized and "beholden" to any one object or subject is key to understanding how to create moods in your design.

Gordon McNee, a Scottish designer based in San Francisco, created a film about his personal experience with a degenerative eye condition. The intention of this film, *20/400*, was to educate people about the eye disease keratoconus. This was done through narration and visual experiences (see Figures 4.3–4.6).

In these frames, many saturated colors are placed over images of a busy street. These colors are intended to reinforce the emotions that are being expressed. They compensate for the lack of clarity and detail within the image. They also heighten the "internal awareness of seeing." The message is that when certain areas of vision are impaired, they are compensated for by others.

figures 4.3–4.6

In this section of the film *20/400* saturated colors were used in order to add information where visual details are minimized.

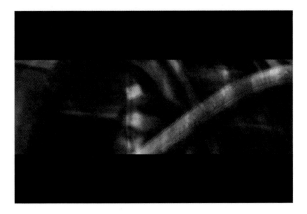

4.5

4.6

Using Color

Design is about conveying a message, and although being true to reality is important, so is creating an emotional image. The mid-nineteenth century marked a pivotal point in art history. That's when people began to represent objects in a way that was more about the momentary experience with the image than the image itself. Painters, sculptors, and poets all over Europe moved away from trying to represent the tangible world, and moved toward the use of form and color as a means of conveying feeling rather than rendering reality. Art became about the expression of emotions. Where previously it was used to represent reality, it now was attempting to reveal new, more abstract realities, reaching into the subconscious, the heart, and the soul. If a painting was about the sadness of war, the emotion was expressed with harsh contrasting colors in their purest form as opposed to photorealistic battle scenes of horses, flames, and dying people.

These same modernist ideas translate to web and interactive design. Ancient Forest Rescue, an activist group established to save old growth forests from clear cutting, needed a small web site to state its mission and its cause (see Figures 4.7 and 4.8). The purpose of the site is to inform citizens about deforestation happening in the small farming town of San Luis, Colorado. In designing the site, the obvious solution would have been to use green to represent the trees of the forest. However, when the designers thought about the message, they concluded it was more important to convey a sense of urgency to the site visitors. The use of greens and the cliched reference to nature would have been too calming and would have detracted from the message.

4.7

4.8

4.9

4.10

figures 4.7 and 4.8

Sharp contrasting colors and bold shapes create a sense of urgency for the activist group.

figures 4.9–4.12

In the film *20/400*, the artist minimized color within certain sections to allow the viewer to experience the emotions associated with the eye condition that is being discussed.

Instead, flat color fields with bold contrasting lines and dramatic angles create a sense of discomfort. The neutral background blue hues allow visitors to focus on the photography and textual content of the site.

These are fundamental ideas in design, and approaching your work with an open palette will feed you with a never-ending source of ideas and solutions to design problems.

Minimizing Color

Sometimes "pulling" color allows the viewer to participate more with the image. In the case of the film *20/400* by Gordon McNee, color is used minimally to allow the viewer more space to think (see Figures 4.9–4.12).

If the filmmaker had given the viewer all the actual color, the experience the viewer had would be quite different. By minimizing the color, the viewer is given space to "interact" with the image and narration. As a result, the absence of color adds sophistication to the piece.

Color treating photography (duotone, desaturate, colorize, and so on) works well on the web. First of all, the less color in the photo, the smaller the file size will be. Apart from image optimization, treating photos consistently adds a sense of uniformity to the site. Coloring treating photos is a good way to use photography as a textural element of your site, without pulling too much attention away from the main content.

4.11

4.12

Fluent Studios was hired to design a site for an upscale beer company (see Figures 4.13–4.17).

The target audience was "hip" people between the ages of 23 and 35. The photography was all shot at bars in various cities. As every bar had unique lighting situations, the photos from each location looked dramatically different. The designers decided to pull most of the color from the photos and then colorize them with warm reds, oranges, and yellows. Once treated, all the photos held together as a body. The designers succeeded in establishing the appropriate hip, glamorous mood by pulling colors from the treated photos and integrating the same palette into the interface.

4.13

4.14

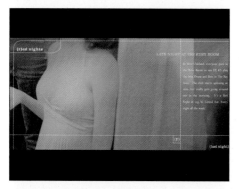

4.15

4.16

4.17

figures 4.13–4.17
Fluent Studios treated all the photography in the site with red and warm toned overlays. The navigation was then designed by pulling color from the photos. The result is a glamorous mood and a sense of uniformity throughout the piece.

Case Study

Studio eg

Studio eg is a company that designs and manufac-
tures office furniture using recycled materials and low
energy manufacturing processes. They pledge a
commitment to "ecologically smart design". The
Studio eg web site (`www.studioeg.com`) is a good
example for how color is used to reinforce the envi-
ronmental friendly aspect that makes the company's
work unique.

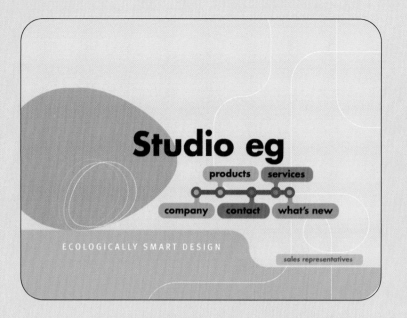

4.18

Soft colors and organic shapes give an earthy feeling to the Studio eg site.

The home page (see Figure 4.18) introduces the palette of the site. Soft, unsaturated colors give a calming effect. The colors are combined with organic shapes and curvy lines to create a serene feeling, suggesting nature. The white out-lined "egg" spins within the larger solid egg. The motion looks like a gear spinning around wel-coming the visitors to the site, which, as it unfolds, becomes a web "recycling machine."

Each section of the site is associated with a dif-ferent hue. The "materials" page (see Figure 4.19) uses oranges, the "components" page

blues (see Figure 4.20), and the "cabling" page greens (see Figure 4.21). The main navigation for the site associates each of these pages with their respective colors. This creates a system and adds another level of logic to the navigation. The color theme remains interesting because it varies from page to page. If all the colors were combined on the same page, the effect would be much less powerful than the isolated color groups from page to page. The monochromatic quality of the individual pages reinforces the soft feeling while the combined overall effect is actu-ally quite colorful.

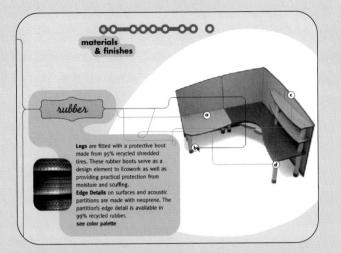

materials
& finishes

rubber

Legs are fitted with a protective boot made from 95% recycled shredded tires. These rubber boots serve as a design element to Ecowork as well as providing practical protection from moisture and scuffing.
Edge Details on surfaces and acoustic partitions are made with neoprene. The partition's edge detail is available in 99% recycled rubber.
see color palette

4.19

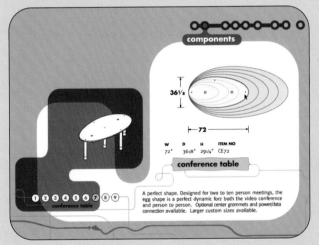

components

$36\frac{1}{2}$

72

W	D	H	ITEM NO
72"	36⅛"	29¼"	CE72

conference table

① ② ③ ④ ⑤ ⑥ ⑦ ⑧ ⑨
conference table

A perfect shape. Designed for two to ten person meetings, the egg shape is a perfect dynamic forz both the video conference and person to person. Optional center grommets and power/data connection available. Larger custom sizes available.

4.20

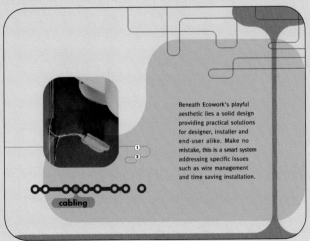

Beneath Ecowork's playful aesthetic lies a solid design providing practical solutions for designer, installer and end-user alike. Make no mistake, this is a smart system addressing specific issues such as wire management and time saving installation.

cabling

4.21

4.19–4.21

Although each page is monochromatic the overall feeling is quite colorful.

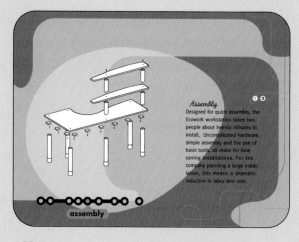

4.22

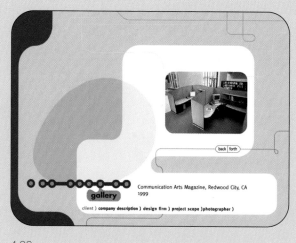

4.23

The color schemes of the individual pages work because they use variations of the same color to break up the space. The assembly page uses brown tones (see Figure 4.22) to create depth within the composition. The background is a light brown, and the main bulbous shapes use the same brown tone in different values. The egg shape is screened back in white. This partial transparency allows for two more variations of the same brown color to show through. The only other color is a sparsely used red, highlighting the image caption and text heading. Similarly, the gallery page (see Figure 4.23) uses varying tones of an icy greenish-blue and light gray.

Aside from color, the shapes, typefaces, and motion used throughout the site add to the overall effect. The site is a good study for how these various design elements can be combined to add mood and personality to a design.

4.22 and 4.23

Different shades of the same color create individual compositions for each page.

Tip:

Tip:
Use the hue/saturation feature in Photoshop to create interesting color effects. Open a photo in Photoshop. Select the entire image and select Image, Adjust, Hue/Saturation. Check Colorize in the Hue/Saturation pop-up window. Drag the Hue slider and see how the color tones of your image change. Drag the Saturation slider to increase or decrease the amount of saturation.

Choosing Your Colors

Now that you know you can choose just about any color for any subject matter, the next step is to narrow your selection to the colors that will best convey the message of your site.

First, you must understand the subject matter. This is one of the most fun parts about being a designer. Each client you have is different, and with every project comes an entirely new range of content. With each project, you get to learn about a whole new field aside from design. One month you may become a semi-expert on the subject of outdoor athletic wear, and the next an aficionado on analytical instrumentation and process chemistry.

Next, you must define your audience. Who will visit the site? A clothing company might ask you

to design its site. The site should look different if it is a retail store for customers rather than an online resource for suppliers. When you determine who will be viewing the site, you can begin to select a palette. For example, an audience of children will generally respond best to bright, contrasting colors (see Figure 4.24). Even within the category of children you can break down color by gender or interest.

figure 4.18

Children respond well to a bright color palette.

As a rule, color combinations that you find in nature generally work quite well (see Figures 4.25–4.27). If you are stuck on your selection, go for a walk and notice the palette of your neighborhood. A look at the outside world will suggest color combinations that you never dreamed possible.

4.25

4.26

4.27

figures 4.25–4.27
Good ideas for color exist everywhere. These palettes were pulled directly from the photos.

figure 4.28

Various color blocks create the navigation for carlsonsolutions.com. Brighter colors are placed in smaller rectangles, and although every navigation element is a different size, each element retains the same importance.

figure 4.29

It's easy deviate from a set palette by using variations of the same colors.

Tip:

Adobe Illustrator makes it easy to create hundreds of variations of the same color. Draw a small solid square and fill it with a color. Pull up the color modification window (Window>Show Color). Select the square. Make sure you are modifying the filled color and go to the color slider. Hold down Shift and drag your mouse along the slider to the right or left (see Figures 4.30 and 4.31). Notice how the color of the square and RGB values change as you move your mouse. When you get a color you like, make a copy of it and soon you'll have numerous variations on your original color—a beautiful integration to your main palette.

Be careful of using too many colors. Color composition is about balance, and the more factors you add to the equation the harder it is to solve (see Figure 4.28). If you only use one color, balancing color within your composition is easy. If there are two colors, you pull the focus back and forth between them. One color is most likely bolder than the other and should probably take up less space. As you add more colors the balance becomes easily disrupted.

Try to keep your palette to a reasonable number of colors. Don't worry, by no means are you limited by any specific number—within each color, you have unlimited variation (see Figure 4.29).

In client design, you will sometimes be limited by a predefined corporate identity. This can be frustrating, especially if you don't like the palette. As a designer, it is your job to make the most of this situation. Think about ways you can use neutral colors or black and white for the background and use the corporate identity colors for accent. Companies hire you to create an image for them and you must be strong with your decisions. It is your responsibility to do what works. Don't let a client's bad aesthetic or predefined ideas hold back your design. If the client still insists on a certain palette, you should back your opinion with technical reasons. For example, small blue type is illegible on a black background.

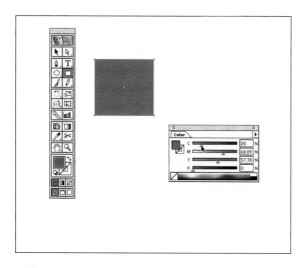

4.30

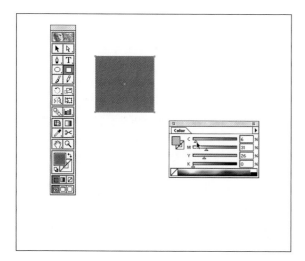

4.31

figures 4.30 and 4.31

You can create countless variations of the same color by holding down Shift while dragging the color bar in Illustrator.

You can explain that with print, you are assured your result—you control the medium—but with the web, you never know what type of monitor the viewer is using. You need to design for a huge range of possibilities, and it's not worth risking losing part of your audience because of technical issues. The best client is one who challenges you to think, yet trusts you to do what you think is best.

How Color Applies to a Web Interface

Choosing color is just the beginning. What you do with the color, and how you arrange it can make a web experience delightful or intolerable.

Background Color

The background color or pattern you choose is the foundation of your page. If you choose a color, it needs to be harmonious with the rest of the colors on your page. The biggest mistake people make is to choose an overpowering background color. If you are choosing a solid color for your background, try to stay in the web-safe palette. (See the section "The Web-Safe Palette" later in this chapter.) You should not feel compelled to stay in the web safe-palette for most of the content of your site, but the percentage of background space on your page is large enough that it makes sense to choose colors in the safe range for this area. Web-safe colors are particularly important for backgrounds because the color will probably backdrop text that needs to be read. A dithering background could distract from the content for users of older monitors.

Background patterns can look beautiful, but if misused they can make it impossible to read a page. When you use a background pattern, keep in mind that you are making a conscious design decision, and have a plan for how it works with the rest of your page.

Fluent Studios designed an interface for a web-based application that enables users to type into fields and receive responses from a server based on key words (see Figure 4.32).

The page required frames, but the designers made sure the different frames merged together seamlessly. To make the design work, they had to rely on a background pattern to present the interface. The design was carefully planned and the page elements were placed within the background pattern.

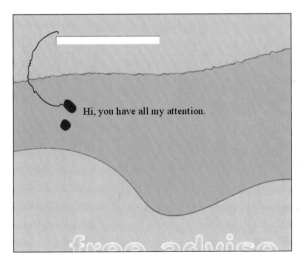

figure 4.32

In this interactive web-based application, background patterns are used to seamlessly integrate frames and help lay out the interface.

Tip:

When you use a background pattern, always specify a background color in your HTML. Choose a color that is dominant in your pattern. When loading, the browser will always flash the background color designated in the HTML before loading the pattern image. If the background image is large, the HTML specified color will show until the image has completely loaded.

Textual Content

When you choose color for type, use common sense. Pick a color that reads well on the background you have chosen. If you are choosing a text color for a large body of copy that contains important information, choose a color that will cause the least amount of stress on the eyes. White type on a black background may look great in your design, but the opposite is much easier to read. Choose colors that contrast one another, but not so much that the type begins to glow. As with the background color, stick to the web-safe palette. Avoid dithering on shapes that are as small and important to distinguish as letters.

Navigation

Color coding navigation is an excellent way to create an interface that facilitates ease of use. Almost everyone can make conceptual associations with colors. Since we were kids we categorized information by color. We had different color folders and notebooks for each class. We put color rings on our keys to distinguish one from the other. It is natural and logical to sort information by color.

People are so adept at finding information by use of color association that we almost have to be careful not to mess up! As you design a site, be very aware of the relationships you make between navigational elements and color. You, the designer, establish the rules for the user. When you deviate from your own rules, the user becomes confused. For example, imagine designing a system where orange text always links you to the glossary. If you decide to make another type of link orange, the user will be confused. When he clicks on the text and ends up

somewhere other than the glossary, he will no longer associate orange with the glossary and the system you created is dismissed.

Using Color to Create a System

Color coding your background and navigation can create a solid system of information architecture. The homepage of carlsonsolutions.com introduces the main navigation of the site (see Figure 4.33).

A different color block in the navigation represents each major section of the site. When you click on one of the words, you go the main page of that section (see Figures 4.34–4.37).

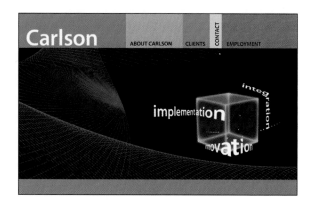

4.33

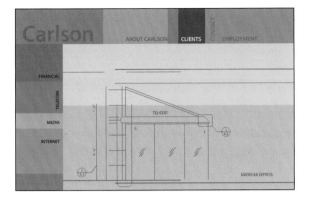

4.34

4.35

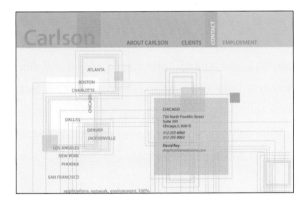

4.36

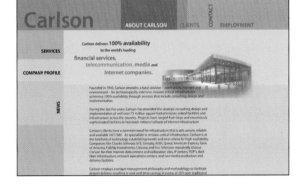

4.37

figure 4.33
Carlson's homepage introduces visitors to the color system used throughout the site.

figures 4.34–4.37
Each section of Carlson's site maintains the color scheme defined by the navigation.

The primary color of the background for each section of the site is taken directly from the main navigation. Notice how the "clients" section is called out by blue navigation (see Figure 4.34). When you click the blue button, you go to the client's main page. All the pages within the client's section are laid out in blues. Notice how the rest of the main navigation changes to various blue tones. If the designer had maintained the same navigational color palette from the home page to this section, the page would look busy and the color would not mix. When you roll over the top-level navigation in any of the main sections of the site, the color that designates that section from the home page reappears, branding a site section with a color. Within each section, the color remains unobtrusive to the composition, yet works as a navigation and information categorization device.

The Web-Safe Palette

We all have our own opinions about the web-safe palette. We love it and we hate it. We use it and we refuse it. One of the scariest parts about publishing your design is that once it is on the web, it is out of your control. Everyone will see it a little differently.

Theoretically, the web-safe palette will be visible on all 256-color monitor systems. If you use a color in the palette, you are assured that a user on a 256-color monitor will not see dithered color. This is particularly important for large background areas and type. If you have a lot of copy that is laid out in small type, you should stick to the web-safe palette for type and background color. If type breaks apart on a dithered background, there is a possibility that the copy will be illegible.

Although using the web-safe palette will eliminate dithering, cross-browser inconsistency, and major color shifts, it does not assure 100-percent consistent viewing for your page. Color is also greatly affected by ambient light, monitor settings, the actual color depth of the monitor, and the type of monitor being used. The best way to check color is to test your work on as many monitors and platforms as possible while you are developing your site.

Most design applications provide you with the web-safe palette. In Photoshop, you can load the web-safe palette through the Swatches window. Click Load Swatches and find the folder Adobe Photoshop>Goodies>Color Palettes and load the swatch Web Safe Colors. If you stick to the swatch colors you will be safe.

The downside of the web-safe palette is that it is extremely restricting, and it is difficult to find the exact colors you want. Most of the colors are highly saturated and difficult to combine. There are few soft colors, making subtle color usage almost impossible.

The best way to decide whether to stick to the web-safe palette is to define your audience. Is your audience a high-tech, hip group? If so, they'll probably have monitors with thousands of colors. If you are designing for a large corporation that anticipates millions of visitors, you should probably go with web safe.

There is no guarantee for how others will see the different colors in your site once it's published. There are too many variables involved. The best thing you can do is to test your work on as many monitors, browsers, and computer configurations as possible during your design process.

Summary

Color is one of the most important elements of your design, so use it wisely. Select colors that will heighten the audiences' interaction with the page. If you are going for clarity, choose subtle background colors with contrasting dark type. If you want to create a mood, choose colors that generate feelings and emotions. Sometimes the least obvious color selection will be far more powerful than one that is expected. Removing all color, or replacing a multicolored image with a limited palette may create mystery and drama. Take time choosing your palette...it may have more of an impact than any other single item in your design.

URLS In This Chapter

- **Carlson Solutions**
  www.carlsonsolutions.com
- **Studio eg** www.studioeg.com

Inspirational Design Model

Matt Owens
one9ine

"…without the personal, the professional would

not be as interesting. Finding the time to do

your own thing and to grow creatively is fun-

damentally important."

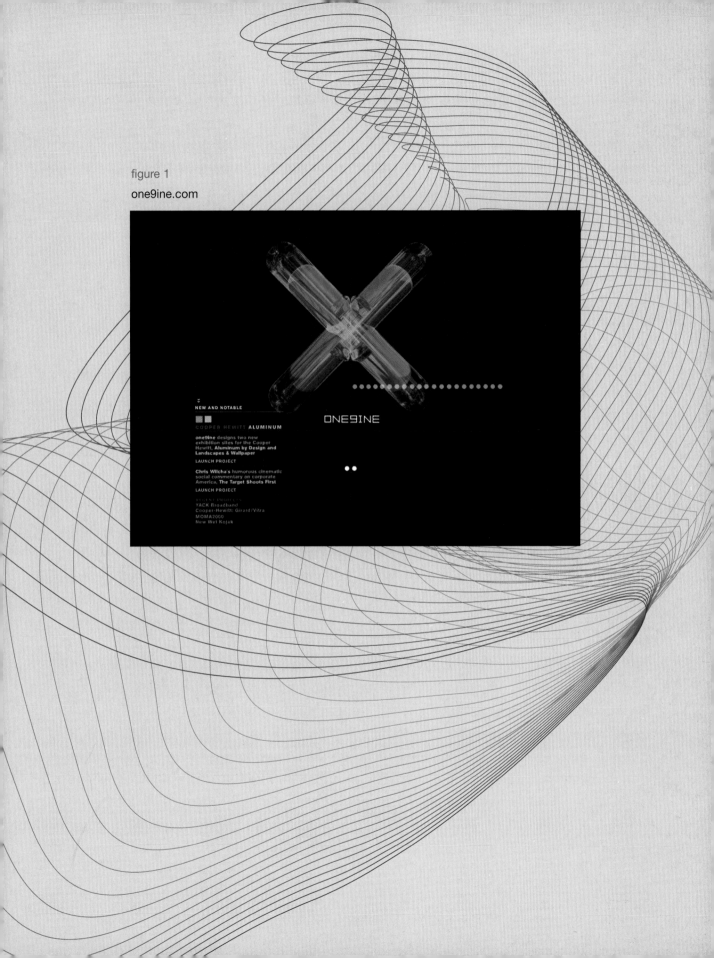

figure 1

one9ine.com

If Matt Owens ever decided to quit the design business, he could have his own talk show. Not the cheesy kind, but a show that would showcase his scathing wit, street smarts, and indie spirit. As a leading designer in the industry and co-founder (with Warren Corbitt) of the design studio, one9ine (`www.one9ine.com`), well-versed Matt can deal his opinion on just about any subject. He hates cubicles. He loves music. He hates "sell outs." He loves New York.

His claim to fame started with his experimental web site, Volume One (`www.volumeone.com`), where his quarterly exhibitions explored various topics with visual and graphical splendor. Considered an "old school" web designer, Matt's work is definitely not just about being interactive. He's immersed in all things design. Matt stresses the importance of being multi-faceted. You can find him move smoothly from designing a web site to designing a book cover. As he discusses the multitude of personal side projects he is working on at the moment, Matt makes it clear that he always has time to hang out with his friends. "I have a life," says Matt.

What inspires you?
My friends, other designers, and the things around me. Being involved in design culture and music and being "out there" and not just in front of the computer is inspirational.

Please tell me more about your studio one9ine.
We are a small design-focused studio that develops projects in multiple mediums.

What's your creative process when you are working on a project? How do you factor in the technology?
I think having a clear design idea in mind and a receptive client are the most important factors. Working with BBH (`www.bartleboglehegarty.com`) we were able to work through content, visual, and technology issues all at the same time. This fluid process allowed us to do more with the materials and in the time frame. It is that mutual commitment to do something interesting that drives as successful project.

How have you found a balance between the work you do for clients and your personal work (volumeone.com, Codex Series, and so on)?
That balance is still hard. I think without the personal, the professional would not be as interesting. Finding the time to do your own thing and to grow creatively is fundamentally important. You have to make that time or both sides of the work (personal and professional) will suffer.

figure 2

one9ine.com

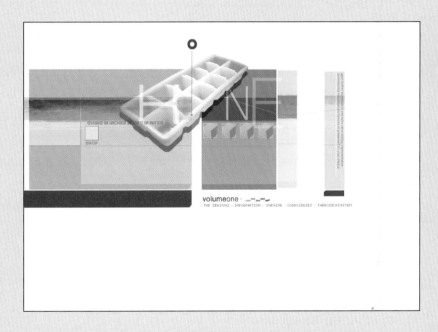

figure 3

volumeone.com—winter 2001

figure 4

volumeone: consumed | perceived

You've been doing quite a lot of speaking at design conferences around the world. Please share with us some of the best experiences of your travels meeting other designers from different places. What are some of the common issues designers are facing today?
We spoke at the IdN Fresh Conference in Hong Kong in February [2001] and had a great time. Hanging out with Amy and Josh from Future Farmers, the OFP, Tubatomic, Deep End, Josh Davis, Tomato Interactive was great. All the people at IdN were amazing as well. It was a big conference, but had an intimacy that I really enjoyed.

Every designer everywhere struggles with doing good work and finding clients that are interested in doing new things.

How do you think Broadband and/or Wireless will change the way in which the digital medium will be thought of and designed for?
Broadband and wireless are expansions of the field. Wireless is amazing, but has major design limitations. Broadband is great, but standards need to be put in place.

Who are your design heroes?
I think Saul Bass and tDR are big heroes of mine.

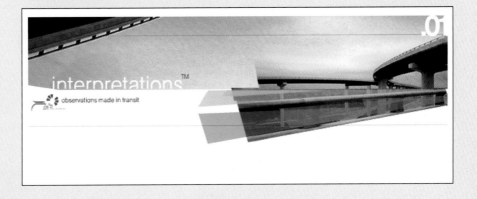

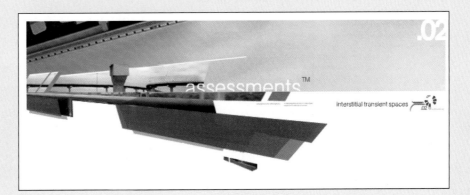

figures 5–7

volumeone: interventions | a study

Do you have any advice that you would like to share with all the aspiring designers out there?

Keep working and learning and doing. You have to be willing to put yourself out on a limb and do new things to keep yourself alive and interested in the work.

What would a "perfect day" at work be like?

A day off! Heh.

If you could be a superhero, who would you be and why?

Not sure...I would rather just be better at what I do...crime fighting seems like a lot of responsibility.

What are three things in the world you can't live without?

My brother, my family, and my art.

Please name a bad habit you have.

Frank insensitivity (I say it like I mean it, but not always in the nicest way).

Matt Owens's URLs:

- **one9ine**   www.one9ine.com
- **Volume One**   www.volumeone.com
- **The Codex Series**
  www.codexseries.com

figure 8
Bartle Bogle Hegarty

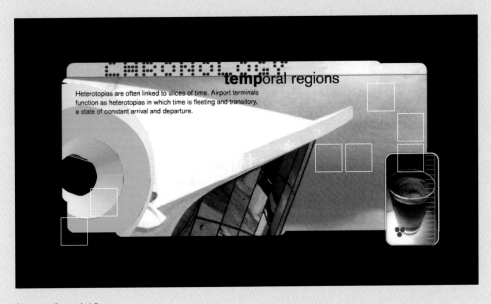

figures 9 and 10

Codex Series 1 CD-ROM, Heterotopia

Part Two

DHTML & Web Interactivity: Make It Move

Personalization

Simplifying with Style Sheets
and Personalizing with JavaScript

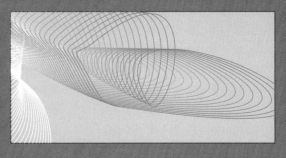

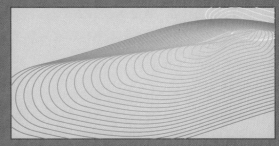

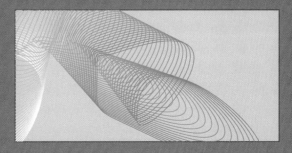

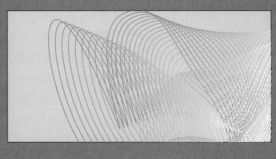

Once you understand the basics of HTML you will have the foundation for learning more complex programming. Understanding how your HTML documents are set up will enable you to add dynamic HTML (DHTML) and JavaScript to your pages.

In this chapter you will learn about style sheets, which allow you to format multiple documents at the same time. They give you better formatting control and more options for typography, enabling you to design layouts that were previously limited with basic HTML.

This chapter also introduces the concept of adding JavaScript to your HTML documents. You don't have to become a JavaScript programmer to benefit from its powers. Simply understanding how HTML references JavaScript and knowing how to place it within your existing HTML code is enough to enable JavaScript functionality. We'll introduce you to some techniques like creating password-protected sites, creative pop-up windows, and working with random elements. We'll also refer you to some sites on the web where you can see examples and copy code from thousands of JavaScript examples.

Style Sheets

Style sheets are a set of rules that tells the browser how to display text and images. You can think of them the same way you think of preferences within an application on your computer. For example, on your hard drive you have a place where you can specify the way your computer desktop appears. You can choose the font and specify how big you want letters to appear, you can choose a color or pattern for your desktop, and you can even select a set of sounds for alerts. You can always change these preferences and a new set of rules will be applied to your whole system. Similarly, style sheets apply rules to multiple places at the same time. Rather than having to write out the code every time you want to reference a header with a specific typeface, font size, and color, you can specify rules once that will effect every header in your document. For example:

```
H2      { font-family: Verdana, Arial,
          Helvetica, sans-serif;
          {font-size: 30pt }
```

This code shows that anytime an `<H2>` header tag appears, it will display the specified rules given in the code. You can see that using these rules saves both coding time on your end and download time for the viewers. Additionally, if you decide you want to change the font size to 20pt, you only have to do it once and it affects the entire document. Depending on how you are using style sheets, it could affect hundreds of documents at the same time.

> ## Note:
> Although you can experience the power of style sheets with the 4.0 browsers, the 4.0 browsers are far from perfect. The 5+ browsers are a little better, but standards of code between the various browsers are still lacking.

Working with Style Sheets

You need to understand some basic concepts to begin using style sheets. A style sheet rule has two parts: the selector and the declaration. The *selector* is the HTML code that links the style to the HTML document, and the *declaration* is the style definition—all the properties and values within the brackets { }.

```
H2 { font-family: helvetica }
```

Here H2 is the selector and font-family; Helvetica is the declaration.

> ## Note:
> If you want to work with style sheets, you need to always close all your paragraphs with the closing `</P>` tag. This is because as you set up rules for paragraphs, the browser needs to know when the selection ends in order to start the next rule.

You can set up as many style sheet rules as you like. They save a lot of time!

Grouping Your Style Sheet Rules

To save space, always group your declarations with their corresponding selectors with a semi-colon. Here's an example:

```
H2      { font-family: Arial;
        Font-weight bold;
        Font-size: 18pt;
        Color: blue }
```

By separating each declaration on its own line, you can easily go back and edit your style sheets. You can also group your rules together.

```
H1, H2, P    { font-family: Arial;
        Font-weight bold;
        Font-size: 20pt;
        Color: red }
```

What this shows is that for every `<H1>`, `<H2>`, and `<P>` tag, the HTML page displays bold, red, 20pt Arial text. By grouping these different HTML declarations, you'll not only find your style sheets easier to edit, but you'll save space in your HTML page as well.

Tip:

You can use the `<SPAN>` tag when you want to display a certain style for your text but do not want to render any particular HTML style (`<B>`,`<H1>`,`<P>`, and so on). The `<SPAN>` tag displays only the declaration you specify in your style sheet, as in the following example:

```
SPAN { font-family: arial }
```

By inserting the `<SPAN></SPAN>` around the area in your HTML document, you ensure that anything contained within (that does not have any other style declarations) the tags displays in Arial.

Adding Styles to Web Pages

It's simple to add style sheets to your web pages. Style sheets can either live in their own document or they can be added straight into an HTML document. Here are some different ways you can add style sheets to web pages:

- **Inline Styles.** For quick style face lifts where your styles live next to your HTML.
- **Embed.** For a single web page.
- **Link.** For the most control where your one style sheet is linked to a number of HTML pages.

Inline Styles

For a quick fix within a page you can add styles inline to your HTML document. This isn't the best use of style sheet properties, but if you just want to add one or two style elements, it works. Here's an example:

```
<P STYLE="color: red; margin-left:
3in; margin-right: 1in">
```

This code replaces one normal `<P>` tag.

Embedding a Style Sheet

To change the face of a single web page, you can embed your styles before the `<HEAD>` of the HTML document. To begin, add `<STYLE TYPE="text/css">` right after the initial HTML tag. Next notice the comment code in the following sample code. Browsers that don't support style sheets simply ignore the style sheet rules. Go ahead and set up your rules within the comment and close it all with a `</STYLE>` tag. Here's an example of an embedded style sheet:

```
<HTML>
<HEAD>
<STYLE TYPE="text/css">
P      { font-family: Arial,Helvetica;
         font-size: 8pt;
         color: #003399 }
</STYLE>
</HEAD>
</BODY>
```

Linking an External Style Sheet

Linking an external style sheet is one of the most powerful aspects of style sheets. You can create one style sheet and link it to a number of HTML pages thereby creating a sort of style template for your site.

First, create the external style sheet with your code:

```
BODY { background: black;
       font-family: arial }
H2   { font-weight: bold;
       font-size: 18pt }
P    { font-size: 14pt }
```

Save this text file with a name and the extension .css. Call this document mystyles.css and upload it to your server.

To link mystyles.css to a web page, add the following line within the <HEAD></HEAD> tags of your HTML page:

```
<HTML>
<HEAD>
<TITLE>welcome to style sheets</TITLE>
<LINK REL="stylesheet"
HREF="mystyles.css" TYPE="text/css">
</HEAD>
```

Note:

You can also use the multiple LINK tags to reference more than one style sheet. Make sure that you test your pages well and check their cascading order. Some rules on different style sheets are liable to clash with each other, which can affect the look of your pages.

The great thing about linking to a style is that if you want to make a simple change to the look, all you have to do is modify the code in one place and upload it again.

Classes and IDs

For more flexibility with style sheets you can further divide them into classes. Sometimes you might find that attributing a style to a <P> tag can get too general. What if you want to change fonts for special paragraphs? You can create different "classes" of <P> tags by separating and naming them in your style sheet and HTML accordingly.

```
<STYLE TYPE="text/css">
     P.a { color: blue;
     font-family: courier }
     P.b { color: red;
     font-family: arial }
</STYLE>
```

You can name the classes anything you want. We've named them simply P.a and P.b. From then on, when you want to use the various styles on the page, you simply activate them within the HTML:

```
<P CLASS="a"> Class A shows up in blue
Courier.</P>
<P CLASS="b"> Class B shows up in red
Arial.</P>
```

By naming the class in the HTML, the style attribute for the specific class tells the browser which variant of `<P>` to use.

> ## Tip:
> Go a step further and you can use the `CLASS` attribute with any HTML tag by leaving out the selector. Make sure to keep the period before the name.

```
<STYLE TYPE="text/css">
.redfont { font-size: 20pt;
          font-color: red;
          font-family: ariel }
</style>
```

Reference any HTML tag with `CLASS="redfont"` and the tag specified will be 20pt Arial in red.

Another way to set up your own specialized rules is with IDs. IDs are similar to classes in that you can set up certain rules in your style sheet and reference them in your HTML. Here's an example:

```
#100  { color: red;
        font-family: ariel }
<H3 ID="100">Red is a bold bright
color.</H3>
```

> ## Note:
> The `CLASS` attribute is used to define styles to elements that are typically reused multiple times in your HTML document. The `ID` attribute is usually used to define a rule that applies to a unique element in your HTML page. A unique `ID` attribute will allow you to access and manipulate that document element using JavaScript (that is, moving a layer).

The Cascade

Style sheets are also called *cascading* style sheets (CSS). This is because with all the intricacies associated with creating different style sheets, the browser reads rules in a certain order. The browser decides which rules in a style sheet are the most important and displays them. This can affect the look of your pages because when the browser finds a conflicting rule, it won't display it the way you want it to look.

This is the order in which styles cascade:

1. **Inline.** Style references within the HTML code.
2. **Embedded.** Style sheet rules embedded in the HTML page.
3. **Linked.** External style sheets referenced in the HTML page.
4. **Imported.** Referencing a style within another style sheet with `@import`.
5. **User.** The browser display settings the user has modified.
6. **Browser default.** The default browser settings.

Unfortunately not all browsers follow this simple order. Navigator and Internet Explorer both have their own kinks when cascading style sheets. As a result, if you find yourself mixing between inline, embedded, and linked styles, make sure you test things properly and don't forget the cascading order.

When it comes to simple HTML tags, such as `FONT FACE`, the style sheet tags can override them. This is because the browser reads the HTML tags first before moving on to the style sheet rules. If there are declared rules that match `FONT FACE`, the style sheet rule wins.

Contextual Selectors

For more options when declaring style sheet rules, you can set up contextual selectors that allow you to have two or more declarations follow the same rule.

```
CENTER B    { color: red }
```

The previous code means that anything that is both centered and in bold appears in red and won't affect other bold text or other centered text. With each declaration separated by a space, you can use contextual selectors not only with HTML tags but also with Classes and IDs.

Style Sheets and Graphics

You've always used graphics and text in your web pages but now you can use them in a way that is impossible with straight HTML. You can layer text and graphics and place them precisely where you want on the page. With style sheets' capability for absolute and relative positioning, a whole new world of possibility is presented for your designs.

You'll also find that the precise control over backgrounds, such as no tiling and transparent backgrounds, will give you a reason to diverge from the standard solid white background we are all so used to using.

Text Over Graphics

Programs like Quark and Illustrator allow us to overlay graphics in creative ways. It is not possible to do this with straight HTML. Relative positioning enables you to position elements such as HTML relative to the position of another element that is its parent element.

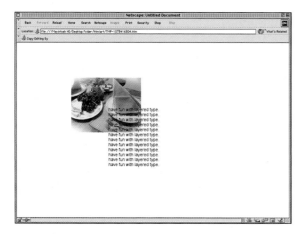

figure 5.1

HTML text layered over a graphic.

In Figure 5.1, the HTML text is layered over the graphic, creating depth in the composition.

To do this, first, we create a CLASS named .positionImage to use for the graphic image. For example, here are the rules to position the graphic:

```
.positionImage { position: relative;
left: 100 px; top: 50 px }
```

The previous code shows that for the CLASS .positionImage the element will appear 100 pixels from the left and 50 pixels from the top relative to the paragraph text. Next, we select the positioning and attributes of the paragraph text:

```
P        { position: relative;
          left: 200 px
```

```
          top: -20 px;
          font-face: arial;
          font-size: 10pt;
          z-index: 1 }
```

The z-index number 1 dictates the layering order of the elements. The higher number 1 ensures that the text will always appear on top of the graphic.

Here's the full code for the HTML page:

```
<HTML>
<STYLE TYPE="text/css">
<!--
BODY    { background: white }
.positionImage      { position:
relative;
                    left: 100 px;
                    top: 50 px }
P                   { position:
relative;
                    left: 100 px:
                    top: -80 px;
                    font-face: arial;
                    font-size: 10pt }
-->
</STYLE>
<HEAD>
<TITLE>text over graphics</TITLE>
</HEAD>
<BODY>
        <SPAN CLASS="positionImage">
        <IMG SRC="images/photo1.gif">
```

```
      </SPAN>
<P>
have fun with layered type.<br>
have fun with layered type.<br>
have fun with layered type.<br>
have fun with layered type.<br>
have fun with layered type.<br>
have fun with layered type.<br>
have fun with layered type.<br>
have fun with layered type.<br>
have fun with layered type.<br>
have fun with layered type.<br>
have fun with layered type.<br>
have fun with layered type.<br>
</P>
</BODY>
</HTML>
```

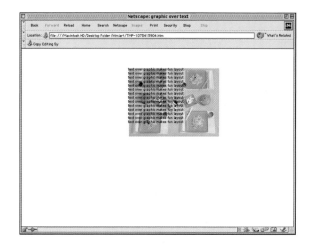

figure 5.2

Overlapping text over graphics with absolute
positioning.

In addition to relative positioning, you can use
absolute positioning to position elements such as
text over graphics on a page. Absolute positioning is different from relative positioning in that it is
independent of any other element on the page.
You can use absolute positioning to position elements anywhere you want. Relative positioning
depends on another element for its position.

In Figure 5.2 the example shows a graphic positioned absolutely on the page. The code works
much the same as relative positioning, except
here everything works independently of each
other because they are absolute.

```
<HTML>
<HEAD>
<STYLE TYPE="text/css">
<!--
BODY { background: white }
.positionImage  { position: absolute;
          left: 200px;
          top: 50px }
P          { position: absolute;
          left: 200px;
          top: 50px;
          font-face: arial;
          font-size: 10pt;
          z-index: 1 }
-->
</STYLE>
```

```
<TITLE>graphic over text</TITLE>
</HEAD>
<BODY>
<SPAN CLASS=positionImage><IMG
SRC="images/photo1.gif"></SPAN>
<P>
text over graphic makes fun layout
<br>
text over graphic makes fun layout
<br>
text over graphic makes fun layout
<br>
text over graphic makes fun layout
<br>
text over graphic makes fun layout
<br>
text over graphic makes fun layout
<br>
text over graphic makes fun layout
<br>
text over graphic makes fun layout
<br>
text over graphic makes fun layout
<br>
text over graphic makes fun layout
<br>
text over graphic makes fun layout
<br>
text over graphic makes fun layout
<br>
text over graphic makes fun layout
<br>
text over graphic makes fun layout
<br>
text over graphic makes fun layout
<br>
```

```
</P>
</BODY>
</HTML>
```

Graphics Over Graphics

After you learn how to layer text over graphics, layering graphics over graphics is a breeze. The addition of the z-index declaration enables you to program the layering order with the highest number as the element on top.

We will start with two graphics, Figures 5.3 and 5.4, which we will layer on top of each other.

With the shape as CLASS .a and the background shape as CLASS .b, we'll find a position that works for the logo to fit nicely in the background shape.

```
<HTML>
<STYLE TYPE="text/css">
<!--
  BODY          { background: white }
  .a            {position: absolute;
                 left: 10px;
                 top: 10px
                 z-index: 1 }
  .b            {position: absolute;
                 left: 300px;
                 top: 150px
                 z-index: 2 }
-->
</STYLE>
<HEAD>
```

figure 5.3

The background image.

figure 5.4

The foreground image.

```
<TITLE> shapes on shapes</TITLE>
</HEAD>
<BODY>
<SPAN CLASS="a"><IMG
SRC="images/bgshape.gif"></SPAN>
<BR>
<SPAN CLASS ="b"><IMG
SRC="images/retro.gif"></SPAN>
</BODY>
</HTML>
```

Because the z-index of the circle is 2, which is higher than the z-index of the large blue graphic, the inside shape appears layered above the other graphic (see Figure 5.5).

To incorporate another element into the web page you can add text or another graphic with a z-index of 3. It will appear above both the other graphics.

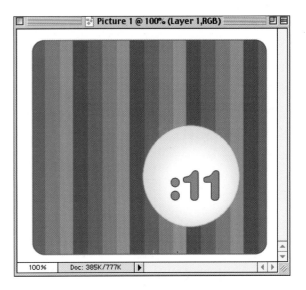

figure 5.5

The foreground graphic is positioned above the background graphic.

Backgrounds

Traditionally, background images tile in the browser window. Using straight HTML you can create backgrounds with the `<BODY BACK-GROUND="img.gif">` tag. Designers have learned to use tiling backgrounds to their advantage, creating stripes, checks, and other tiling patterns. Although this technique can sometimes save download time and is capable of creating interesting effects, we have all at one time or another wished that the background image could also be direct to appear once. Well, now it can!

Here are the properties to use for background:

- **Background-color.** To specify the background color with color name or hex code
  ```
  H2 { background-color: red }
  H2 { background-color: #66ccff}
  ```
- **Background image.** To insert a background graphic
  ```
  BODY { background-image:
  url("image.gif");
       background-color: white }
  ```
  Adding a default background color like white ensures that a background will be there should the image take a while to load or doesn't appear.
- **Background repeat.** To determine tiling of the background graphic
  ```
  H2 { background-image:
  url(image.gif)
       background-repeat:
       repeat-x }
  ```

There are several attributes associated with the background-repeat property:

- **No-repeat.** Background image appears just once and doesn't tile.
- **Repeat.** Background image tiles.
- **Repeat-x.** Background image tiles only horizontally.
- **Repeat-y.** Background image tiles only vertically.

Figure 5.6 illustrates a background with no tile or repeat. The code for this follows:

```
<HTML>
<STYLE TYPE="text/css">
<!--
BODY
background-image:
url("images/bg.gif");
       background-repeat: no-repeat }
--}
</STYLE>
<HEAD>
<TITLE>background no-repeat</TITLE>
</HEAD>
<BODY>
</BODY>
</HTML>
```

You can compare a normal tiling background in Figure 5.7.

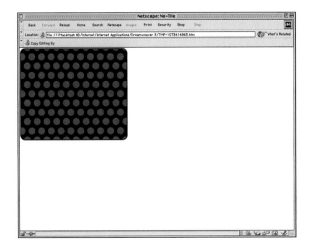

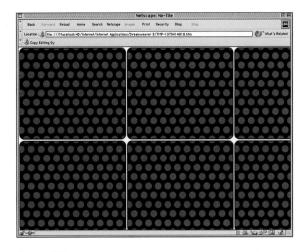

figure 5.6

Background image that doesn't tile.

figure 5.7

Tiling the background image.

JavaScript

JavaScript allows you to add special features and enhance the interactivity of your web pages. Using JavaScript you can add personalization and individualization to the pages you design. The first thing you should know about JavaScript is that it is not at all related to Java. JavaScript is much easier to learn than Java. By the time you finish reading this chapter you will have no problem adding simple JavaScript to your pages.

JavaScript allows you to do the following:

- Control the behavior of the browser (pop-up windows, display alerts).
- Process and store data (add functionality to a form; count site visitors).
- Add enhanced interactivity to a page.

- Get browser information (detect browser configuration; plug-ins installed, and so on).
- Save and retrieve information about your site visitors with "cookies".

Objects, Properties, and Events

JavaScript is an object-oriented programming language. This means that it deals with objects relating to the browser. These objects include browser windows, forms, graphics, and any other object that relates to the browser. All of these objects have properties. For example, the browser window has a specific size, a place it appears on the monitor, scrollbars, and browser buttons. JavaScript allows you to modify the properties of the various objects.

Events happen when a user interacts with a page. You go to a web site and the page loads. You roll over a graphic; you click on a graphic; you leave the page. These are all events. In JavaScript you assign things to happen when the user initiates these events. The duties that are related to the events are assigned in the head of your document. When an event happens the instructions are called. These instructions are called *functions* or *behaviors*. A function can be called many times. Here's an example: You can write a function in the head of your document that says a certain sound plays when you roll over a graphic. In the body of your HTML document you call this code you wrote in the head every time you want the sound to be played with the roll over of a specific graphic.

This is all you need to understand to enable simple JavaScript functions on your page. It may sound like a lot, but with a little bit of practice you'll have it down in no time.

A Word on Syntax

In the first part of this chapter you learned how to code style sheets by using the `<STYLE TYPE...>` `</STYLE>` tag in the head of your document. You then learned how to call your style code in the body of your document. JavaScript works in a very similar way. The first part of the script appears in the head of your document. This code is surrounded by the `<SCRIPT LANGUAGE= "JavaScript">` `</SCRIPT>` tag. Any JavaScript you write in the head of your document must appear within this code.

You can write as many different statements as you please within the `<SCRIPT>` `</SCRIPT>` tags. Each statement should end with `;` (semi-colon) and a hard return. The script will be executed in a sequential order. You can have multiple pairs of `<SCRIPT>` `</SCRIPT>` tags in your document; just remember to keep your code as clean as possible. JavaScript is case sensitive, so we recommend keeping it all in lower case. Finally, like HTML, JavaScript ignores multiple extra spaces.

JavaScript and the Browser Window

Using JavaScript you can tell the browser to appear and behave in many different ways. We'll start out really simply.

Creating an Alert Message

Let's say you want the browser to pop up an alert message when the user arrives at the web page. To do this we use the `onLoad` event. This event initiates an action as soon as the user arrives at a page and it has loaded. A list of commonly used events is detailed in Chapter 7, "Dynamic Web Animation." Here is the code used to pop up an alert message:

```
<HTML>
<HEAD>
<TITLE>Alert!</TITLE>
    <SCRIPT LANGUAGE="JavaScript">
        function popUp(message){
        alert(message);
        }
```

```
        </SCRIPT>
</HEAD>
<BODY BGCOLOR="#FFFFFF"
ONLOAD="popUp('Warning! You are
entering a funky design zone!')"
BACKGROUND="images/stripesbg.gif">
</BODY>
</HTML>
```

The result of this code is illustrated in Figure 5.8. Take a minute to examine the way the code was written. The function is stated within the script tags in the head of the document. The `onLoad` action is placed in the body tag. `OnLoad` signifies the event; alert calls the function or behavior. The part in parenthesis, in this case `('Warning! You are entering a funky design zone!')`, is the property we are telling the alert message to take. Figure 5.9 visually diagrams this logic.

figure 5.8

A JavaScript alert message.

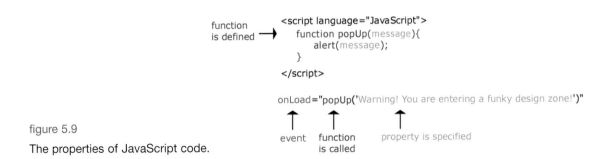

figure 5.9

The properties of JavaScript code.

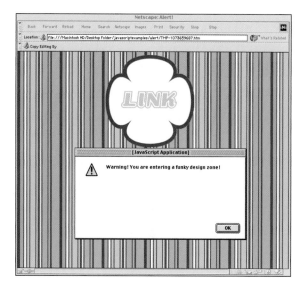

figures 5.10 and 5.11

Two alerts are generated from the same JavaScript function.

This next example illustrates how you can call the same function multiple times. In this example the onLoad action brings up the same alert message as the first example. Another alert message is brought up when the visitor clicks on the link. The sequence of events is illustrated in Figures 5.10 and 5.11.

```
<HTML>
<HEAD>
<TITLE>Alert!</TITLE>
        <SCRIPT LANGUAGE="JavaScript">
                function popUp(message){
                        alert(message);
                }
        </SCRIPT>
</HEAD>
<BODY BGCOLOR="#FFFFFF"
ONLOAD="popUp('Warning! You are
entering a funky design zone!')"
background="images/stripesbg.gif">
        <CENTER>
                <P>
                <A HREF="url.html"
ONMOUSEDOWN="popUp('why are you
leaving me?')"><img
src="images/linkout.gif" width="234"
height="234" border="0"></A>
        </CENTER>
</BODY>
</HTML>
```

Tip:

`alert()` is a predefined function in JavaScript and can be called directly from an event handler like `onLoad`. As such the above code can be simplified to look like:

```
<HTML>
<HEAD>
<TITLE>Alert!</TITLE>
</HEAD>
<BODY BGCOLOR="#FFFFFF"
ONLOAD="alert('Warning! You are
entering a funky design zone!')"
BACKGROUND="images/stripesbg.gif">
        <CENTER>
            <P>
            <A HREF="url.html"
ONMOUSEDOWN="alert('why are you
leaving me?')"><IMG
SRC="images/linkout.gif"
WIDTH="234" HEIGHT="234"
BORDER="0"></A>
        </CENTER>
</BODY>
</HTML>
```

You will notice, because we can directly call the alert function, we no longer need the `<script></script>` tags to write a custom function.

Pop-Up Windows (Basic)

Pop-up windows can be used creatively in your interfaces. With HTML, the only way to open a new window is by using the `target=new` tag within an `href`. Using this method for popping up windows severely limits your design. You have no control over the size of the window where it pops up or how it appears. Using JavaScript you can create windows that are specific sizes with specific attributes, merging them cleanly into your design.

Fluent Studios designed a companion site for a TV documentary on the California power crisis for KQED, San Francisco's public broadcast station. The site has an area that showcases video clips from the film. The clips are displayed in pop-up windows that are accessed by clicking on graphics in the main HTML window (see Figure 5.12). The following is the code the designers used to create the pop-up windows:

```
<HTML>
<HEAD>
<TITLE>Open Window</TITLE>

<SCRIPT LANGUAGE="JavaScript">
<!--
    function openBrWindow
    (theURL,winName,features){
        window.open(theURL,
        winName,features);
    }
//-->
```

```
</SCRIPT>
</HEAD>

<BODY BGCOLOR="#FFFFFF">
<A HREF="#"
ONCLICK="openBrWindow('fightbackmov.
html','videowindow','toolbar=no,
location=no,menubar=no,scrollbars=no,
resizable=no,width=400,height=500')">
<IMG SRC="images/watchstory1.gif"
WIDTH="149" HEIGHT="75" BORDER="0"
name="Image1"></A>
</BODY>
</HTML>
```

In this code there are three different properties being defined in the `function` tag in the head of the document (`theURL,winName,features`). Each of these corresponds with the properties specified in the `image` tag. Each property is stated within the parentheses (`'fightback-mov.html','videowindow','toolbar=no, location=no,menubar=no,scrollbars=no, resizable=no,width=400,height=500'`). The first two are pretty obvious. `fightbackmov. html` is the URL that will open in the pop-up window. `videowindow` is the name of the window. The last one is a little more complex. All the words in this property define the various features the window will have. The features themselves are self-explanatory. Notice in Figure 5.13 what the same exact pop-up window looks like if we specify yes for each of these features. The window now has all the features of a default browser

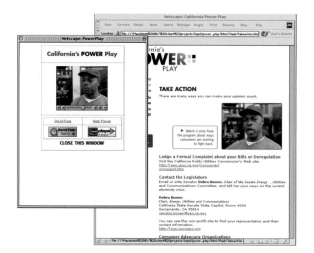

figure 5.12

A window pops up to display the movie clip.

figure 5.13

A pop-up window with all the default browser features.

window—the toolbar, the area for typing the URL, and so on. Fortunately, by specifying no for these features we don't have to be distracted by excessive navigation.

Note:

Like the `alert()` function, the `window.open()` function can be called directly from the event handler, and the pop-up window code is very often written using the following code:

```
<HTML>
        <HEAD>
                <TITLE>Open
Window</TITLE>
        </HEAD>


        <BODY BGCOLOR="#FFFFFF">
                <A HREF="#"
ONCLICK="window.open('fightbackmov
.html','videowindow','toolbar=no,
location=no,menubar=no,scrollbars=
no,resizable=no,width=400,height=5
00')"><IMG SRC="banner1.gif"
WIDTH="149" HEIGHT="75" BORDER="0"
NAME="Image1"></A>
        </BODY>
</HTML>
```

Close Window

In some cases, it is nice to provide users with a Close Window button. The code the designers used in the Power Play site for the Close This Window button is as follows:

```
<a href="javascript:;"
onClick="window.close()"><img
src="images/vidclosewindow.gif"
width="147" height="25"
border="0"></a>
```

Because the close window function is a predefined JavaScript function the code can be called directly from the event handler in the body of the document within the `<A HREF>` tag.

Pop-Up Windows (Advanced)

Now that you understand how to pop up a window and how to control the various window features, you can really begin to get creative with how you use them.

Full-Screen Browser

One of the most frustrating things about web design is that there are so many different variables that make up the way each individual sees a site. Mac or PC, Netscape or Internet Explorer, hundreds, thousands, or millions of colors, Flash or no Flash—the variables go on forever. Another variable that you may not have even thought about is the monitor size and how the browser sits proportionally in the monitor. Figures 5.14–5.16 illustrate a number of ways the same

5.14

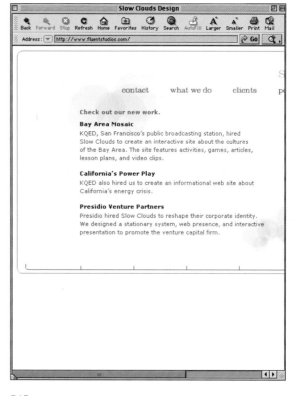

5.15

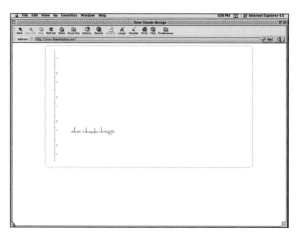

figures 5.14–5.16

The same browser window opened in various proportions on one monitor.

5.16

browser appears on one monitor. As you can see, the entire composition depends on the proportions for how the user has opened their browser. Also, many times the user will have multiple windows open behind the browser. This can distract from your design. Using JavaScript, you can resize the browser automatically so it fills the monitor. The following code will make a new window pop up and scale to the size of the monitor when you click on the image:

```
<HTML>
<HEAD>
<TITLE>Full-Screen</TITLE>
<SCRIPT LANGUAGE="JavaScript">
<!--
    function myFullscreen(where) {
        if (where=="html") {
            var sWindow=
            "webpage.html";
        }
        else {
            var sWindow=
            "webpage.html";
        }
        window.open(sWindow,
    'thestage','width='+(screen.
    width-10)+',height='+(screen.
    height-55)+',top=0,left=0');
    }
//-->
</SCRIPT>
</HEAD>
<BODY BGCOLOR="#FFFFFF">
```

```
<A HREF="#"
ONCLICK="myFullscreen('flash')"><IMG
SRC="images/popup.gif" BORDER="0"></A>
</BODY>
</HTML>
```

In the code, `webpage.html` is the page that will be opened in the new browser window. Just because you can fill everyone's monitor with a browser doesn't mean the HTML of your pages will scale to the same size. You still need to code your page so that it will look nice in all different size windows. The best way to do this is by using tables that expand by percentages or by centering everything.

Remote Controller

The web site shown in Figure 5.17 uses a remote control-type device for the navigation. (In this experimental site the user navigates with the zeroes illustrated in the left window.) When you click on one of the lines of zeroes in the pop-up window, the main web page changes. Targeting between windows works very much like targeting frames. The first step in creating a web remote controller is popping up the controller window as the main HTML page loads. To do this you use the `onLoad` action. The following code will make the controller window pop up as the main page loads.

```
<HTML>
<HEAD>
<TITLE>Remote Controller</TITLE>
```

```
<SCRIPT LANGUAGE="JavaScript">
<!--
    function
    openRemote(theURL,winName,
    features) {
        window.name="main";
        window.open(theURL,
        winName,features);
    }
//-->
</SCRIPT>
</HEAD>
<BODY BGCOLOR="#FFFFFF"
ONLOAD="openRemote('navigation.html',
'navigation','toolbar=no,location=no,
directories=no,status=no,menubar=no,
scrollbars=no,resizable=no,width=206,
height=400')">
</BODY>
</HTML>
```

In the preceding code, a new window of 206×400 pixels opens with the page navigation.html. The first part of the code names the original browser window "main." It is necessary to name the original browser window so that it can be targeted later. Now that the remote is open, you can click on the navigation to make the page in the main window change. Here's the code:

```
<HTML>
<HEAD>
<TITLE>Floating Navigation</TITLE>
</HEAD>
<BODY BGCOLOR="#FFFFFF">
<A HREF="blue.html"
TARGET="main">hello </A>
</BODY>
</HTML>
```

In this example, when you click on the word "hello," the main browser window updates with the page blue.html.

Placing a Window in a Specific Location

At times you may want a window to pop up in a specific place on the monitor. Using the following code, you can specify the exact x and y coordinates for where the window will open. In this example when the user clicks on the image hello.gif, a window that is 200×200 pixels opens up 400 pixels from the left and 300 pixels from the top on the monitor (see Figure 5.18).

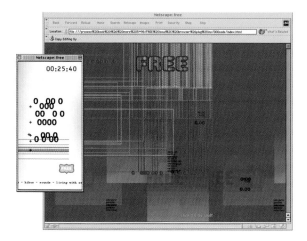

figure 5.17

The navigation is in a "remote control" pop-up window.

```
<HTML>
    <HEAD>
    <TITLE>Place Window</TITLE>
        <SCRIPT LANGUAGE=
        "javascript">
            <!--
            function windowB()
            {
            windowB =
window.open("pink.html","windowB",
"width=200,height=200,toolbar=no,
menubar=no,status=no,scrollbars=no,
resizable=no,left=400,screenX=400,
top=300,screenY=300");
            }
            // -->
        </SCRIPT>
    </HEAD>
    <BODY BGCOLOR="#084B6D">
```

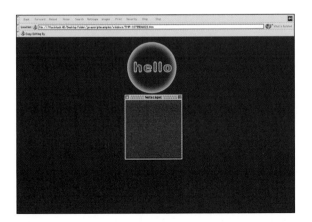

figure 5.18

A window pops up in a specified position on the monitor.

```
    <CENTER>
        <A HREF="#"
ONMOUSEDOWN="windowB();"><Img
Src="images/hello.gif" BORDER=0></A>
        </CENTER>
    </BODY>
</HTML>
```

Shaking Browser Window

Another fun trick is the 'earthquake' trick. This trick uses the `moveTo(x,y)` function to move the window after it has popped up. By feeding different coordinates each time we call the `moveTo (x,y)` function, we can move the pop-up around the desktop.

```
<HTML>
    <HEAD>
    <TITLE>Shake Window</TITLE>
    <SCRIPT LANGUAGE="javascript">

    coordinates=[400,300,600,300,
    600,400,400,400,400,300,600,300,
    600,400,400,400,400,300,600,300,
    600,400,400,400,400,300,600,300,
    600,400,400,400,400,300,600,300,
    600,400,400,400];
    <!--
        function windowB()
        {
            windowB =
window.open("navigation.html",
"windowB","width=200,height=200,
toolbar=no,menubar=no,status=no,
scrollbars=no,resizable=no");
```

```
              moveWindowB(0,1);
        //for (var i=0; i<
coordinates.length;i=i+2){
              //
setTimeout("windowB.moveTo(coordinates
["+i+"],coordinates["+eval(i+1)+"])",
750);
        //}
        }
        function
        moveWindowB(x,y){
        //alert(x);
              windowB.moveTo
              (coordinates[x],
              coordinates[y])

              if (x <=
              coordinates.length
              /2){
setTimeout("moveWindowB
("+eval(x+2)+","+eval(y+2)+")",
50);
              }
        }
// -->
</SCRIPT>
</HEAD>
<BODY BGCOLOR="#084B6D">
        <CENTER>
              <A HREF="#"
ONMOUSEDOWN="windowB();"><Img
Src="images/hello.gif" BORDER=0></A>
        </CENTER>
     </BODY>
</HTML>
```

Opening Two Windows

The site illustrated in Figure 5.19 has a postcard generator. The opening postcard page presents six different postcard selections. When you click on the icon of choice, the main page switches to the postcard customization page and two small windows pop up (see Figure 5.20). One window provides background pattern choices and the other one is a stamp detail. The code for making two windows pop up at the same time is as follows:

```
<HTML>
     <HEAD>
     <TITLE>Pop Up Twice</TITLE>
     </HEAD>
           <SCRIPT LANGUAGE=
           "Javascript">
           <!--
              function
openaa(documt1,h1,w1,documt2, h2, w2)
{
        myWindow=window.open(documt1,
"background","toolbar=no,location=no,
directories=no,status=no,menubar=no,
scrollbars=no,resizable=no,width=
"+w1+",height="+h1+"");
myWindow2=window.open(documt2,"stamp","
toolbar=no,location=no,directories=no,
status=no,menubar=no,scrollbars=no,
resizable=no,width="+w2+",
height="+h2+"");
```

```
self.location="customize.html";
                    }
               //-->
               </SCRIPT>
        <BODY BGCOLOR="#EFE7C6"
BACKGROUND="postcardbg.gif">
        <A HREF="Javascript:
openaa('background.html',150,200,
'stamp1.html',135,100);"><IMG SRC=
"banner1.gif" WIDTH="65" HEIGHT="60"
BORDER=0></A>
        </BODY>
</HTML>
```

By now you should be pretty familiar with how
the JavaScript works. In this example, function
`openaa(documt1,h1,w1, documt2, h2, w2)`
describes `window1html` page, `window1` height,
`window1` width, `window2html` page, `window2`
height, and `window2` width. In the code for the
image in the body of the document, we write
`<a href="Javascript:openaa('background.`
`html',150,200,'stamp.html',135,100)">`.
Each of the properties stated in parentheses
relates to the function as it is stated in the
JavaScript code.

By now you should have enough experience
writing JavaScript and popping up windows that
you can find and work with other pop-up tricks
that are available on the web.

figure 5.19

A web site that displays different choices
for postcards.

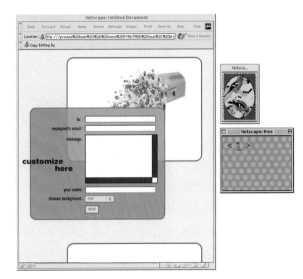

figure 5.20

The main page changes and two windows pop up
simultaneously when a selection is made.

Password Protect Your Site

At times you may want to prevent surfers from entering certain pages or sections of your web sites. There are thousands of different scripts with varying levels of security to protect your site. The example we are giving is by no means the most secure. A hacker would be able to get through this barrier pretty quickly, but your average surfer would be blocked. The more complex the code, the more security you get. We didn't want to get too complicated because this is still an introduction to JavaScript. In other words, don't use this code to protect top-secret information.

Here is the code for a really simple password-protection system:

```
<html>
<head>
<title>Secret Stuff</title>

<script language="JavaScript">
<!--
function passprotect(path) {
var password = prompt("Please Enter
Password:", "");
if (password) location.href = path +
password + ".html";
}
// -->
</SCRIPT>
</head>
```

```
<body bgcolor="# #006666"
onLoad="javascript: passprotect('')">

</body>
</html>
```

This script is set up so that when the web page loads, a window pops up prompting the visitor for a password (see Figure 5.21). The password for this script is the name of the HTML page you are trying to get to minus the .html extension. For example, if the HTML page that you are trying to access is called mysecrets.html, then the password would be mysecrets. If there is no mysecrets.html page name in the folder, the user will get an "unable to find file or directory" message. If you are creative with the way you name your HTML pages, no one will be able to guess where they are going.

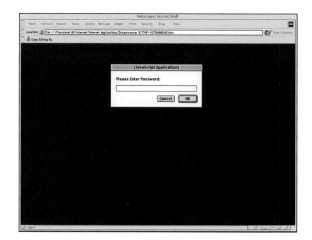

figure 5.21
A password-protected site.

Clients often like their work to be password pro-tected while it is in development. Using this code you can keep your clients work available for review on your site, yet accessible only to them. You can really customize this feature for your clients by making a bumper page with the pass-word of their choice. Perhaps they want their password to be star88 but the page you want to direct them to is called testing.html. Create an HTML page called star88.html. Use this auto-matic page refresh code to make them automat-ically go from star88.html to testing.html:

```
<HTML>
<HEAD>
<TITLE></TITLE>
<META HTTP-EQUIV="Refresh" CONTENT="1;
URL=testing.html">
</HEAD>
<BODY bgcolor="#FFFFFF">
</BODY>
</HTML>
```

The preceding code refreshes the page to a new HTML page after one second. You can use this code in other instances. The number 1 in CONTENT="1" specifies that the browser will refresh in one second. If you change the number to 5, it refreshes in five seconds. You can use this simple refresh code to flash a news mes-sage or graphic before redirecting a site visitor into a web site.

Working with Random Elements

Adding a little bit of random behavior to your pages makes each visit to a site a little different. Loading random graphic elements or sound can be a nice feature for a site that is frequently visited. It keeps the experience fresh, and makes it seem like someone is updating the pages even if they aren't.

Displaying a Random Background Pattern

We'll start out simple. This code makes a ran-dom background pattern appear every time you load the page. Here's the code:

```
<HTML>
<HEAD>
<TITLE>Random Background</TITLE>
<SCRIPT LANGUAGE="Javascript">
<!--
    function bkgrnd() {} ;
    bg = new bkgrnd () ;
    n = 0
    bg[n++] = "images/image1.gif"
    bg[n++] = "images/image2.gif"
    bg[n++] = "images/image3.gif"
    bg[n++] = "images/image4.gif"
    bg[n++] = "images/image5.gif"
    rnd = Math.floor(Math.random() *
n) ;
    tmp =  '<BODY BACKGROUND="'
+bg[rnd]+ '"'
        +' BGCOLOR="#FFFFFF">'
```

```
  //-->
</SCRIPT>
</HEAD>

<SCRIPT LANGUAGE="Javascript"><!--
document.write( tmp )
 //--></SCRIPT>
</BODY>
</HTML>
```

You can list as many or few background images in the script as you please. If you want more than five, just add sequentially below the `bg[n++] = "images/image5.gif"` line.

Embedding a Random Sound

Sounds add a whole new feeling to your design; however, hearing the same sounds over and over can drive you crazy. The last thing you want is for someone to leave your site just because they are sick of the sound! This code will play a random sound each time the page is loaded:

```
<HTML>
<HEAD>
<TITLE>Random Sound</TITLE>
</HEAD>
<BODY BGCOLOR="#FFFFFF">
<SCRIPT LANGUAGE="Javascript">
<!--
    function sound() {
    } ; s = new sound() ; n = 0
    // - Sound Database -
    s[n++]= "sound01.mp3"
```

```
s[n++]= "sound02.mp3"
s[n++]= "sound03.mp3"
s[n++]= "sound04.mp3"
s[n++]= "sound05.mp3"
s[n++]= "sound06.mp3"
i=Math.floor(Math.random() * n);
if (navigator.appName.indexOf
("Microsoft") != -1){
        document.write('<BGSOUND
        SRC="'+ s[i] +'"> ')
    }
else if
(navigator.appName.indexOf
("Netscape") != -1){
        document.write('<EMBED
        SRC="'+ s[i] +'" HIDDEN=
        TRUE AUTOSTART=TRUE> ')
    }
//-->
</SCRIPT>
</BODY>
</HTML>
```

Note:

Depending on browser and compatibility, not all sound types will play automatically—you may need plug-ins or helper applications. In the preceding code you can use as many sounds as you wish, just keep adding them to the list of sounds. You can use different sound types as well—we used the .mp3 extension in this example, but you can use .wav and .mid sounds too.

Loading a Random HTML Page

If you really want variation for your visitors, you can have an entirely different HTML page load each time you come to a site. It's simple: The hardest part is coming up with a bunch of different HTML pages to choose from. Here's how you do it:

```
<HTML>
<HEAD>
<TITLE>Load a Random Page</TITLE>
<SCRIPT LANGUAGE="Javascript">
<!--

    function randomwebpage() {
    } ;
    p = new randomwebpage() ;
    n = 0
    p[n++]= "a.html"
    p[n++]= "b.html"
    p[n++]= "c.html"
    p[n++]= "d.html"
    p[n++]= "e.html"
    i=Math.floor(Math.random() * n);
    self.location.href=( p[i] );
//-->
</SCRIPT>
</HEAD>
<BODY BGCOLOR="#ffffff">
</BODY>
</HTML>
```

Copy the code above into an HTML page. If it is the home page you want to randomly rotate, then name this page index.html. Like the previous examples, you can have as many HTML pages as you want to choose from. Simply continue the list below `p[n++]= "e.html"`. When this page loads it will immediately refresh itself with one of the pages in the list.

Moving Ahead with JavaScript

We have only scratched the surface of the vast world of JavaScript that lives on the web. By now you should be able to go to a JavaScript site and easily integrate other people's code into your pages. Almost any code you want exists somewhere on the web and is available for you to use. These are some good resources for code and tutorials:

- www.scriptsearch.com/ JavaScript/Scripts/
- builder.cnet.com
- www.jsworld.com
- cgiarchive.com
- javascript.internet.com
- www.javascript.com

Summary

Using what you have learned in this chapter, you can add a whole new level of sophistication to your web pages. Style sheets give you flexibility and control over the appearance of your pages. They provide an easy and efficient way to make large scope design changes on the fly. They make organizing any size site a breeze. Adding JavaScript to your pages completely changes the user experience. All of a sudden the web seems much more personal and each surfing experience becomes unique.

Inspirational Design Model

Stella Lai and
Krister Olsson
Tree-Axis

"A talking rabbit jumped out from behind

the tree and told us that if we named our

company tree-axis we would make a lot

of money."

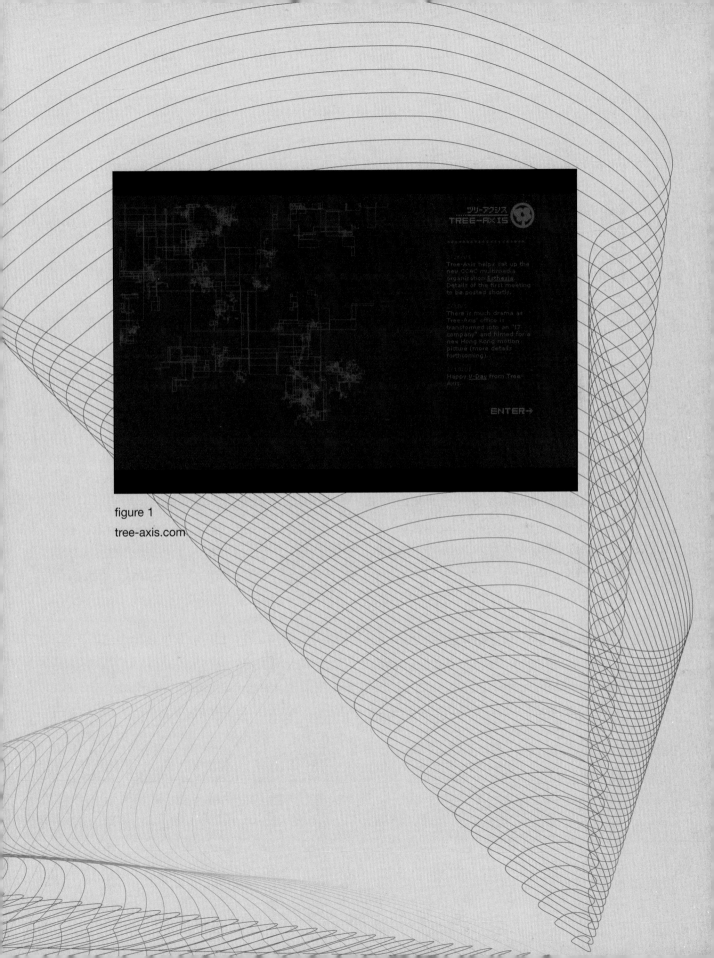

figure 1
tree-axis.com

Stella Lai and Krister Olsson could be deemed the next dynamic duo. In the tradition of the great duos, such as Hepburn and Tracey, or Astaire and Rogers, dynamic duos possess a power that is illuminated even stronger when together. Stella and Krister, co-founders of the design studio, tree-axis, possess that special "one-two punch" with their creative and technical expertise.

Together they have tackled work for such clients as MTVi, AOL, and Saachi & Saachi, exploring new interactive mediums for online games. Together they have fun. Together they are an inspiration.

What inspires you?

Stella and Krister: Everything!

Please tell me more about your design studio Tree-Axis. How did you come up with the name? What kinds of projects do you work on?

Stella: One day Krister and I were walking through the forest when we saw this really old redwood tree. A talking rabbit jumped out from behind the tree and told us that if we named our company tree-axis we would make a lot of money.

Krister: Uh, yeah. We like to work on projects that target the consumer space. Things like games as well as mildly-intensely interactive hyperkinetic design. The most interesting things we've done have been for clients like MTV, Nike, and Gatorade. Of course we have a more mellow, contemplative side (for example, the piece we did for the Remedi Project).

Our gentler work tends to be more for promotion, for non-profit projects, or for ourselves.

What's your creative process when you are working on a project? How do you factor in the technology?

Stella: We [Stella and Krister] work as a team, so often times design ideas come out of code Krister has been playing with, and vice versa. Sometimes Krister will hit a wall in a project early on, with clients wanting something that hasn't been done before, that looks virtually impossible. This often creates a new path for exploration, and potentially, a new project. For example, for a project for MTVi, Krister needed to develop a mechanism which allowed graphics to be uploaded from a Shockwave application to a server without any extras. This was similar to a feature request he had run into before when doing work for Disney. By the time the MTVi project rolled around, he had a working solution based on his explorations.

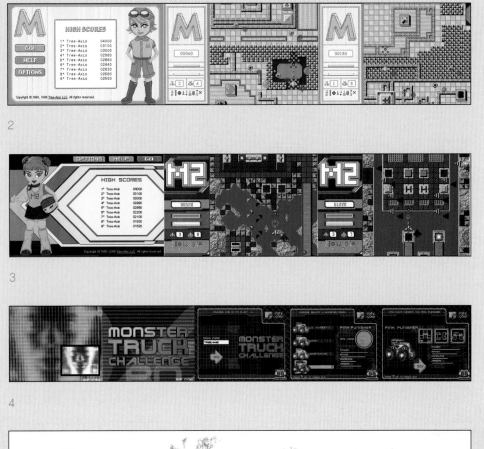

2

3

4

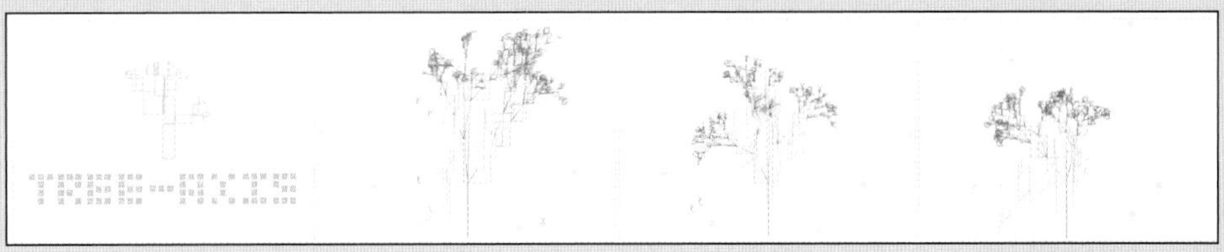

5

figures 2 and 3

Games developed by tree-axis

figure 4

MTV Monster Truck Challenge

figure 5

The Remedi Project, 2000 Summer
Exhibition

figure 6

A typical tree-axis storyboard

What's your dream project?

Stella: To create a new media lab for kids, with the opportunity to design everything from the interior to the print materials. And of course the many interactive installations and toys.

Krister: Developing interactive work, either online, or offline, for one of my non-print/web/multimedia/etc. design heroes (that is, fashion or architecture heroes), with complete creative control (or as much as possible!), with a comfortable time frame and a budget big enough to support my many excesses.

How do you think Broadband will change the way in which the digital medium will be thought of and designed for?

Stella: Broadband, eh?

Krister: I'm kind of curious about how the proliferation of Flash sites will affect search engines. As the web becomes more dynamic (sites being Flash or backend or something else driven), it is evolving into more of a collection of sites from a collection of pages. In some ways it's frustrating; it can become more difficult to find what you are looking for. Broadband will probably exacerbate the situation.

Who are your design heroes?

Stella: John Maeda and right now, Murakami Takashi.

Krister: John Maeda. Mostly for his ability to create a powerful synergy between design and programming. Rei Kawakubo: for her completely uncompromising nature, and her ability to build such a powerful brand (Comme des Garçons) using very little marketing. Also, her ability to enhance her own work (without diluting it in any way) by forming partnerships with people in other areas of design expertise (interior design, furniture design, etc.).

Do you have any advice that you would like to share with all the aspiring designers out there?

Stella: Be cool, stay in school. Say no to drugs. D.A.R.E.

Krister: No.

If you could be a superhero, who would you be and why?

Stella: I want to be Doraemon. He is not really a superhero, but a blue cat. He has a magic pocket on his tummy and there are all kinds of toys inside: a time traveling machine, isolation bubbles, a virtual space enlarger... and so on.

Krister: I'd be LinguisticsMan, able to speak every language in the known universe.

What are three things in the world you can't live without?

Stella: My cat Pupi, sugar, and my motorcycle.

Krister: My cat Isis, travel, and a grab bag of other things and people.

Please name a bad habit you have.

Stella: I'm hyperactive. Is that a habit or disorder?

Krister: I am easily irritated, particularly when Stella is hyperactive.

Tree-Axis URLs:

- **Tree-Axis** `www.tree-axis.com`
- **The Remedi Project**
  `www.theremediproject.com`
  (2000 Summer exhibition)
- **MTV Monster Truck Challenge**
  `www.tree-axis.com/relocated/`
  `MTV.com/rr.html`

figure 7

Tree-Axis workshop

On Writing Bios:

Krister Olsson, Technical Director. Aside from being a cutting-edge programmer, Krister is also a shape-shifter. Shape-shifting is neither a skill nor a hobby, because he can't control what physical form he takes. It happens suddenly, in the morning, before breakfast. It doesn't affect his work unless he meets with a client in the form of an ice cream truck or a front-end loader. He cannot, can *not,* travel through time. We can't stress that enough.

Stella Lai, Creative Director. Somewhere in the Library of Congress there's an ancient text describing the appearance, in 2500 BCE, of a giant cat to the peoples of the Hawaiian Archipelago. Legend has it this cat devoured some 50,000 pineapples and then died of indigestion. In her more lucid moments, Stella claims to be a reincarnation of this cat.

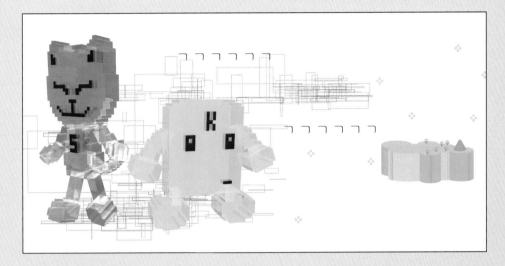

figure 8

Book cover design

Flash Design Principles

Studies in the Interactive Space

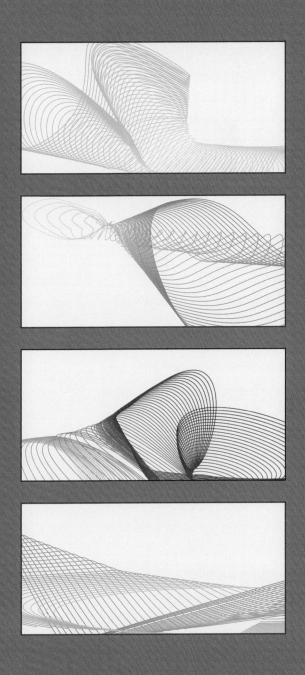

As Flash becomes one of the standard tools for web design, there are certain aspects of designing for Flash that differ depending on the project you are doing. This chapter covers three aspects of Flash design taken from three different projects: a screensaver, a game, and a sitelet (or micro-site). Each project brings together design and technical issues and shows you how client objectives come into play. It's all a game of balance.

Before We Begin...

Every designer—beginning or experienced—knows that not all clients are web savvy. Clients often see something they like on the web and want it on their own site without really evaluating whether it fits their audience, how it stretches their web budget, and how long it might take to implement.

And there's much going on that's exciting in web development these days—especially where Flash is concerned—that most of us would like to add the latest-and-greatest technologies to our sites if our budgets supported it. However, web enthusiasts sometimes have a set vision of what they want, but know little about the realities of making it happen. That's where you come in. The primary sections in this chapter will help you evaluate what's possible and what's needed so that you can balance those realities against what your client wants.

Screensavers

Screensavers are simple eye candy animations that you can design and create easily in Flash, especially if you are a beginner. Some web sites like to offer screensavers as a free download, in order to brand themselves or advertise a special event. Screensavers are most popular off entertainment web sites such as movie or game sites.

When you begin a project that involves a screensaver, you may find yourself wondering where to get started. The key is simple. Just know that screensavers are activated when a computer is idle. Therefore, depending on what the goals of the screensaver is, make sure you keep the following in mind:

- Animations should be simple and looping.
- Keep file size low for download and processor purposes.
- No interactivity. (Remember, if they move their mouse, the computer goes back to their desktop!)

For the Barbie.com site, three different screensavers are available for download from the calendar area. You'll find the download area at www.barbie.com/activities/calendar/downloads/screensaver.asp (see Figure 6.1).

Here we will go through the steps on how to create a Flash screensaver with one from this site. The Barbie screensaver has a distinctive look, as you can see in Figure 6.2.

figure 6.1

You can download three screensavers from the Barbie.com site.

figure 6.2

This Barbie screensaver created in Flash.

Note:

The additional software required to create a Flash screensaver is ScreenTime Media's ScreenTime for Flash. If you are creating both Mac and Windows versions of screensavers, you will need both the Mac and Windows versions of the software. You can download the trial versions of the software from the ScreenTime Media web site (`www.screentime.com`).

The Design Concept

The Barbie.com site you see today launched in the summer of 2000. Since the new site was filled with interactive games and activities, the screensaver's purpose was to be an additional element that would play off the fun nature of the site and would be a great way to continue the Barbie brand offline.

It was a necessary for this screensaver to be a minimal download off a 56K modem. Therefore, I had to keep in mind that it wasn't just the Flash SWF file size that I had to consider, but how big it would be as a projector file. A Flash projector adds a lot more in terms of file size because it needs to add in Flash Player elements.

It's important not to get too carried away with a screensaver. Because most of the site has really rich, interactive scenes and activities, the screensaver's purpose is to be consistent with the design and imagery of the site. However, it isn't something that needs to entertain someone since it's on when the computer has essentially been inactive for a number of minutes. Okay, so watching the flying toasters on a screen can be entertaining, but see how something so simple can do its job so well?

Simple is the key here—and, most importantly—fun. The animations didn't need to be too complex. For assets, I decided on the Barbie-illustrated artwork that we had gotten from the client. They were already in vector format so I knew they would work great in Flash. We narrowed it down to three different screensavers: Two were of flowers and one was illustrated candies. We will go through the making of the candy screensaver here.

The animation would be a simple fade-in of the Barbie logo with visions of cute candies popping up all around the screen. They would zoom out and fade while new ones fade in and repeat the cycle.

Making It in Flash

Because the animation is so simple, it's really simple to make in Flash. To begin with, we need to make sure this movie works within the proportions of a users screen. Since one of the great things about Flash is that it has scales, you can make your movie been essentially any size.

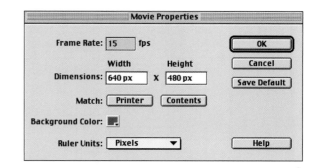

figure 6.3
Choose settings at the lowest common denominator to make sure the largest possible audience will be able to view it.

But it's best to start out with the lowest common denominator, either 640×480 or 800×600 to ensure that no animation will get cut off the screen if a user has a lower resolution (see Figure 6.3).

Start by laying out all the assets for the Flash movie in your library. There are four different candies and each one is its own movie clip. Each of these four movie clips will be on its own layer.

Now we can start animating each candy movie clip and place all the elements over the main timeline (see Figure 6.4). Because it's easy to get caught up in the animation phase of the project, as I'm working and tweaking animations, I typically export test SWFs to check the file size. Once it meets both design and file size standards, I can move on.

Of course, to ensure that the movie will play full screen, use the FSCOMMAND in Flash to make the movie full screen (see Figure 6.5). To do so, go to your Frame Actions palette and type in the following:

```
fscommand ("fullscreen", "true");
```

Now that everything is done, we can create a projector file of the Flash movie. (See Figure 6.6.) Because we are making a Mac Screensaver now, we will make a Mac projector.

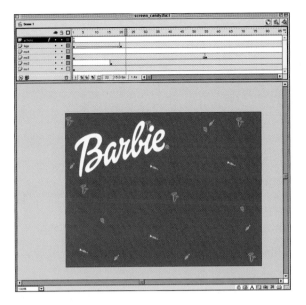

6.4

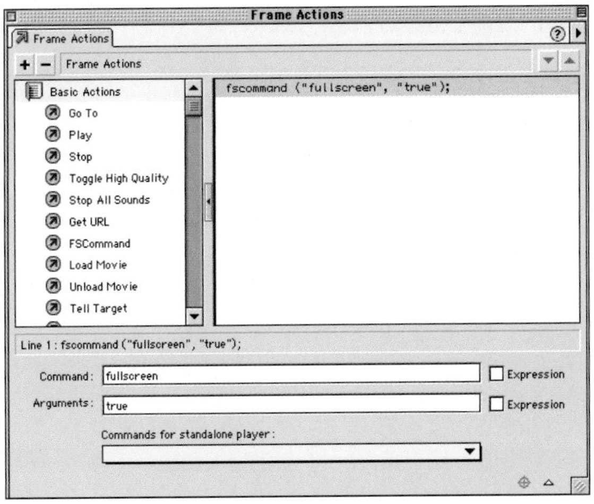

6.5

figure 6.4

Adding the elements to the timeline.

figure 6.5

FSCOMMAND ensures that the movie will play full screen.

figure 6.6

The created projector file.

screen_candy

6.6

Start up the ScreenTime for Flash application and choose Preferences to customize the screensaver. As Figure 6.7 shows, you can have the screensaver quit on mouse moves/clicks and keydowns, have the screensaver expire at a certain amount of time (good for promotions), include a mute button for screensavers with sound, and choose the language option.

We are going to add the Barbie logo to further brand the screensaver. This logo appears when users click on their screensaver preferences (see Figure 6.8). You will also choose the settings that control the way the screensaver operates (see Figure 6.9).

Now from the File menu, choose Convert Projector and select the projector file from your hard drive (see Figure 6.10).

Once it has been successfully converted, you will see the final dialog box (see Figure 6.11).

The final output will be a screensaver control panel that can be placed in your system folder (see Figure 6.12). You'll want to test it out to see how it works on various machines and processor speeds.

In checking the file size, the screensaver is 406K and when stuffed as a self-extracting file is 180K, which takes less than a minute to download on a 56K modem.

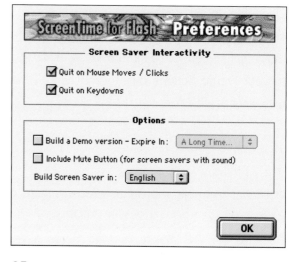

6.7

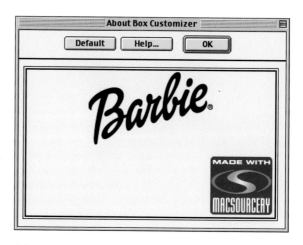

6.8

figure 6.7
Setting screensaver preferences.

figure 6.8
The Barbie logo.

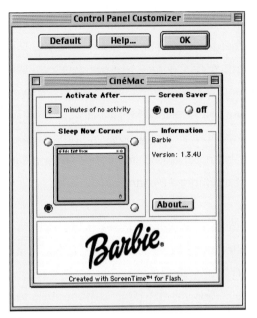

6.9

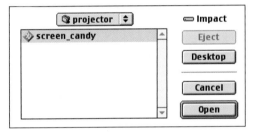

6.10

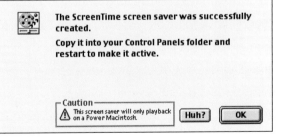

6.11

candy screensaver

6.12

figure 6.9

The settings for the way the screen-saver behaves.

figure 6.10

Choosing the projector file for the screensaver.

figure 6.11

The conversion was successful.

figure 6.12

The finished screensaver object.

Summing Up Screensavers

The screensavers on Barbie.com are popular downloads and work well with the desktop wallpapers and Barbie browser that users can download. You can check them out at `www.barbie.com/activities/calendar/downloads/`. Adding these extra items to your site is a fun addition and a great way to brand a site.

The wallpaper and screensavers are easy to create and make available the web, and your users will find the download steps easy to follow. The best thing is that your custom-designed wallpapers or screensavers will appear in front of the users each time they sit down to work with their computers. That continual reminder of your company may be worth its weight in marketing gold—try it and see!

Games

Games are one of the most popular destinations on the web today. Creating a game, though, doesn't have to be a complex mess of variables. One of the most important steps is the concept and planning stages to game development.

When it comes to brainstorming for games, one popular format is to use classic game concepts—whether from real world activities or classic video games—and add your own spin or twist to it to make it different. For instance, you can have a classic Concentration-type game for matching items but take on a different format like the "Shoe Hunt" game by having the shoes be hidden in a messy room. You can find the Shoe Hunt at `www.barbie.com/Activities/Games/Shoe_Hunt/`.

Shoe Hunt uses fun animation techniques to allow players to look for the missing shoes; just as in Concentration users match identical cards. The game is set up in three different levels, so that users of different experience levels can play. For example, in level 1, when the user rolls the mouse over an object (such as a box top, or even the cat), the object moves to reveal a hidden shoe, if there is one. This room layout and matching shoes give the game a level of novelty and fun, while keeping with a concept that users are familiar with.

Keep in mind the following things when designing a game:

- Make sure the flow of the game is mapped out and assets are organized.
- Create functionality prototypes to make sure ideas can actually work.
- Test, test, test!

In this section, we'll be going in depth into the creative concepting and technical development for the "Let's Baby-sit Baby Krissy" game from Barbie.com (see Figure 6.13). You can find this game online at `www.barbie.com/activities/care_share/Babysit/`.

figure 6.13

The Baby Krissy game.

It is said that designing computer games for young girls is a challenging task. The team of designers and developers at SBI and Company who have been working on developing these since 2000 have found that it can be fun as well.

Game Design Concept

The concept behind the game was to introduce a "nurturing" activity for the "Care n' Share" section of the site in the summer of 2001. One of the decisions was to have a game center around the doll, Baby Krissy, who is Barbie's baby sister. Since this game was targeted to a younger audience of girls aged 4–7 years old, the concept of the game was important. Most of the young girls needed a concept that they could understand and were familiar with in order to interact and play on the computer. We decided that the concept of a babysitting game worked best in this context because we would then be able to create an interactive story around it.

The game was to be an interactive experience of babysitting Baby Krissy that would take the user though three fun, interactive scenes leading to a final payoff screen: a babysitting certificate that could be printed out. Through team brainstorming, lists of possible activities for Baby Krissy, such as eating and sleeping, were listed out. For more game play, it was decided that the three scenes would be randomly picked from a poll of six scenes to keep the game fresh as users came back to the game.

The popularity of the game was so high among the young girls that we developed more scenes based on email feedback to be added into the game for 2002. The new scenes that were added to the mix were the beach, grocery, and playground scenes.

Figures 6.14 through 6.19 show the six scenes in rotation:

Each individual scene has "on-click" animations (animations that play when the user clicks on it), which take users through the tasks of helping Baby Krissy eat, sleep, play, and so on. After the user has completed two tasks, the next button appears and the user can choose to stay (and explore some Easter egg sounds and animations) or move on to the next scene. A voice and text instructions help young girls who can't read understand how to play the game.

figure 6.14

The bathtub scene.

figure 6.15

The beach scene.

figure 6.16

The dressing scene.

figure 6.17

The feeding scene.

figure 6.18

The grocery scene.

figure 6.19

The playground scene.

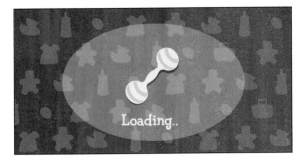

figure 6.20

The loading scene.

figure 6.21

The end of the game—a babysitting certificate.

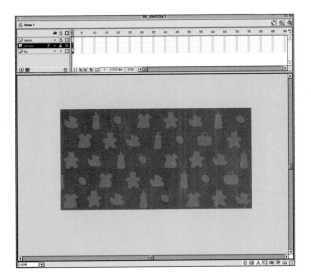

figure 6.22

The shell movie in Flash.

Each scene has a loading sequence that plays when the scene is downloading in the background (see Figure 6.20). The game is optimized for 56K modems and each scene is an average weight of 100–150K. To make the loading scene fun, users can interact with it by rolling over the rattle and seeing it shake.

The final ending screen gives young girls a sense of satisfaction and completion to their fun by getting an official babysitting certificate, which proudly displays their name (taken from the intro scene) and Baby Krissy herself (see Figure 6.21).

Flash Development— Randomizing Scenes

Before Flash development starts, a clear plan for the architecture needs to be in place. Lead Flash designer David Warczak ensures the team's game development consistency by creating a shell movie (see Figure 6.22). A *shell movie* is the Flash game's "level 0" movie—a movie that has all the basic properties and background laid out and has the scripts that bring in the other movies to be layered on top of it.

"The movie levels can be very useful in creating rich online gaming experiences in Flash," explains David. "By using a 'shell' SWF as a backstage for the gaming interface, variable values can be easily captured, stored, and passed to the other SWFs as the user progresses through game play. The result is a richer, more customized user experience, even in games that have no back-end component."

In the Baby Krissy shell movie, the randomizing script that chooses which three scenes the user will be playing with is present, along with the loading of the intro, loading, and final screens (see Figure 6.23).

By using an array in Flash, you can create your own functions. In this case we are setting up the randomization of the scenes. Listing each of the six scene names sets up the array "activities." Make sure you include the .swf syntax because these are the names of the Flash movies that will be loaded into the shell.

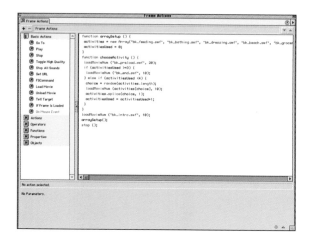

figure 6.23
The randomization of scenes script.

```
function arraySetup () {
    activities = new
Array("bk_feeding.swf",
"bk_bathing.swf", "bk_dressing.swf",
"bk_beach.swf", "bk_grocery.swf",
"bk_playground.swf");
    activitiesUsed = 0;
}
```

The second part of the script dictates the order and loading of the scenes as well as the loading, intro, and final screens. The function also checks to make sure that three scenes are chosen through `activitiesUsed`; once it becomes greater than four, it moves it the final ending screen.

```
function chooseActivity () {
    loadMovieNum ("bk_preload.swf",
    20);
    if (activitiesUsed >=3) {
        loadMovieNum ("bk_end.swf",
        10);
    } else if (activitiesUsed <4) {
        choice =
        random(activities.length);
        loadMovieNum
        (activities[choice], 10);
        activities.splice(choice, 1);
        activitiesUsed =
        activitiesUsed+1;
    }
}
loadMovieNum ("bk_intro.swf", 10);
arraySetup();
stop ();
```

By randomizing scenes, games can be kept fresh so that users can have a unique experience each time they come back.

Flash Development— Sound Objects

Now let's look more closely at an individual scene and how to set up the movie and work with sounds. Here we will be working with the Baby Krissy feeding movie (see Figure 6.24).

When working with individual animations, it's a good idea to have them within a working movie clip. In each Baby Krissy scene movie, for consistency across Flash designers, the movie clip `activities_anim` held all the animations for that movie. This ensured that if things needed to be edited, everyone would know where all the clips would be.

The sound object is a powerful attribute in Flash that can allow you to script and play sounds on cue without being tied to a timeline.

Working with the radio in the movie, let's go into the radio movie clip (see Figure 6.25).

figure 6.24

The Baby Krissy feeding movie.

figure 6.25

The radio movie clip.

In the library, go to the Sounds folder and high-light music.aif as you see in Figure 6.26.

From the top-right corner choose Options and then choose Linkage. Enter the name "music," which is then the same name used in your script. Make sure that the Export for ActionScript and Export in first frame are selected (see Figure 6.27).

Going back to the radio movie clip, we will add the action to the invisible button so that when the radio is clicked on, the music will play.

```
on (release) {
    gotoAndPlay ("on");
    _root.music.start(0, 400);
}
```

The first element in parentheses is the secondOffset argument, which allows you to have the sound start to play at a specific second point in the file. Since here we want it to start at the very beginning, we have it set to start at 0 seconds. The next argument sets the looping, which here is set to 400.

figure 6.26

The library.

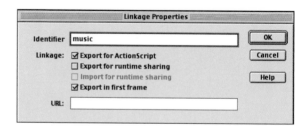

figure 6.27

The linkage property from the library.

figure 6.28

The final Baby Krissy game on the Barbie.com site.

Summing Up Games

It is important throughout the design and development of your game to never lose your key concept. Sometimes it is easy to get pulled into the nitty-gritty details and wind up making a game more complex, but that doesn't necessarily make it better. Sometimes it can take your concept and goals way off track.

Make sure you go through a complete testing process with various browsers and systems to ensure that all the bugs are detected and can be fixed before the launch. More importantly, ensure that the end flow and experience for the user is a good one. Figure 6.28 shows the final scene in the Baby Krissy game.

Sitelets

Sitelets (some use the word microsites) are essentially self-contained mini web sites that link off a main site into its own popup browser window. Sitelets are extremely flexible because they allow more freedom in terms of design (you aren't constrained by the look and feel of the main site) as well being a special outlet for targeted messaging. Sitelets can be product demos, marketing campaigns, contests, games, or promotions. That's why multimedia elements such as Flash, audio, video, and animations work so well in a sitelet because these elements are all self-contained within their own shell.

Keep in mind the following things when designing a sitelet:

- Keep navigation to a minimum; remember, it's a sitelet, not a web site.
- Know the target audience for the sitelet and make sure the technology involved fits that demographic.
- Maintain consistency if the sitelet is part of a larger marketing campaign.

We'll explain how to create a sitelet by using the Dockers® Mobile Pant™ sitelet as an example (see Figure 6.29). The sitelet is linked off the main Dockers site off a promo ad on the middle right (see Figure 6.30).

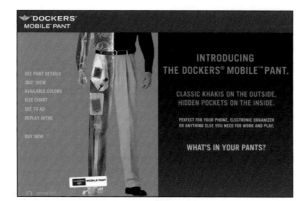

figure 6.29

Dockers' sitelet home page.

figure 6.30

Dockers' homepage.

Sitelet Design Concept

The goal was to design a sitelet to coincide with the introduction of the Mobile Pant™ from Dockers. The client wanted a sitelet that would convey a sense of innovation and appeal to its target audience of 25–40-year-old techie males.

Conceptually, the sitelet needed to work in tandem with the television and print campaigns being done by another agency. Michael Chichi, Interactive Creative Director at SBI and Company, headed up the project. "In the introduction sequence to the sitelet, we borrowed the musical score from the TV spot, and some screen grabs," explains Michael. "We sequenced them as in the commercial, and added some Flash animation over top with type to give it a more cinematic and dramatic effect, and to set the stage."

Figures 6.31 through 6.35 show the introductory sequence to the Dockers' sitelet.

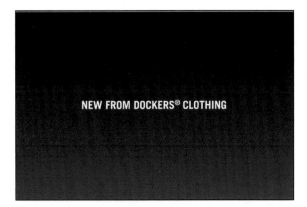

figure 6.31

figure 6.32

figure 6.33

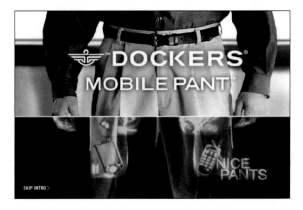

figure 6.34

figure 6.35

The rest of the sitelet was aimed to allow the audience to go deep into what makes the Mobile Pant so special and noteworthy (see Figures 6.36 and 6.37). "We utilized the metaphor of an X-ray machine (also borrowed from the marketing campaign), to reveal features of the pant such as the 'Hidden Zip Vault Pocket,'" describes Michael.

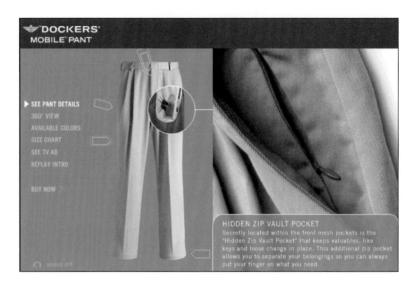

figure 6.36

The hidden zip vault pocket.

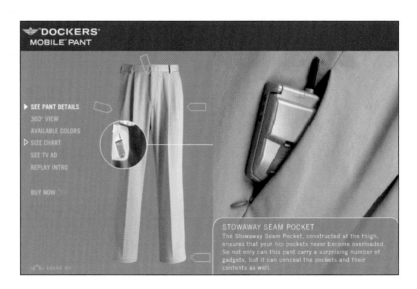

figure 6.37

The stowaway seam pocket.

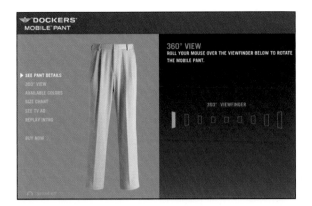

figure 6.38
360-degree view.

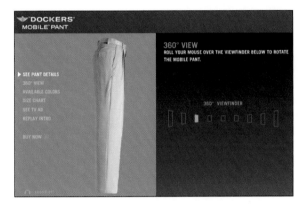

figure 6.39
Another version of the 360-degree view.

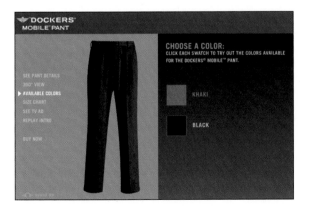

figure 6.40
Displaying the pants in another color.

Other sections include interactive 360-degree views and color charts, where you could interactively rotate the pant to see all angles or change the color (see Figures 6.38 through 6.40).

Flash and HTML

One of the clear advantages of using Flash to author web sites, especially sitelets, is that all of the disparate elements can be much more integrated—everything from sound, animation, type, photography, and interactivity. This allows for quick turnaround and implementation, as well as a seamless end-user experience.

When the goal of a site is provide an experience that entertains and educates, Flash provides a much more compelling experience than that of flat HTML. Flash is also more appropriate when a sitelet is not too text-heavy, and is aimed to be more experiential than informational.

But to make sure that you are truly building that seamless experience, HTML does come into play. As the framework for all the Flash movies, it's important to see how each section is going to work with the others and what would work well to create a seamless experience.

Because one of the sections was going to be "See TV Ad," there had to be a seamless way to move between the Flash movie and the QuickTime video clip of the commercial (see Figure 6.41).

> ## Note:
>
> There could have easily been another pop-up window to play the QuickTime movie, but it would only give the user more browser windows open. It's important to maintain the concepts of good usability and to ensure optimum user experience.

Because the navigation needed to be in Flash, the page structure was broken up into four frame quadrants (see Figure 6.42).

Frameset 1 is the branded masthead that also serves as an advertising space for within the sitelet. When the Mobile Pants Sweepstakes was in effect, a special callout was in this area to drive users to enter the sweepstakes. Frameset 2 holds the Flash navigation. Framesets 3 and 4 actually work together as the main area of the site. All of the Flash movies in the sitelet cover the area of Framesets 3 and 4. Only in the TV section does Frameset 4 appear.

When users come to this section and click on the TV commercial image, the QT movie will start to play seamlessly and the experience is not interrupted (see Figure 6.43).

Flash Promotions

As a part of the sitelet, a sweepstakes section was created (see Figure 6.44). Instead of doing the usual entry form, the team decided to create a game following the X-ray theme, where users

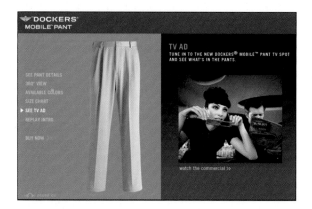

figure 6.41
Displaying the TV Ad section.

figure 6.42
Frameset breakdown.

figure 6.43
TV commercial playing.

had to find the hidden items that were in the secret pockets of the Mobile Pants. Of course, since the goal was to make entering easy, the game portion of it was optional and users could click the button "Enter Sweepstakes Now" to go straight to the entry form.

I photographed each of the items—the cell phone, Compaq IPAQ, and car keys—and we recorded their respective sounds that would alert the user to scan the pants and find the item. To start, the cell phone would zoom up and animate as a ringing sound continued. Only when the user finds the ringing cell phone in the pants (noted with thin blue lines animating out) and clicks it, will it stop and descriptive content on the pocket itself will be revealed on the right. The same goes for the beeping IPAQ, and the jingling car keys. After the car key sequence, the user is automatically taken to the entry form.

Because this idea was following along the whole X-ray scan theme, we decided that we would use the same mask of the pants and x-ray version, but make the mouse trigger the circle viewer to move around the pants.

To do this in Flash, we used the same movie templates that we did for each of the sections and added a few smart clips so that the game could activate and allow the user to interact.

The top-left corner holds the mouse tracker movie clip called "maskscript." The maskscript

figure 6.44
The sweepstakes section.

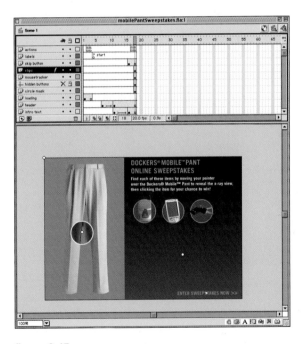

figure 6.45
The sweepstakes Flash movie.

targets the "tracker" movie clip that lies in the center of the masked circle. In this Flash movie, the mouse cursor in this area disappears and is replaced by the masked circle.

The maskscript has 2 frame actions the first one controls the area in which the mouse can go (see Figure 6.46).

```
startDrag ("/tracker", true);
if (getProperty("/tracker", _x)<=190) {
    setProperty ("/mask/xray", _y,
    185-(getProperty("/tracker",
    _y)));
    setProperty ("/mask", _x,
    getProperty("/tracker", _x));
    setProperty ("/mask/xray", _x,
    110-(getProperty("/tracker",
    _x)));
    setProperty ("/mask", _y,
    getProperty("/tracker", _y));
}
```

The second frame loops the sequence with the following:

```
gotoAndPlay (1);
```

As for the mask itself, it can be tricky to line things up in Flash (see Figure 6.47). One of the best rules of thumb is to use the "work in place" function of Flash. By clicking on the movie clip on the stage, the movie will take you to that specific movie clip with the background of the main movie grayed out in the back. Then you can successfully line artwork up and make sure movie clip animations work correctly on the main stage.

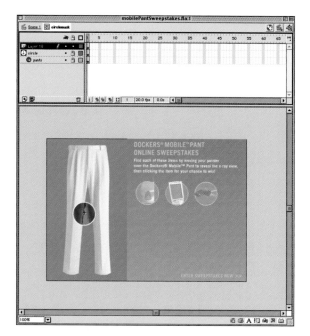

figure 6.47

The masked movie clip.

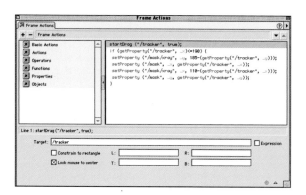

figure 6.46

Mouse tracker script.

By revealing the mask as in Figure 6.48, you'll be able to see where all the hot spots are in the pockets of the pants. Then you'll be able to create the invisible buttons and small animations that will appear once each of the items are activated. Once the items are placed correctly in their respective movie clips and on the stage, the sequence of the phone ringing, IPAQ beeping, and keys jingling begins and users will have an interesting way to sign up for a sweepstakes.

Summary

This chapter introduced you to the basics of adding Flash to your sites. By focusing on three different types of projects—screensavers, games, and sitelets—you were introduced to the design and implementation of Flash animations. Now you can apply the basics to your own ideas, throw in some creativity, and have fun.

URLS In This Chapter

- **Barbie** www.barbie.com
- **Dockers** www.dockers.com

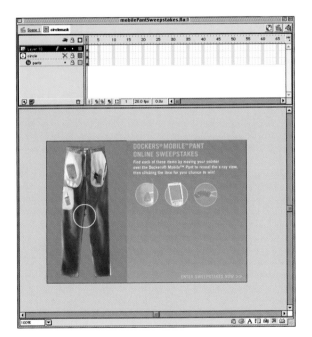

figure 6.48

The masked movie clip revealed.

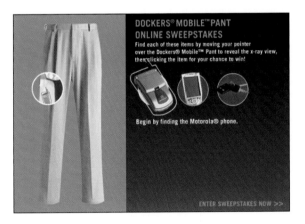

figure 6.49

Final working sweepstakes movie.

Inspirational Design Model

Keith Cottingham
Artist

"I ask my own questions and create my own problems, and then develop the best way to materialize these ideas. I research photographic images, read books on history and cultural anthropology..."

figure 1

Triplets

Constructed photograph

Archival Fuji color coupler print

You are probably already familiar with the work of Keith Cottingham. From the Apple OS X logo to the Apple QuickTime logo, Keith's commercial work showcases his 3D/digital expertise as well as his creative talents. Some would be already content with the body of work and the list of clients that fill his resume. Not Keith.

More impressive is Keith's personal work—his art, and his drive to push the boundaries on what is deemed "digital art." With his photorealisitic creations that he brings to life with a computer, the end result is something that carries a more traditional art aesthetic. Keith spends countless hours that lead into sleepless nights and weeks, perfecting his ideas and honing his vision. It is his vision and his journey of exploration that make him an inspiration to us.

What inspires you?
Life.

You have created some amazing pieces of art that are created on a computer, but look real like photographs or paintings. How would you describe the technology you use to create these realistic images?
I choose photography for its historical constraints to realism and choose painting for creative writing. I use these two methods together to write fictions based in the real world. The technology I use is standard for someone lucky

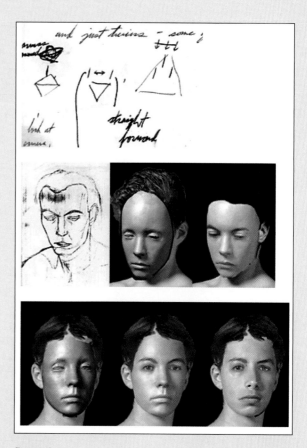

figure 2
Triplets
Creative process

enough to be in my economic sphere. These tools cost: Either one has to have money or knowledge to borrowing software.

I use the tools and methods of advertisement and entertainment. My work is shown as a 2D image, but my work starts as sculpture. I try to make work that occupies space and events.

Some of the work starts as traditional wax sculptures. These sculptures are then digitized into 3D models, while other objects start directly in 3D software. Within 3D software, parts are combined, posed, animated, and rendered as a still image. These renderings then act as underpaintings for original and/or historical photographic material to be painted on top of. When all is done, the digital files are printed as photographic prints.

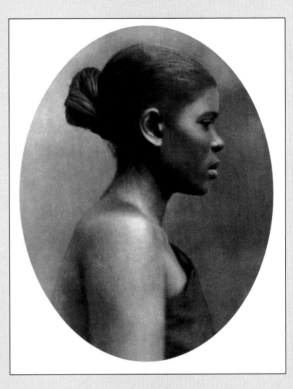

3

figure 3

Portraits (Female Adult #1), 1998
Constructed photograph
Albumen print

figure 4

Landscapes (Animal Sculpture), 1999
Constructed photograph
Gelatin print out print

4

figure 5

Botanicals (Leaves #1), 1999
Constructed photograph
Platinum/palladium print

Please tell us how you get prepared for a project. What's your process? How do you do research?

I ask my own questions and create my own problems, and then develop the best way to materialize these ideas. I research photographic images, read books on history and cultural anthropology. I design personalities, architecture, botanical, and so on, by photographing source material, sculpting in wax, drawing, constructing environments in 3D programs, and montage in 2D programs.

What are some of the new art pieces you are working on? (Tell me what you are researching now—for example, you had mentioned once about researching a person's collarbone/neck structure.)

I've been working on my current project for five years. It's a large series, over forty photographs, presented as traditional genres: portraits, architecture, landscapes, and still lives. Using digital and traditional art techniques, I craft fictions into illusions of a material world.

The images work individually with their separate concerns, and as a group, form a pictorial survey of a fictional existence, set in a period fused from the past, present, and imaginary. Landscapes and buildings become sets. Subjects become actors. They are documents of nowhere, of no time, of nobody, but of constructed possibilities based in the real.

These works imitate the process of becoming real by realizing a human world. We shape and perceive the world egocentrically, with our imaginings acting as mirrors, reflecting back to and drawing onto our lives. We not only mold thoughts into actions and objects, we mold ourselves. As nature, culture, and history continue to fall into a resource well, we gleefully rush towards a place where mystery is further reduced and buried underneath the appearance of the rational.

figure 6
Landscapes (Tree), 1999
Constructed photograph
Gelatin print out print

I'm hoping this work will act as a magical looking glass, revealing unfamiliar glimpses of spirit enshrouded within our designed world and selves, and in doing so, unbury the mysterious that lies beneath the surface of the familiar.

Do you have any advice to the people out there who are interested in getting started with 3D and art?
Go to museums, read books, and spend time on the web looking at work done by others that you admire and hate. Read about their creative process, what influences them, what their goals are, and what tools they use. Get yourself some

software and read the manuals. Take art, history, politics, and any classes that interest you or learn on your own. The important thing is to push your traditional art skills and concepts. Lots of people have skills and talents, and the world is populated with billions of ideas, but forward explorations are not as readily found.

We all work differently, and there is no best way to create, but being old fashioned, this is what I strive for.

Take your ideas, question them, love and hate them, push them, rest, then push them further. Expand your ideas to make them more complex and then simplify them. Repeat this a few times. After a few weeks or months, start working them out materially, and let yourself get lost in the creative idiosyncrasies of your chosen material. Pay attention to accidents that are given to you that might lead to new directions. If your ideas are coming to life, taking you to an exciting place, keep going. If the work takes a wrong turn for the worst, stop, take a rest, refocus, and start again.

We live in a world saturated with monotonous change—a world where accelerated motion, color, and sound tends to deaden us instead of inspire us. There is so much noise; it's very difficult to rise above the cultural pollution. We all have to pay rent, so work will be work. But with personal art and heightened commercial work, you need to be honest, considerate of others, and try not to add to the cultural waste pile. In our current art world, where art is product sold in boutiques, called galleries, art can and should ultimately be about exploration. An exploration that takes us outside of our everyday in order to bring us back into an everyday with a deeper appreciation of life's beauty, mystery, and humor.

7

If you could be a superhero, who would you be and why?
None. I'm already amazed by what we are and what we are capable of.

figure 7

Exploration (Junk), 1999
Constructed photograph
Platinum/palladium print

figure 8

Portraits (Female Youth #1), 1999
Constructed photograph
Gelatin print out print

8

What are three things in the world you can't live without?

Creative inspiration, good health, friends.

Please name a bad habit you have.

Relating to work, my worst habit is perfectionism. I put too much pressure on my work. I'll sit on ideas for months if not years to make sure they hold up before I even start working on them.

Keith Cottingham URL:

- **Keith Cottingham** www.kcott.com

On first jobs:

I graduated from college during a recession, and took temporary jobs. After a few years, I bought a "Learning Illustrator" book and I studied the program for two days on a rented Macintosh. With a very bad portfolio, along with examples of my artwork, I got a temp job at PacBell making maps for phone books. With no timecards, no manager yelling at me, taking breaks when I wanted to, I knew I was moving up in the world. After this, a freelance job at Landor & Associates became a paying school for the commercial arts. During this time, I created a series of three artworks, had some shows, and formed relationships with some galleries. After Landor, I worked at CKS/Partners for eight years. Now, into the void, I continue my art.

Dynamic
Web Animation

Dreamweaver & DHTML

CHAPTER 7

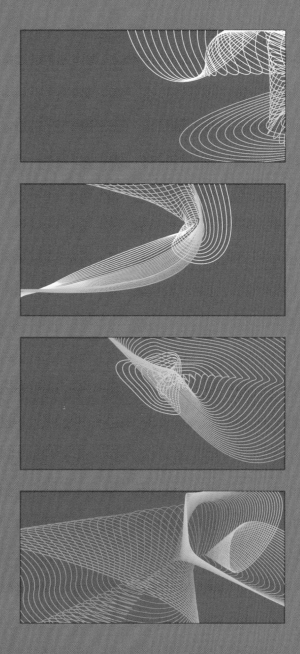

Designers who learn to hand-code HTML are often shocked when they are introduced to Macromedia Dreamweaver. The first thing they think is, "Why did I ever bother learning HTML?" The answer is simple. Learning HTML makes learning Dreamweaver easy and it enables you to utilize the features of Dreamweaver in a way that no HTML novice would ever be able to do. Dreamweaver makes it easy to program a web page; however, understanding why Dreamweaver seems to have limitations for your design and knowing what is and isn't allowed in HTML will allow you to use Dreamweaver efficiently and effectively.

This chapter is not going to teach you all the functions of Dreamweaver. Dreamweaver is a fantastic tool and there are books that focus entirely on the program. We have chosen to write about the elements we think are the most useful in adding to the interest of your design. Toward the end of the chapter we talk about the integration of Fireworks (another Macromedia HTML generating application) into your Dreamweaver documents.

Don't Forget About HTML

Dreamweaver writes all your code—that's why we use it! One of the best parts about Dreamweaver is that your code is always available. New code is written for every object you set on your page. It's simple to flip back and forth between the code on your page and your composition. Just select View>Code. You can also access your code by pressing F10 on your keyboard. If you keep referring to your code, you will not only learn more about writing HTML, DHTML, and JavaScript, but you will be able to modify the code in ways the tools of Dreamweaver would never allow. The best thing you can do when you are learning the things we talk about in this chapter is keep referring to your code.

Using Layers in Dreamweaver

As you learned in Chapter 6, "Flash Design Principles," layers allow designers to have precise control over the placement of images, text, or really *anything* on the page. Whereas tables allow some control of your design, layers allow for complete and total precision. Using Dreamweaver you can preview what you are designing as you bring images and text on to the page. Writing code requires that you keep checking in the browser to see how things are looking. With Dreamweaver, you do need to check in the browser, but not nearly as often. The preview window within the Dreamweaver application allows you to get a pretty clear idea of the composition your code is generating before you open it in the browser. Using this feature will allow you to have a much better idea of what to expect when you do look in the browser.

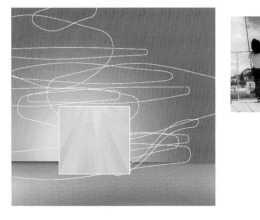

7.1

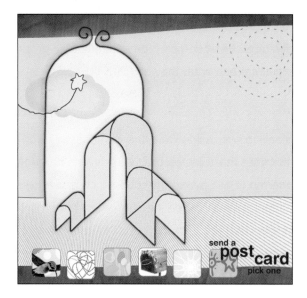

7.2

7.3

figures 7.1–7.3

The web site Free uses layers to stack multiple transparent gifs. The result is a unified composition made of many parts.

Dreamweaver makes it simple to create, manipulate, and even animate layers. Layers can contain anything that you find in regular HTML. This includes, text, formatted text, graphics, plug-ins, forms…you name it. If you can put it on an HTML page, you can put it in a layer. Some web sites depend entirely on layers to make nice compositions (see Figures 7.1–7.3).

Working with Layer Properties

Layers, like all the elements of your page, have distinct and unique properties based on what they are doing. You can access the properties dialog box in Dreamweaver by selecting Window>Properties. Then, select your layer. Notice how the property specifications change to that for layers. The following section describes what some of the different layer properties are and what they do.

Layer Name

Many things, aside from the content they contain, that make layers unique. A layer's name is referred to as *Layer ID*. By default, Dreamweaver names a layer based on the order in which it is created. The first layer you create is called Layer1. You can change the default layer name by typing a new name in the Properties dialog box.

When you begin naming layers, keep a few guidelines in mind. It is a good idea to name your layers based on the content they contain. You can't begin layer names with numbers and they cannot contain spaces. Dreamweaver won't even allow you to name them like that. (Remember, its not that Dreamweaver can't handle certain naming systems; it's the code that's created that won't function in the browser if you don't stick to the coding rules of DHTML.) You can always change the name of your layer, but be careful. If you have referred to that layer with any other actions, they will not be carried forward with your new layer name.

Left and Top (L, T)

L and T refer to the distance in pixels from the left and top edges of your page. L and T represent the same thing as x and y coordinates.

There are three ways to position layers on your page. For designers, the most logical positioning technique is to drag layers into position by selecting and dragging. Another way is to select the layer and use the arrow keys on your keyboard to nudge it around. The third, most precise, way is to type the left and top coordinates in the properties box (see Figure 7.4).

Note:

The screenshots used in this chapter were generated from a Mac interface. The interface varies between platforms but the steps described remain the same.

Z-Index

The Z-index defines the stacking order of your layers. A number defines the Z-index. The lowest number is 1. A layer with a Z-index of 1 is the bottommost layer on the page. Any other layer, if placed in the same place as the layer with a Z-index of 1, will overlap the layer with the lower Z-index. The topmost layer on the page is the layer with the highest Z-index (see Figure 7.5). You can change the Z-index by typing a number in the Properties dialog box or by dragging one layer above or below the other in the Layers window.

Visibility

By default, all your layers will be visible when the page loads. You have control over when your

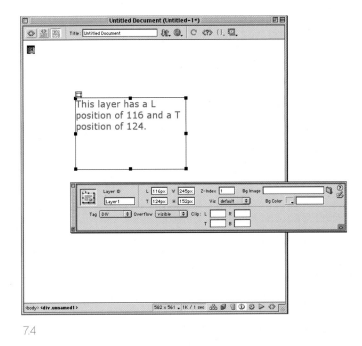

7.4

figure 7.4

The L and T distances are defined by the distance in pixels from the left and top of the screen. The numeric values are typed in the Properties dialog box.

figure 7.5

The Zeros have a Z-index of 2. The S has a Z-index of 1. The layer with the higher Z-index appears on top of the other.

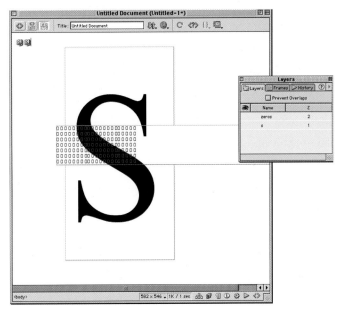

7.5

layers are visible. For example, you can load the page hiding all the layers and make layers show based on how the user interacts with the page. You can also have layers appear or disappear based on the amount of time that has elapsed since the page loaded.

You use the Properties dialog box to set the type of visibility you want. By selecting default, the layer will show. If you select Inherit, the layer inherits the visibility of its parent. This is only relevant if the layer is nested within another layer. If it is not, it will take the default of the page, visible. You can also select visibility for layers that are hidden within your preview window. This means you can select the type of visibility the layer will have in the browser window, while keeping it hidden and out of your way in Dreamweaver's preview window. Visible means it shows, hidden means the layer will not show when the page loads. Just because the layer does not show doesn't mean you don't download the content in the layer. You download everything at the same time, it's just temporarily invisible to the eye.

You can choose the type of visibility with the Properties dialog box or in the Layers window. To change the type of visibility using the Layers window, click on the eyeball icon. Notice how the eye closes. If you click again the eye disappears. An open eye means the layer is visible, a closed eye means it's invisible, and no eye means it takes the default (usually visible) (see

Figure 7.6). If a layer is invisible, you can still select it by selecting the layer in the layer window. To change the visibility of all the layers simultaneously, click on the main eye icon at the top of the layers box. It is important to know you can assign visibility to layers. You will learn more about controlling visibility using behaviors later in this chapter.

Height and Width

You can specify the height and width of a layer by typing the pixel dimension in the Properties dialog box (see Figure 7.7). You can also change the size of a layer by dragging it by the resize handles on the sides or the corners. It's a good idea to keep the size of your layers to about the size of the content they contain. Layer boxes tend to get in the way when they are much bigger than the content they contain.

Background Image and Color

Layers can be different colors and can have different tiled images as backgrounds (see Figures 7.8 and 7.9). Specify the color of your layer by selecting a color from the Bg Color box in the Properties window or by typing a hex value in the Bg Color selection space.

Background images in layers work the same way they do for the entire page. They will tile to fill the layer's specified size. You can type in the path to the background image in the Properties dialog box or you can click on the folder icon and retrieve the image from your hard drive.

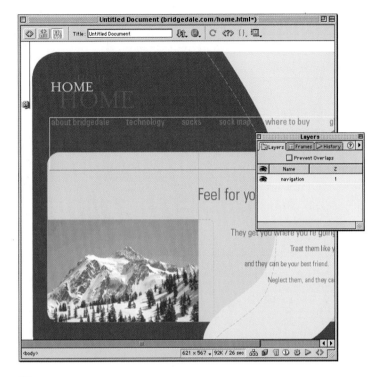

7.6

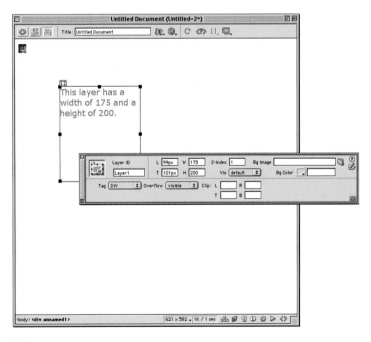

figure 7.6

The layer "navigation" is set to be visible.

figure 7.7

The layer's width and height are specified in the Properties box.

7.7

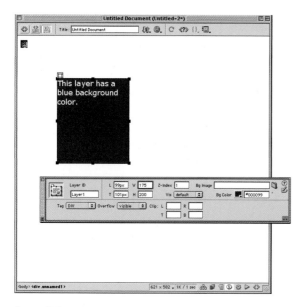

figure 7.8

The layer's background color is specified in the Properties dialog box.

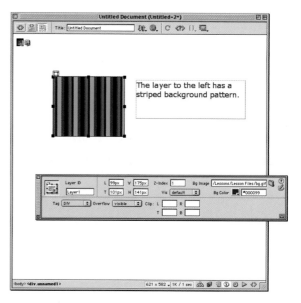

figure 7.9

The layer has a background pattern.

Working with Layers

There are a couple of ways to create a layer on the page. The easiest way is to drag a layer right from the Objects window (Window>Show Objects) onto your document. Select the layer icon and bring your mouse over the document. Drag your mouse to draw the layer. You can always resize and reposition the layer once it is on the page.

The other way to create a layer is by selecting Insert>Layer. A layer with the default size specifications from your preferences will be created on your page.

When you create a layer, notice the yellow box that appears in the top left corner of the page (see Figure 7.10). The yellow box is a layer marker, and every layer will have its own layer marker. It will not show up on your web page. It is only there to show you how many layers you have. If you select the layer marker, you will also select the layer itself. If you don't like having the layer markers visible, choose View>Invisible Elements; you can swap between having them visible and invisible. Do not delete the layer markers unless you want to delete the entire layer.

If you want text in your layer, go ahead and start typing in the layer. You can make the same modifications to the text as you can in regular HTML: size, color, font, and so on (see Figures 7.11 and 7.12). Text will wrap with the size of the layer. For wider columns of text, give the layer a larger width. You can also copy paste text from other documents into layers.

To place an image in the layer, select inside the layer and choose Insert>Image. Follow the dialog window to select the image you want. The image will appear within the layer. You can insert any type of Web image (gif, jpeg, animated gif, transparent gif, and so on) An animated gif will not animate in the Dreamweaver preview window. You must preview the page in a browser (by pressing F12) to see it animate. You can place a Flash file in the layer by selecting Insert>Media>Flash. If a layer contains a Flash movie, the Z-index will not act true to its designation. Even if a Flash movie has the Z-index of 1, it will always be the topmost layer.

7.10

7.11

figure 7.10

The yellow box is a layer marker.

figure 7.11 and 7.12

Interesting compositions are made by layering text in layers for an experimental web site.

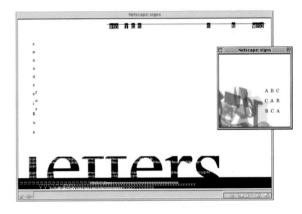

7.12

Now you have the knowledge to compose your page any way you like using layers. Experiment with moving them around the page. Play with stacking layers. What happens when you put a transparent gif over a layer filled with text? Make compositions layering text alone. Once you understand how to manipulate and use layers for layout purposes, you can move on to using them as a means for adding more sophisticated interactivity to your pages by using behaviors and timelines.

Using Behaviors

Behaviors allow you to design pages with more complex interactivity. Behaviors can be applied to the entire page, an image, or simply text. Behaviors work using JavaScript and the behaviors that are available vary from browser to browser. A list of behaviors and events that are commonly used by designers, and the browsers that handle them has been outlined later in this chapter.

Simply stated, a *behavior* is the combination of an event and an action. Logically speaking, the event happens before the action: The user clicks on an image and a new window pops up; a page loads and a plugin check is performed.

You don't need to learn how to write the code for behaviors, but it's a good idea to understand what's going on. The action is what is ultimately going to happen. The event is the thing that triggers the action. JavaScript defines the action in the head of your document. All the actions for a single page are spelled out in code at the top of your page.

When the page loads, everything is set to happen. It will take an event to trigger an action. Until it is triggered, the action sits all spelled out in the head of your document. An event is what calls the JavaScript action and makes something happen. The event is defined next to the image or text it is associated with in the body of your HTML. An event tag can be thought of similar to an `<a href>` tag. It, like the `<a href>` tag, is placed side-by-side with the tag of the object to which it is associated.

Any event can trigger multiple actions. For example, rolling over an image may make two other images appear and a browser window pop-up (see Figures 7.13–15). The actions will happen in the order called.

If you are copying JavaScript actions from a Dreamweaver document to another HTML document you must copy both parts of script to make it work. Copy the JavaScript from the head of your document as well as the event code from the body. When copying code from the Web into Dreamweaver, be sure to copy both parts of the code (head and body).

JavaScript is a fairly extensive programming language and Dreamweaver only has a specific set

7.13

7.14

7.15

figures 7.13–7.15

Different lines of the poem appear in different places based on which layers you roll over.

of JavaScript code that it comes with. There are thousands of sites on the web that offer JavaScript code. Programmers who don't mind if you copy their code established many of these sites. Using the web as a resource, you should be able to do anything you want in JavaScript.

That's enough on the back end of behaviors; although important to understand, they are more fun to work with! Remember to keep checking your code by using View>Source. Referring to the source as you design will help you understand behaviors and JavaScript quickly.

Applying Behaviors to Images

To use behaviors, you must familiarize yourself with the Behavior inspector. You can access the Behavior inspector by going to Window> Behaviors. The Behaviors palette is quite simple. You will notice four main components: the + symbol for adding behaviors, the − symbol for deleting behaviors, and the lists of events and actions you have assigned to your selected object.

Select an image on your page. Keeping the image selected go to the Behaviors palette. Select the + symbol and you can see all the behaviors that are available for your image. Any of the behaviors in black can be used, but the grayed-out behaviors are not available for you at the moment.

The first behavior you should familiarize yourself with is the "Show events for" behavior. This feature enables you to select what platform you want to make your page function for. The most recent browsers (4.0 and later) can handle more behaviors.

Many of the common behaviors are described in the Common Behaviors chart in the Dreamweaver manual. Once you understand what the different behaviors do and how you trigger them, applying behaviors to your pages is a breeze. In the following example, we are going to apply the pop-up browser window behavior to the action of clicking on an image. For this example, we will look at a site that Fluent Studios designed for KQED, San Francisco's public TV and radio broadcast station.

KQED wanted a site separate from their main site that would act as an online resource for teachers and students. The site contains infor-

Common Events

The following is a list of behaviors and browser capabilities that designers most commonly use:

- **onClick** (Netscape 3, 4, Internet Explorer 3, 4, 5). When the user clicks on then releases the mouse button.
- **onDblClick** (Netscape 4, Internet Explorer 4, 5). When the user double-clicks the mouse button.
- **onKeyDown** (Netscape 4, Internet Explorer 4, 5). When the user presses any key.
- **onKeyPress** (Netscape 4, Internet Explorer 4, 5). When the user presses then releases any key.
- **onLoad** (Netscape 3, 4, Internet Explorer 3, 4, 5). When the document finishes loading in the browser.

- **onMouseDown** (Netscape 4, Internet Explorer 4, 5). When the user presses the mouse button.
- **onMouseOut** (Netscape 3, 4, Internet Explorer 4, 5). When the user rolls the mouse off a specific object.
- **onMouseOver** (Netscape 3, 4, Internet Explorer 3, 4, 5). When the user rolls the mouse over a specific object.
- **onMouseUp** (Netscape 4, Internet Explorer 4, 5). When the user releases the click of the mouse.
- **onResize** (Netscape 4, Internet Explorer 4, 5). When the user resizes the browser window.
- **onSubmit** (Netscape 3, 4, Internet Explorer 3, 4, 5). When the user submits a form.

mation about the many cultures that make up the Bay Area. Because the audience was made up of teachers in public schools, the site had to be designed to fit the smallest monitors. The designers wanted the interactive portion of the site to feel completely separate from the main KQED site.

In addition, since they were designing for such small monitors, they wanted to make sure their design made the best use of the space. If they placed the site in the main browser, about a quarter of the image area would have been taken away by the browser window (see Figure 7.16). Instead, they decided to have the site come up in a pop-up window. That way, they could maintain control of the entire space, ensure all monitors showed the same thing, and, most importantly, remove the browser interface from the space.

figure 7.16

The 640×480 screen size makes it impossible to view this site in a normal browser window.

Fluent Studios wanted the window to pop up when visitors clicked on the Bay Area Mosaic icon on the home page. Follow the example by bringing your own image into Dreamweaver. Select the image from which you want the action to occur. With the image selected, select the add action (+) in the Behaviors palette. Select what you want to have happen from the actions—in this case, Open Browser Window. Upon selecting, an Open Browser Window dialog box pops up. Enter the HTML page that will be in the pop-up window in the URL to display field. Specify Window Width and Window Height. In the case of the KQED site, the window width and height were 625×420, sized to fit perfectly at 640×480 screen resolution.

Under Attributes you can specify how you want the window to appear. You can check for location field, toolbar, and so on. In the case of the KQED site, the designers wanted to maximize the area for the content so they did not check any boxes under attributes. The final option in the dialog box is Window Name. Naming windows is very similar to naming frames. Use the window name to target that window later from other HTML documents.

After you have specified everything for your pop-up window, select OK and the action is almost complete. Notice in the Behaviors dialog box that there is now information under Events and Actions. The action should say Open Browser Window. Under Events it says (onMouseDown).

Dreamweaver guesses what you want the action to be. In this case, it is correct—we do want the action to happen upon clicking the image. But suppose, for a moment, that we want the action to happen upon rolling over the image. Select the pull-down menu next to the event to get a list of all the available events for this action. Select onMouseOver. Notice how the text in the event column has changed to onMouseOver.

Vanessa Sterling, a designer and former design student at the California College of Arts and Crafts, designed a site that used multiple pop-up windows for her Graphic Design Thesis Project (see Figures 7.17–7.20). "The objective of my thesis statement was to communicate how connected one object can be. By taking one single object, in this case a sweater, I wove in countless connections by using the Internet as a

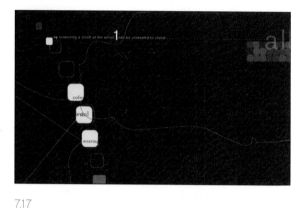

7.17

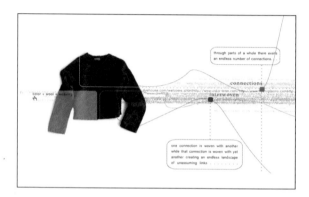

7.18

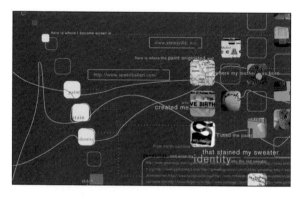

7.19

7.20

figures 7.17–7.20
Layers of information heighten the concept of interconnectivity.

vehicle. Through the Internet, it was possible for me to virtually connect to the most obvious connections... the concept being that there are an infinite amount of aspects connected in some way to this one sweater."

The pages show the piling of information. The objective was to increasingly layer information almost filling the page.

By applying behaviors to images, Vanessa was able to reveal multiple layers of information. The presence of all the layers piling on the screen at the same time reiterated her concept that everything is connected.

Tip:

Sometimes the action or event you want will not be selectable in the Behaviors palette. Usually this means you have the preferences set for earlier browser versions. To change this, select the + button and choose Show Events for 4.0 and Later Browsers. Oftentimes doing this will enable you select the events or behaviors that were previously screened back. If you still can't select what you want, that action probably isn't available for the object you have selected to put the event on.

Changing or Deleting Behaviors

To change a behavior, select the object you want to change. Open the Behaviors window. Double-click the behavior you want to change from the behaviors list. A window will pop up allowing you to edit the previous specifications. To change the order of behaviors, select the behavior and move it up or down the list with the arrow keys. To delete a behavior, select it and click the – icon.

Technique: Swap Image

The Swap Image action allows you to swap out one image with a different one. The JavaScript works by replacing one image with another in the `<img src>` code. In order to work, both images must be the same size. If they are not the same size, the image that is swapped in will stretch to fit the dimensions of the original image. Depending on the proportional difference, the stretching may look very strange. The Swap Image action works very well for creating rollovers (see Figure 7.21).

Create two images, the same size, that you want for a rollover. For this example we created one image with the text "rollover" in black and one image with the text "rollover" in red (see

Figure 7.22). Bring the graphic that represents the original state, in this case the black graphic, into Dreamweaver. To keep things clean, make sure the image you want to swap out is in the same folder as the original image. Select the image. In the Behaviors window select Swap Image. The Swap Image dialog box pops up (see Figure 7.23). Type the source of the image to be swapped or go get it directly by clicking Browse…. If you haven't yet named your image it will show up in this window as "unnamed `<img>`."

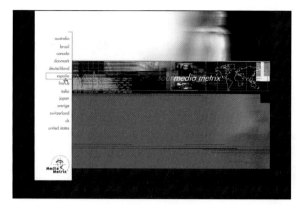

7.21

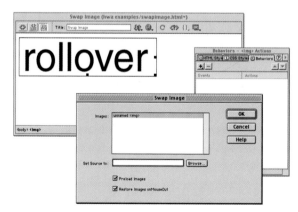

7.22

figure 7.21

The Media Matrix site uses a combination of swap image rollovers and Flash to create a sophisticated interface.

figure 7.22

Begin implementing Swap Image by creating the two rollover states the exact same size.

figure 7.23

The Swap Image dialog box.

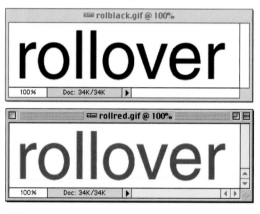

7.23

By default, the Preload Images and Restore Images onMouseOut boxes will be selected. Preload Images means that the rollover image will be preloaded when the page is loaded. It is a good idea to preload images with the page. Not doing so can cause a delay in the rollover action. Restore Images onMouseOut means that when you roll off the image, the original image will come back to replace the rollover. If you want the rollover image to stay visible, do not check the Restore Images box. Select OK and the Swap Image dialog box closes.

The Behaviors window has been updated with the new information. The default event for Swap Image is (onMouseOver). If this is not the event you want select a different event from the pull-down menu. You will notice that an (onMouseOut) SwapImageRestore has been added to the window. Don't delete it. This is the code that tells the original image to come back when you roll away.

The Swap Image action can be used with image maps. The California Power Play web site required navigation using JavaScript rollovers. The designers created 10 different images for swapping—each one with a different state of an active rollover. The original image, the navigation with no selection, was brought into Dreamweaver. The designers' image mapped the image and gave each section of the map a link in the Properties box as well as a behavior.

Using Behaviors and Layers Together

Using what you have learned so far in this chapter, you can now work with applying behaviors to layers. In this example we will make rolling over the image of the number "1" show the word "one" in another place on the screen. After we get that to work, we'll make rolling over the word "one" hide the number "one" and show the image "2."

Sound tricky? It's not. Begin by inserting all three graphics into the document. Next, place each image in its own layer. Name the layer so that it describes what it contains (see Figure 7.24). Next click the eye icon so it is closed for the frames you want hidden (see Figure 7.25). Closing the eye makes the layers invisible upon loading the page.

The next step is telling the "1" to show the layer one when the mouse rolls over the "1." Open the Behaviors window. Select the image "1." Be sure to select the image itself, not the layer containing the image. In the Behaviors window select Show-Hide Layers. The Show-Hide Layers window lists all the layers in your document.

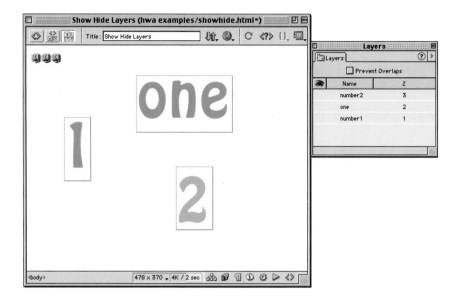

figure 7.24

Stay organized by naming your layers by the content they contain.

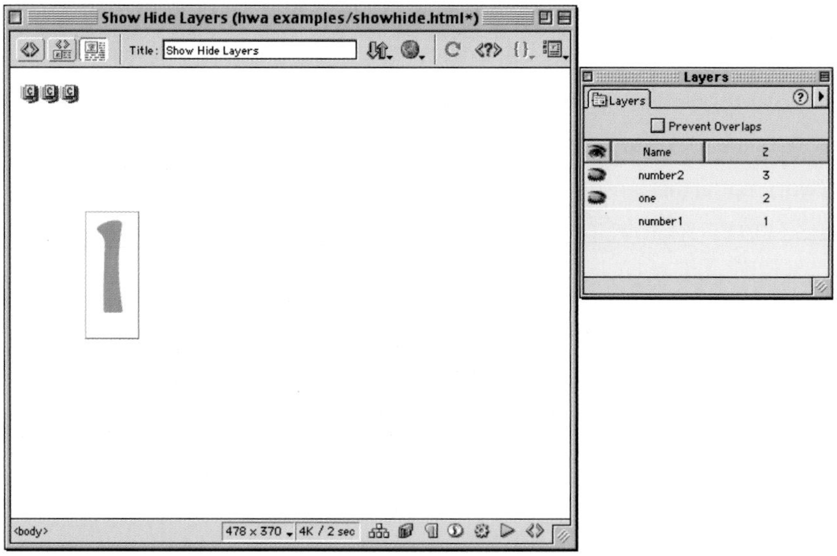

figure 7.25

The closed eye indicates that the two layers are invisible.

Highlight layer "one" and select Show (see Figure 7.26). You do not need to select Show or Hide for the other layers. Leaving them as they are will keep them at their onPageLoad visibility. In this case, layer "number1" will stay showing and layer "number2" will remain hidden. The only layer we are affecting is layer "one." Select OK.

If you preview the page in the browser, rolling over the number "1" should make the word "one" appear (see Figure 7.27). Rolling off the number 1 does not make the "one" disappear. We did not specify any roll off action so the layer will remain visible. If you click the Reload button on the browser, it will disappear again.

figure 7.26

Show is selected for layer "one."

figure 7.27

The layer "one" shows on the rollover of layer "1."

Now that that's working we'll take it one step further. Select the "one" layer from the Layers window. When you select the layer, Dreamweaver temporarily makes the content visible, even though the eye icon is closed (see Figure 4.28). Because the layer is visible, you can select the actual image. With the image "one" selected, go to the Behaviors window and select Show-Hide Layers. This time make layer "number1" (Hide),

"one" (Show), and "number2" (Show). Select OK. Preview the page in the browser to make sure it works.

Knowing the basic concepts of showing and hiding layers enables you to use the technique to create more interesting interactivity (see Figure 7.29). You can make any number of layers do anything on any action. The possibilities are unlimited!

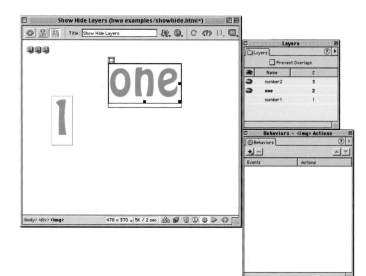

figure 7.28

Even though the eye is closed, when the layer is selected you can see it.

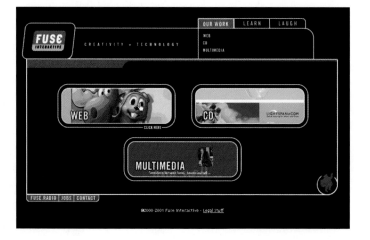

figure 7.29

The Fuse design uses Show-Hide Layers to reveal different information based on where you roll over.

Case Study

Sharon Coon, designer

Sharon Coon is a graduate of the California College of Arts and Crafts (CCAC) in Oakland and San Francisco. The graphic design school at CCAC has a thesis requirement in which students are challenged to expand the way they think about graphic design and asked to think deeply and conceptually about their work. A thesis committee critiques students as they push boundaries and bring a heightened sense of meaning to their design work. Students are encouraged to work in mediums they are not familiar with and to use mediums in inventive and thoughtful ways that have not been explored before.

7.30

The interactive journey begins from this screen.

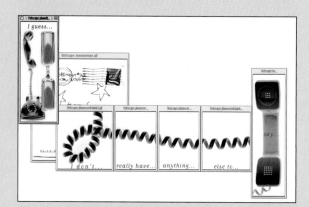

7.31

Windows are programmed to pop up in very specific places on the screen. They merge together to create one illustration.

Sharon came to the class with the experience of having moved across the country to a place quite different from where she was raised. Her move made her think about all she had known in the past and what she was learning and experiencing in her new life. Sharon's thesis became a poetic journey of her experiences. The project had a starting point, but as it unfolded, the order and ending were undetermined.

Sharon's concept required a medium in which the person experiencing the poem could interact with images and words, each experience unfolding in a different way. The web proved to be the perfect medium.

Although the web would be the perfect place for this interactive journey, Sharon was at first intimidated by the medium. Her design foundation was with print and the technical expertise required to implement her concept was daunting. However, thanks to Dreamweaver, Sharon was able to make a beautiful site that articulated her ideas perfectly. By the end of the course, Sharon was a web-design wiz. Not only did Dreamweaver allow her to create her site, but by reading the code Dreamweaver generated, she even began to learn to hand-code and understand HTML herself.

The result was an amazingly beautiful, conceptually rich thesis project.

The following is an interview with Sharon.

Describe your thesis project.

My project was basically about designing a hypertextual poem. I was trying to illustrate how each individual word in a poem has its own string of meaning, which relate to other experiences and meanings, and essentially create a massive network of all the feelings and ideas that went in to the poem.

What made the web a better medium than any other did?

The web was ideal for this project because it allowed me to express my ideas in a non-linear format, which is exactly what I wanted to do. It allowed me to combine word, image, motion, and sequence all in one medium.

How did Dreamweaver help you in creating the site?

I used Dreamweaver for pretty much every aspect of this site. I used it to set pop-up window sizes and locations, create links between pages, and general page properties.

How did Fireworks help?

I used Fireworks to "chop" up my images and to create tables so that I could link specific areas in Dreamweaver.

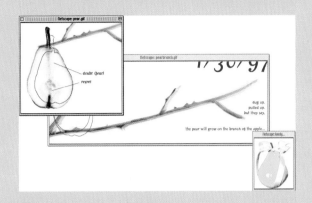

7.32

Visitors click on image-mapped words to get to new information.

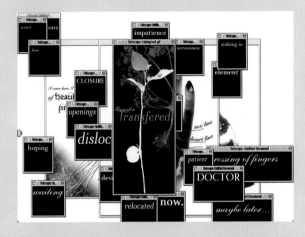

7.33

Pop-up windows bombard the user, each containing unique words and phrases that make up the poem.

How do you work with the web personally versus professionally?

For personal projects, I tend to disregard any issues of download time. I'll just use huge, full-color objects and not worry about it. In my work, image size and download time are always issues that must be considered.

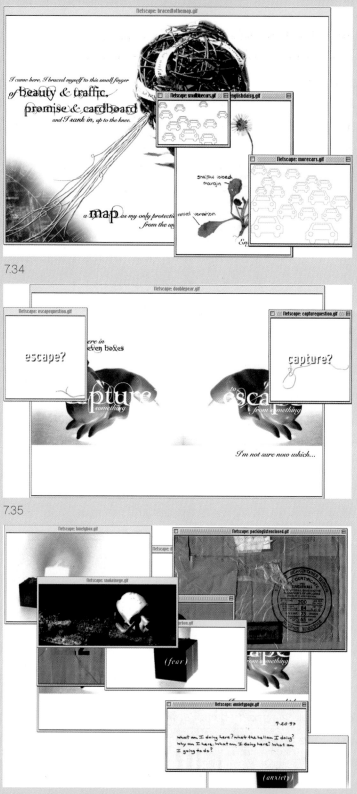

7.34

7.35

736

7.34–736

The site unfolds to several different places, each unique in content and visuals. The experience depends on the path taken.

OnLoad

The onLoad behavior allows you to place an action to the page that occurs the second the page loads. onLoad can be used for a variety of purposes, including checking a plug-in, checking a browser version, and redirecting the page to a different URL. Another (sometimes annoying) use is a pop-up window that pops up with the page.

The onLoad behavior is set similar to the other behaviors in Dreamweaver. The following example will redirect a visitor from one page to another. To apply onLoad, open the Behaviors palette. Select the document body. (Confirm that it has been selected by looking at the title of the Behaviors window.) Press the (+) add action button and select Go to URL. Type the page you want to go to in the URL dialog box and select OK. That's it. Visitors will now go directly to the assigned page.

When you are using onLoad for URL redirection, be aware that the `<body>` characteristics of your page will be visible, if just for a second. Give your onLoad page the same background color as the page to which you are redirecting. This will avoid any abrupt graphic flash.

Check Browser

The Check Browser behavior enables you to send visitors to different HTML pages based on what browser type and version they are using. For example, if you create a site that uses complex behaviors, you may be losing potential site visitors using earlier versions of browsers. You can send people to different versions of the site based on what works best with their configuration.

The check browser behavior is attached to the body of your HTML page. To perform Check Browser, click on any empty part of your Dreamweaver document. This selects the entire body. You can confirm that you have the body selected by looking at the title bar in the Behaviors window. It should say Behaviors - `<body>` Actions.

Click on the + icon and select Check Browser. The Check Browser window will pop up (see Figure 7.37). Type where you want visitors to go based on their browser and version. For example, perhaps you want everyone using Netscape Navigator 4.0 or later to stay on the page and all other versions of Netscape to go to a different URL. In the field next to Netscape Navigator, you would type 4.0. Pull down the menu that reads Stay on This Page. To specify where all other URLs should go, pull down the menu. Otherwise, select Go to URL. Then, specify the specific URL in the URL field at the bottom. Fill in your specifications for Internet Explorer the same way, and then do the same for all other browsers. If you want visitors on older browsers to go to a third alternate URL, select Go to Alt URL and type the alternate URL at the bottom.

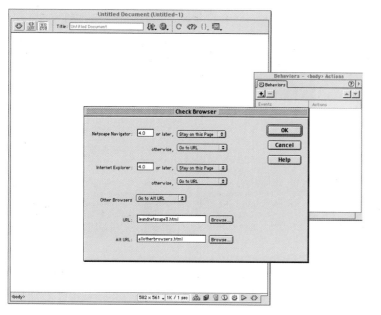

figure 7.37

The Check Browser dialog box.

Check Plug-In

The Check Plugin behavior is used to check whether a user has a specific plug-in installed. For example, if someone did not have the Flash plugin installed on their computer, and they came to a Flash page they would get the image of the broken plug-in. This is not something you want your site visitors to ever see. If they do not have Flash installed, you want to do one of two things. Either send them to a page that directs them to get the Flash plug in, linking them to Macromedia's site, or send them to an alternate web site.

To perform a Check Plugin, select the body of your page. Select Check Plugin from the Behaviors dialog box. Select the plug-in you

want to search for. If it is not in the pull-down list, type the exact name and version of the plug-in in the field. Type the URL to direct to if the plug-in is found. If you want to stay on the same page, don't type anything. Type the URL you want to direct to if it is not found. Click OK.

Before you actually use the Check Plugin you should know that plug-in detection is impossible on Internet Explorer on a Macintosh. This can cause some frustration. A visitor using that configuration will always be defaulted to the "you need to download Flash" page.

There are a few work-arounds for this problem. One way is to place a graphic on your "Get Flash" page that reads, "If you know you have

Flash, click here." Clicking would obviously re-direct the visitor to the appropriate Flash page. The site Vector Zone used this technique (see Figure 7.38). Another work-around is to first check Browser. If the visitor is coming from Internet Explorer with a version higher than 4, you can be pretty sure he has Flash installed and you can redirect him to the Flash page. This work-around is definitely risky, but does avoid visitors having to see the get Flash page. If you are searching for a plug-in other than Flash, the first work-around is recommended.

figure 7.38

The graphic directs you to click in a certain space if you know you have Flash.

Creating Rollovers in Macromedia Fireworks

It can become very production-intensive design-ing navigation with rollovers for every item. Sometimes Dreamweaver is a perfect tool for coding your swap images; however, in certain instances, Macromedia Fireworks is better. Take for example the Power Play web site navigation (see Figure 7.39). Almost every word on the nav-igation has a rollover state. Fireworks makes chopping up a graphic, giving it the behaviors, and placing it properly in a table quite easy.

Using Photoshop, create a document that con-tains three layers. One layer should be a solid, filled with the background color of the naviga-tion. In the case of the Power Play site, this was white. Layer 2 should be the up state for the nav-igation. The up state is always the state of the

figure 7.39

The Power Play web site uses a navigation with mul-tiple rollovers.

image with no rollover. Name this layer "Up." The third layer should be a copy of Layer 2. Name this layer "Over." Fill the duplicate of Layer 1 with the color you want for the over state (see Figures 7.40 and 41). Save the document, maintaining the layers.

Open the PhotoShop file in Fireworks File>Open. Select Maintain Layers in the dialog box that appears. Your PhotoShop file will open up within the Fireworks interface. If the Layers and Frames windows are not open, open them (Window>Layers). Select the Frames tab. Click the Add Frame icon at the bottom of the Frames window (see Figure 7.42). Now click back on the Layers tab. Select the layer "over" (see Figure 7.43). Select all (Ctrl+A/Cmd+A) and copy (Ctrl+C/Cmd+C) the content of the "over" layer. Select the Frames tab. Select Frame 2 and paste (Ctrl+V/Cmd+V) the image into frame 2 (see Figure 7.44). Now, go back to the Layers window. Select Frame 1 from the pull down directly below the Layers tab. Turn off the "over" layer in frame one by clicking on the eye icon. The layer should turn off.

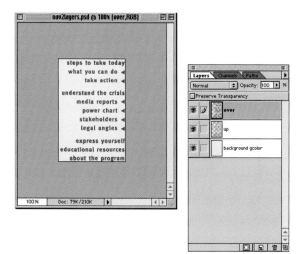
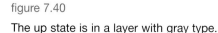

figure 7.40

The up state is in a layer with gray type.

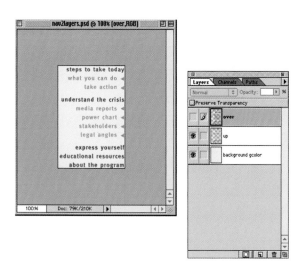

figure 7.41

The over state is in a layer with red type.

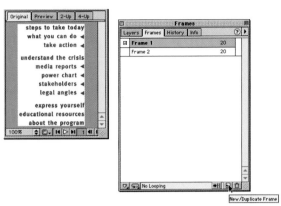

figure 7.42

Click the icon at the bottom right to add a frame.

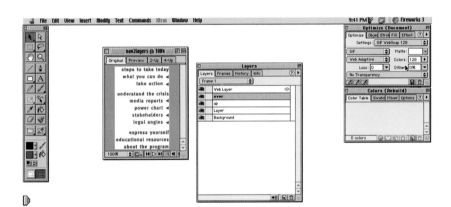

figure 7.43

Select just the over state.

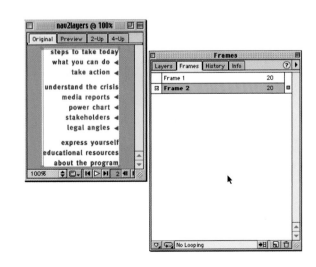

figure 7.44

Paste the over state into frame 2.

Select the slice tool from the tool palette (see Figure 7.45). Draw slices on the image separating each rollover (see Figure 4.46). In slicing, you are literally cutting your image into multiple smaller images. Try to keep the cuts as close together as possible. Continue mapping the cuts until you have each rollover designated.

Now it's time to add the behaviors. Open the Behaviors palette: Window>Behaviors. Does it look familiar? Select the (+) add action key and select Simple Rollover. Fireworks will cut the

graphics up, and write the code for the rollovers of the entire navigation. If you had had a third frame with another color, that would have become the hit state. For this example, we are using up and over. Now, click in the Behaviors window to the URL tab. With your first slice still selected, type the URL for the link in the text field. Click the (+) symbol next to the URL field and notice how the URL appears in the column below (see Figure 7.47). Click on the next slice and repeat the process for every slice.

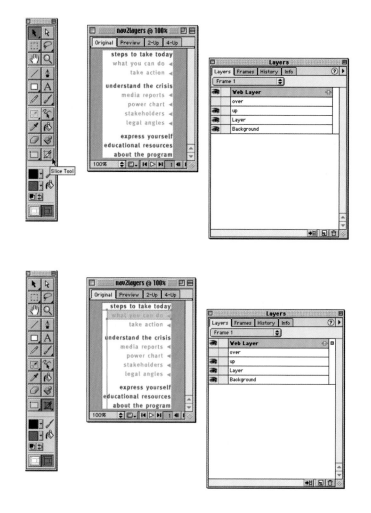

figure 7.45

The slice tool.

figure 7.46

Draw a slice.

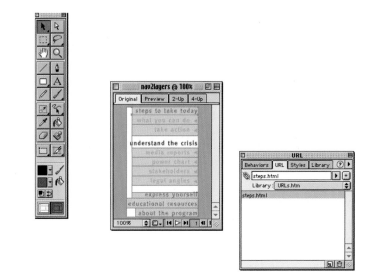

figure 7.47

Designate the URL link.

When you are done, select File>Export. Create a new folder for the export. Depending on how many rollovers you have, you may end up with a lot of images. Select Export. That's it—you're done. Well, almost done: You still need to bring it into Dreamweaver.

Open Dreamweaver. Select Insert>Interactive Images>Fireworks HTML. The table containing your rollover navigation and all the code that goes along with it imports right into your Dreamweaver document.

Summary

As you can have learned, Dreamweaver can help you turn your basic HTML code into sophisticated JavaScript. This chapter only touched on the surface on the capabilities of Dreamweaver.

Using the basics we have described here, you can now add just about any JavaScript to your HTML pages. Remember though, that Dreamweaver won't *always* do *all* the work for you. It is important to understand HTML in order to incorporate more advanced code in you sites. Be creative with the tools and you will discover unlimited possibilities.

URLS In This Chapter

- **HTML and Web Artistry**

  www.htmlartistry.com/urls/signs

  www.htmlartistry.com/urls/ccacds4

  www.htmlartistry.com/urls/venessa

  www.htmlartistry.com/urls/sharon

- **Media Matrix** www.mediamatrix.com
- **KQED** www.kqed.org

Inspirational Design Model

Julie Beeler
Second Story

"We are interactive storytellers...We provide

the characters, the stage, music, information,

images, and animation that visitors use to

weave their own story."

figure 1

secondstory.com

The combined creative talents of the folks at Second Story are matched only by their warm and personable nature. No one represents that better than Julie Beeler, co-founder and Studio Director. While overseeing all of the creative development of projects in the studio, Julie also seems to maintain a positive energy and outlook for the future.

Maybe it has a bit to do with that clean, crisp Portland air, or the fact that being in their 100 year-old renovated warehouse space is almost like being in a ski lodge, that makes Second Story's imaginative spirit come alive in their work and life.

What kinds of projects do you work on at second story?
Second Story works on entertaining and educational content-based projects. For the past six years we have focused on projects that allow us to create media-rich, interactive experiences. We've staged over 40 immersive, informative, and enduring interactive experiences for the web and other electronic media.

The Studio is a multi-disciplinary team of creative artists, producers, writers, animators, and programmers dedicated to entertaining, educating, and inspiring their audiences through storytelling innovation. Each experience is crafted from the ground up, allowing for the creation of an original and fresh structure and design that best presents the story and delivers the greatest impact.

We are interactive storytellers, but for years, we wrestled with the idea of what that meant. In this medium, the story no longer flows in one direction, from the one to the many. We provide the characters, the stage, music, information, images, and animation that visitors use to weave their own story. The narrative is only visible in hindsight, when we piece together the visitor's path through our work—the path that was their history, their story. This is the second story.

What inspires you and the team?
I am inspired by the content of each of our projects and the range and diversity of all the different projects we work on. I enjoy immersing myself in a subject and understanding it to such a degree that it can be pulled apart and dissected and then have fun gluing it back together. It is inspiring just working in the interactive medium itself, the immediacy of the medium as well as the interaction by the visitors is really fulfilling.

It is great fun to put something out there and have people interact with it in a meaningful way in that they are learning something and being entertained at the same time.

What's your creative process when you are working on a project?

Our creative process starts with immersing ourselves in the content, which includes everyone in the studio. We gather as many materials as possible on each subject—photographs, interviews, writing, video—and immerse ourselves in the content. Each project starts by doing endless research and learning as much as we can about the subjects of our projects. For each project the content dictates the interactive experience. The content doesn't just dictate the visual art direction, but more importantly the site architecture, structure, information design, interface, and navigation.

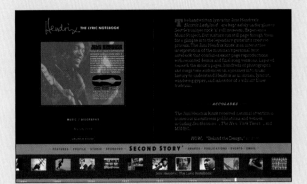

figure 2
secondstory.com

Second Story has a great reputation of creating some amazing projects that are both artistically and technically innovative, utilizing some of the most cutting-edge technologies. How do you and your team find balance between the creative and technical aspects of the medium? Has it been a challenge? A frustration?

Balancing both the technical and creative aspects of creating interactive stories is what we love. Many times we are driving by the technology restraints and it is within these restrictions that we love to find creative, innovative solutions—both technical and visual. It is fun to place such incredible challenges on yourself, and many times the technology on the web is very limiting compared to technology in other mediums. It is these challenges that force us to come up with creative, innovative solutions to our designs. We always build our projects from the ground up; we start at the bottom of the project, deep down in the content, and create a concept for the site. The concept integrates all levels of the process; we think about everything and the concept driving each aspect of the project.

Then we define a structure and framework, as well as the information design and navigation and interactivity, and then we start to paint in all the visual graphics.

Your recent project on Mummies for Discovery Online was a new foray for you into the world of broadband. Please tell us more about it. What were the challenges you found?

We have continually pushed our sites into the realm of broadband by delivering media rich components whether it is animation, audio, video, etc. With *Unwrapped: The Mysterious World of Mummies* for Discovery we officially had the opportunity to develop for highspeed Internet connections. Working with Discovery.com gave us the opportunity to really push the web's capabilities by building a site that could only be experienced via broadband. We were working to define true interactive broadband content by delivering a deep media-rich experience that goes beyond typical streaming-video.

Designing for a broadband audience allowed us to maximize the storytelling potential of interactive media, meshing a cinematic experience with user-driven responsiveness. Creating *Unwrapped* was a great opportunity to break down traditional notions of what's possible with interactive content. The web allows us to combine storytelling devices from many diverse media into a seamlessly integrated experience that becomes as emotive and immersive as film or video, as escapist as a CD-ROM game, as information-rich as print, as democratic as television, and yet more intuitive and personal through its meaningful interaction.

figure 3
2020 Green

We believe that when staging stories, interactive media need not always be in the service of traditional media. The web can be an extremely powerful and engaging medium when the content is original and not derivative from TV or film. As a result, we take advantage of the web's inherent interactivity to stage educational entertainment that is immersive and uniquely user-driven.

Who are your design heroes?

Now this isn't an easy one for me. I am inspired by many artists, architects, writers, and so on, but don't really have a design hero. My inspirations are always changing and are so broad that I can't really capture them. I guess in the end this question made me realize that I am not really a "designy" person.

Do you have any advice that you would like to share with all the aspiring designers out there?

I don't really see myself having any advice for designers. I just feel that if you are passionate about what you do it will show in your work, and your passion, drive, and dedication towards whatever it is you do, just has to make it fun. I couldn't imagine not loving what you do.

If you could be a superhero, who would you be and why?

I don't really have any, but when I was a kid I always would pretend that my sister and I were the Wonder Twins and we could change into anything we wanted. Whatever we dreamed up we could become and we would act them out together.

What are three things in the world you can't live without?

Books, quilting, and my dogs. (Cheesy answer, aye?)

Please name a bad habit you have.

Picking at my fingers and making them bleed.

Second Story URL:

■ **Second Story** www.secondstory.com

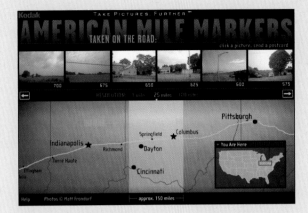

figure 4
Kodak's American Mile Markers

On the art of quilts:

I love to make quilts. I took up quiltmaking eight years ago while living in Berkeley, CA. I love working but I found myself sitting in front of the computer for too many hours on end and at a certain level I wasn't completely "creatively" satisfied with creating art via the computer, so I started making quilts. I love the quiltmaking tradition; the history, folklore, and storytelling aspects of creating quilts were very powerful, and I love abstracting things to such a degree that you have to take them apart and put them back together. I enjoy all the math, precision, and strategy behind piecework and, more than anything, I love putting a contemporary spin on traditional quilting patterns.

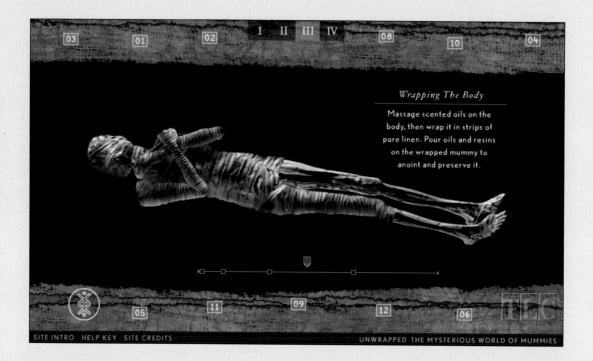

figures 5 and 6

Discovery's Mummies Unwrapped

7

8

figures 7 and 8

**History of Recorded
Sound**

figure 9

**Hendrix—The Lyric
Notebook**

9

Multimedia

Moving Forward with Video and Sound

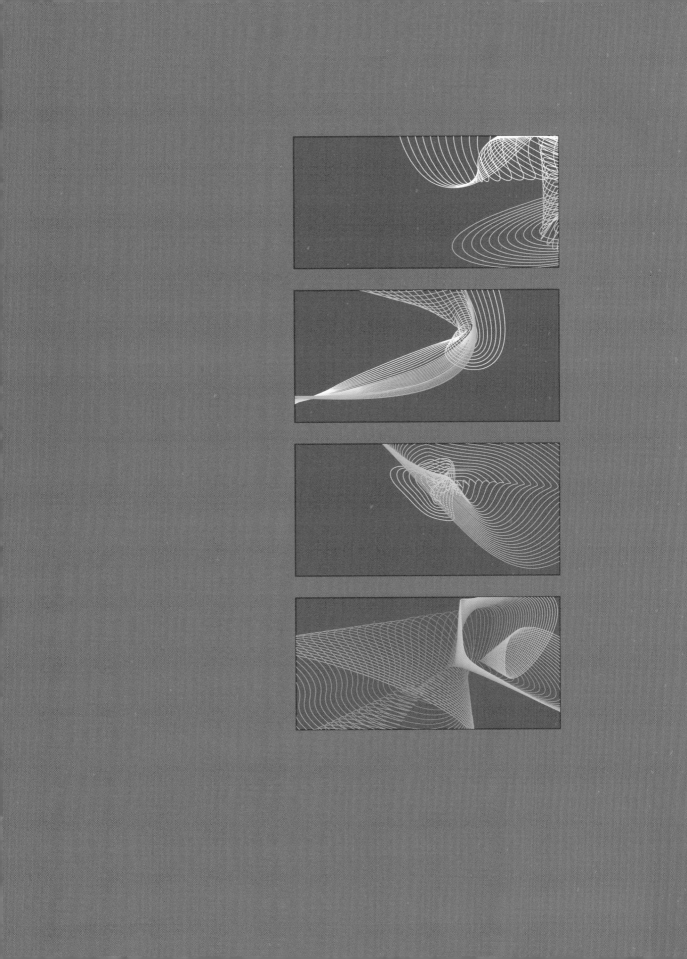

How would you like to make your own digital film and publish it straight to the web? What if you could make your pages sing, your characters move, and your visitors want to stick around and explore your site? As technology changes and the available bandwidth increases (meaning that more data can be transmitted in shorter periods of time), video and sound will become increasingly important in the design of your sites. Not only will visitors expect to see video and hear sound on the best sites, but you will find that these engaging elements will be easier to create and manage than ever before. The best news is that you won't have to wait for the next web generation in order to enjoy the advent of usable video and sound—they are available on the web today, in a variety of formats, presenting a wide range of possibilities.

This chapter will prepare you for the Broadband future. We'll show you the video and sound techniques that you can use today and will also prepare you for building the sites of the future. Apple's QuickTime is currently the video player of choice for both Macs and PCs because it works the best cross-platform. It also has some of the best image quality of all movie players around and has full sound support, ensuring that you get the full effect for the video and sound elements you use. Next we'll show you the WildForm Flix Player (www.wildform.com), which can help convert some of your QuickTime movies into the Flash SWF format for easy,

seamless integration into your Flash sites. Finally, we will cover the importance of sound and how it plays an integral part in the design process. We'll cover techniques in optimizing sound for the web, as well as show off the Beatnik player tool.

Planning Video and Sound

But before we go shooting off in the direction of eye-popping video and attention-getting sound, a few considerations are in order. Although the golden age of Broadband is almost here, the reality is that the many users aren't yet on the cutting edge of technology. This means that web sites with major video clips and complicated sound files may be so painfully slow in loading that your users may be jumping ship before the page fully loads.

For this reason, think carefully about how you plan to use video and sound before you begin adding those elements to your site. Here are a few questions to help you determine what you need right now and what you'll want to add as bandwidth allows:

- How will video and/or sound improve your site?
- Will your site visitors expect to find video and sound?
- Do you currently have digitized video or sound files you intend to use?

- How large are the media files you will be working with?
- How will this increase your download times?
- Is there a way to optimize or compress the files to make them more manageable?
- How fast is the computer of your average user?
- Is adding video and sound practical for your audience?

Note:

The examples and techniques in this chapter are illustrated using a Mac. Most of the software mentioned is cross platform, with the exception of Macromedia SoundEdit 16.

Using QuickTime for Video Work

One of our favorite programs for displaying video content on the web is the QuickTime Player, available from Apple (`www.apple.com/quicktime`). The player itself will allow you to work with not only video, but sound, animation, graphics, text, music, and even 360-degree virtual reality (QuickTime VR) in which you can pan around images. QuickTime will allow you to view media directly in your browser window as well.

As a site developer, you'll like using QuickTime Pro because you'll be able to do things like use Macromedia Flash in your QuickTime movies, import and edit movies from your digital camera, and export media objects into literally dozens of different file formats (see Figure 8.1).

Tip:

QuickTime 5.0 works with the following browsers on both Macintosh and Windows systems: America Online version 3.0 and later, Microsoft Internet Explorer version 3.x and later, Netscape Navigator 3.x and later.

figure 8.1

The QuickTime Player has a familiar look and feel.

Here are some of the benefits of using QuickTime:

- QuickTime helps stream in files so that users don't have to wait for the whole movie to load in order to play.
- It supports over 200 kinds of digital media such as GIF, AVI, and MPEG, as well as its own QuickTime movie format MOV.
- The QuickTime player is free, which means that virtually anyone will be able to load and play your video and sound files after they've installed the player.
- QuickTime is flexible and upwardly compatible, so that media objects created in one version of QuickTime are playable in all subsequent versions.
- The Media Skins feature enables you to create different looks and customize your media display.

Note:

For more detailed information on QuickTime specifications, please visit `www.apple.com/quicktime/`.

The QuickTime player is easy to understand and use. The controls are all visible in the media display, which means users will easily recognize familiar controls and be able to run your media files without having to learn new techniques and tools. At the top of the QuickTime player, users will see the name of your site, beneath which the six QuickTime menus—File, Edit, Movie, QTV,

Window, and Help—appear. In the center of the player is the display window; and along the bottom are the status/loading bar and the player controls, which users will easily recognize.

Capturing or Digitizing Video

When you have a specific video segment you want to use—and you have the capability to capture it yourself—your creative options are limited only by your imagination (and, perhaps, your budget). One sophisticated tool for capturing and editing web video is Final Cut Pro, another Apple product currently available for Mac systems only.

Note:

To find out more about Final Cut Pro, see the product information on the web at `www.apple.com/finalcutpro/`.

Here are the steps for capturing video using Final Cut Pro:

1. Connect your digital video camera to your computer via firewire.
2. Start up Final Cut Pro.
3. From the File menu, choose Log and Capture (see Figure 8.2).
4. The Log and Capture dialog box opens. The digital video output from your camera will be visible in the dialog box window.
5. To capture sequences or the whole video, make sure you start at the right cue point. When you are sure you are at the right

point, press the play button and then click the Now button in the capture area on the bottom right (see Figure 8.3).

6. When you have reached the final point of the video, press the Esc button to stop the capture.

7. Now you can start editing your movie (see Figure 8.4). You can add special effects such as fades or dissolves, or even further cut and move sequences.

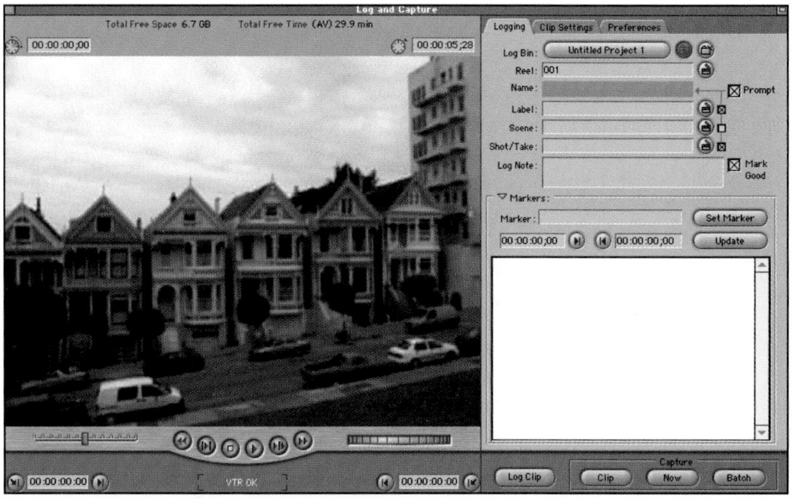

figure 8.2

Video output displayed in the Log and Capture dialog box.

figure 8.3

Capturing the video.

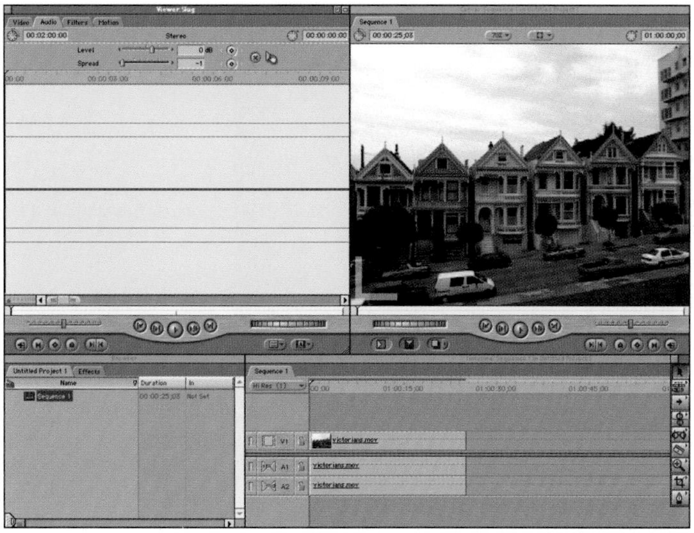

figure 8.4

Editing the movie.

8. Save your final working file so that if you need to go back to your raw movie, you can re-edit it without having to start all over (see Figure 8.5).

9. Save the captured movie (see Figure 8.6). You can specify what kind of file type, movie size, and quality you want for the file.

10. Final movie is viewed in the QuickTime Viewer (see Figure 8.7).

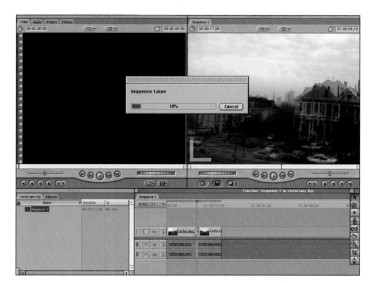

figure 8.5
Saving the video sequence

figure 8.6
The captured movie.

figure 8.7
The final movie displayed in QuickTime Viewer.

Digitizing Video

You can capture regular video and transfer it to digital if you have a video card in your computer that allows for a connection to your VCR.

Sometimes on projects, clients may ask for you to digitize existing broadcast commercials or training sessions for use over the web. You can do this type of capturing easily with Adobe Premiere, a video editing software program available for both Windows and Mac systems.

> Note:
>
> To find out more about Adobe Premiere, visit them on the web at www.adobe.com/products/premiere/main.html.

Here are the steps:

1. Open Premiere (see Figure 8.8). If you are working with Premiere 6, you will have an opening dialog box appear letting you choose which format you will be out-putting for the movie. Because we are making a movie for the web, we will choose Multimedia.

2. Choose File, Capture, Movie Capture (see Figure 8.9).

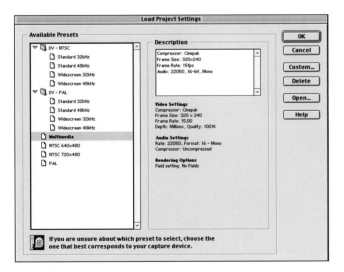

figure 8.8

Starting the Premiere work session.

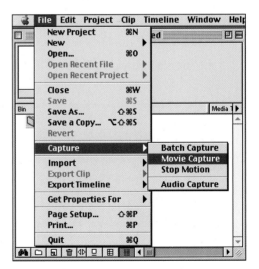

figure 8.9

Starting the capture process.

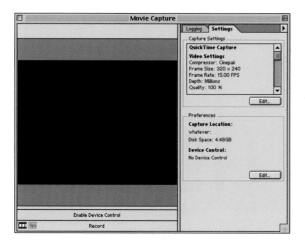

figure 8.10

Play back the VHS tape and capture the digital video.

3. Finally you'll be presented with the Edit window where you can play back the VHS tape and can "capture" the session (see Figure 8.10).

4. Save the video by choosing File, Save As; then type a name for the file and choose the format you want.

Tip:

For more technical information on Digital Video, download the DV Primer PDF off the Adobe web site here. It's a great resource to help you get started in Digital Video: www.adobe.com:80/motion/events/ pdfs/dvprimer.pdf

Compressing and Optimizing Video

Because video and sound files can demand a lot of download time, it's a good idea to compress your videos in order to better optimize them for the web. This will make your site visitors happy. One of the best tools out there now for this is Cleaner 5 (formerly Media Cleaner Pro).

Note:

For more information on Cleaner 5 or to try out the free downloadable demo, visit the product's web site at www.discreet.com/ products/cleaner/.

What this program does is read through the whole movie once and then it begins to rebuild it according to your settings.

We will be using a clip we just digitized from a runway video of fashion designer William Reid that was used for his web site. The video clip uncompressed is 20MB right now—a file that's really too big to put up on the Web.

With Cleaner's easy-to-use wizard, even if you don't know much about digital video production, the software helps guide you along the process so that you can best optimize your movies. You can start the Settings Wizard by going to the File menu and choosing Windows, Settings Wizard (see Figure 8.11). The first screen of the wizard enables you to choose the type of video output you want to prepare. Your choices are WWW, CD-ROM, DVD Video, Kiosk, DV Camera, or Still Picture.

The only problem with the wizard is that you give up some of the control of the program. When you choose to compress and optimize the files yourself instead of relying on the wizard, you have the opportunity to tweak the output for maximum value and low file size.

Here are the steps for compressing and optimizing your video files in Cleaner 5:

1. Open the program and drag your QuickTime movie into the interface. You should see the name of the movie appear. If you are optimizing multiple movies, multiple lines will appear.
2. Next, click on the movie settings and a dialog box will appear so that you can choose the optimization settings (see Figure 8.12).
3. Because this will be a QuickTime movie over the web, we can actually choose which type. We will choose optimization for streaming QT over a 56K modem. With the tabs on the right side, you are able to further optimize each setting such as image (size, quality, and so on) or sound (see Figure 8.13).

figure 8.11

The Settings Wizard walks you through the steps for choosing the settings that are right for your output.

figure 8.12

The dialog box you'll use to optimize the video.

4. Finally, whether you choose to optimize via advanced or wizard settings, you will read the final settings dialog. Press the play button to start the encoding process. As the movie starts to encode, you'll see the actual encoding process happen within the encoding window. The process window will document the entire process (complete with a visual graph) of the breakdown of the movie that is being optimized (see Figure 8.14).

We started with a 20MB movie to being with and now, after a few minutes of encoding this three-second movie, it's only 400K.

figure 8.13

Click the tabs on the right to choose what you want to optimize.

> ## Note:
>
> You'll notice with digital video that it will take a long time for movies to optimize. Just remember the larger the movie in file size, the longer it will take to optimize (sometimes a few hours). That's why on long projects it's a good idea to let your computer run the optimization process overnight.

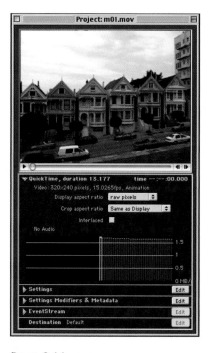

figure 8.14

After encoding is complete, Cleaner 5 begins the optimization.

Embedding QuickTime

You'll use the `<embed>` tag to run QuickTime movies—and other media files—on your site. Embed enables your site's visitors to view or hear media files created in all sorts of applications, as long as they have the application or plug-in they need. For example, consider the following line of code:

```
<EMBED SRC="victorians.mov"
width="320" height="240"
AUTOPLAY="true"></embed>
```

In this line, the SRC is the media object (this can be an absolute or relative address); the width is the width of the object's display and height is the height of the object's display. The AUTOPLAY tag tells the page to play the media object automatically when the page is opened.

Note:

If you want your pages to be compatible with both Internet Explorer and Netscape Navigator on PC and Mac systems, you need to use an <OBJECT> tag along with the <EMBED> tag (for IE 5.5 and later versions).

Tip:

The newest version of QuickTime, version 5.0, includes the Darwin Streaming Server, which enables you to provide streaming media to Linux, Windows, Solaris, and FreeBSD systems.

QuickTime and Flash

Macromedia Flash is one of the world's most popular graphics and animation authoring application in use today. Flash enables you to design and deliver animation, presentations, and more on your site without causing huge drains on system resources or hogging users' bandwidth. The Flash format (SWF) is compact and widely supported, allowing you to include vector, bitmap, and interactive elements in your animations and make your animations accessible to the widest possible audience.

Because Flash works with media created in many different applications, you can use it to incorporate in your QuickTime movies formats that QuickTime wouldn't ordinarily support. To do this, you simply import the Flash (SWF) file that includes them as a new track in your QuickTime movie. To add a Flash track to your QuickTime movie, follow these steps:

1. Open your QuickTime Player as usual.
2. Open the File menu and choose Import.
3. Navigate to the folder storing the Flash .swf file, select it, and click Convert.
4. Save the movie file as a self-contained movie.
   This adds the Flash track to your QuickTime movie, and now you can work with it as you would any other track in your media production.

Wildform Flix—Convert Video to Flash SWF Format

To easily make SWF files from video, you can use the Wildfrom Flix application, shown in Figure 8.15 (www.wildform.com).

We will be using a QuickTime video clip from Daniel Jenett and will convert that QuickTime video to a SWF file (see Figure 8.16). With a SWF file, you can easily add video within a Flash interface, even adding variables so you can control it via action scripting.

When you first open the Wildform Flix application, an easy-to-use four-tab interface appears: Files, SWF, Audio, Video (see Figure 8.17). Select your video by clicking on the Input field's Browse button. This will select your source file that you want to convert to SWF. If you are including this Flash video as a part of a larger flash site, you can also rename the movie for consistency in the output field. If you leave it blank, the default SWF name will be the name of the QuickTime video.

For your convenience, there are preset encoders for various bandwidth outputs. If you want a little more control, you can follow each tab at the top to control specific settings in the SWF, Audio, or Video areas.

figure 8.15

The Flix application.

figure 8.16

The QuickTime movie.

figure 8.17

The Flix interface.

We will choose to customize our own since this video is pretty short and doesn't have any audio. By clicking on the SWF tab, you will see that you have a range of options to add to the SWF file (see Figure 8.18). Here is also the place where you can add custom variables for action scripting purposes. We will just loop the movie and set the frame rate to 12 (the same as the QuickTime movie).

Since we don't have any audio in this movie, we can skip it. But it is good to note that the Flix player will not only help compress your audio to different bit rates but also export it out to a separate AIF or MP3 file.

Next we will go to the video attributes by clicking on the Video tab. From here we can set the quality of the video, much like setting the image quality in Photoshop. Here we will choose 60 (see Figure 8.19). You can play with the output setting to get the optimum quality and file size balance.

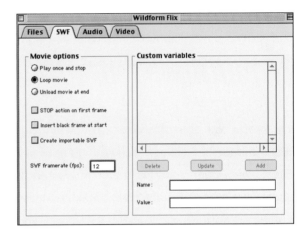

8.18

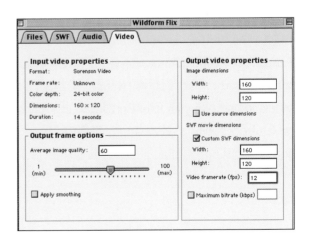

8.19

figure 8.18

Controlling the SWF attributes.

figure 8.19

Setting the video quality.

Finally, go back to the main Files tab and click on the Encode button. You'll see a dialog box appear as you wait for your movie to transform into a SWF file (see Figure 8.20).

Now you have a SWF file that you can use within your Flash movies (see Figure 8.21). The Flix player can also export the accompanying HTML (check the HTML button before you encode) so that you can also upload it on your site right away if you want!

QuickTime Skins

We live in the age of changeable everything. Want to trade in the black face-plate of your cell phone for a tiger-striped version? Interested in getting a different look for your pager, changing the appearance of your desktop, or altering the way your Media Player looks? All those things are possible—and easy—no matter what your medium. You simply swap face-plates or skins to get a different look.

QuickTime 5 also offers Media Skins, which enable you to customize the QuickTime player that appears when visitors watch or listen to media objects on your site. But QuickTime skins go a step beyond the conventional ones, giving you the option of changing not only the look of the player but altering the way it functions, as well.

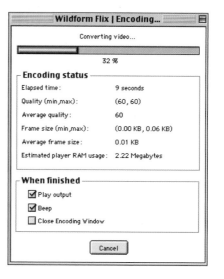

figure 8.20
Encoding process.

figure 8.21
The final SWF movie playing in a browser.

This means that you can create a player that is any size and shape, and you can create it using literally dozens of different file formats that are supported by QuickTime. You can rearrange the controls, if you like, to present your visitors with the right navigation tools for your media.

And perhaps the thing is that the players are delivered to your site visitors along with the content, which means that you can customize not only the media experience you want your site visitors to have but also the player you use to give them that experience.

You could, for example, display the video segment of your newest racing bike shown in a player designed to look like the reflector mirror of a biker's helmet. And you can do all this using AppleScript to automate the process of adding the skins to content. The possibilities are endless—and can be used to directly reinforce whatever you want your site visitors to remember most about you.

QuickTime skins could be well on their way to be the next wave in Internet advertising. Take the Dido "Hunter" single, for instance, where design studio Graphico created a customized interface to promote the artist's new single (see Figure 8.22). (195.92.224.73/dido_hunter) The Dido-branded "skin" also includes three other sample audio to help to promote the artist and gives users a chance to sample some of her music before they buy.

figure 8.22
Dido "Hunter" video in its customized shell.

Adding Sound to Your Sites

Finding sites that make good use of sound is still a bit like finding a needle in a haystack—but your site can be one of the trend-setters. The sound you use might be little more than an eight-note melody or it might be the entire voice-over to your client's latest TV commercial.

How will you use sound on your web site? Here are just a few ideas:

- Attach a sound to a user action, such as a button click or a menu selection.
- Play an audio clip of the corporate jingle.
- Add voice-over elements for demos.
- Offer an online sample of an artist's latest CD.

Background of Sound

The earliest web sites, of course, were lucky to display black text on a white background, let alone include sound. Today's web sites can include things we didn't even dream about a decade ago—whether you want to listen to a symphony, hear the soundtrack of a new movie release, listen to a live Internet radio broadcast, or hear the CEO's recorded speech from the annual meeting, you can now find it on the web. For you as a developer, that means that the sky—or the bandwidth—is the limit when it comes to including sound on your sites.

When the Internet first began to spread to the masses (escaping the university clutches of white-coated engineers), the need for sound wasn't apparent. People were interested in the transmission of data, which usually meant text, if not simply bits and bytes. The introduction of the web brought with it the first graphical interface and the easy point-and-click navigation that was missing in the text-based world of commands that had run the Internet before that point.

Once the graphical nature of the web caught on, developers began creating new, exciting, and increasingly interactive ways of communicating with and engaging web visitors. Slick new buttons, friendlier interfaces, inviting graphics, effective animations, and more became first attention-getting devices and then standards on well-designed, engaging sites. As the visual appeal of the web improved and designers came to understand more about what web users wanted and needed to see, sound played more of a role in informing and entertaining visitors. Not only for entertainment purposes, sound design on the web is a major issue now for making sites accessible to the visually disabled.

1995 was a big year for sound on the web, with the launch of Radio HK, the first 24-hour Internet radio station, and the introduction of RealAudio, by RealNetworks, the first audio player plug-in that enabled web visitors to play sound on the web.

Today RealAudio has been through multiple versions and is now RealPlayer (you can check out the latest version on the web at `www.real.com`). RealAudio was one of the early players that offered streaming technology. *Streaming* refers to the way in which media data is sent—streaming over the Internet continuously as the audio or video plays. Other popular media players today include the QuickTime Player and the Windows Media Player.

What's driving sound on the web today? Although sound use is still limited by the large sizes of most sound files (even most compressed files take up quite a bit of space), and streaming technology helps reduce the time delays users sometimes experience in playing sound files, much of sound's popularity on the web today comes from downloadable music offered by artists of all types. Users looking for

MP3 downloadable files—music files they can download and burn to their own CDs, play on their computers, or use with their MP3 players—flock to the web in search of the latest music.

Similarly, Internet radio has become a big draw, with literally thousands of radio stations broadcasting live online. Technology has made it possible for you to listen while you work with relatively little trade-off in system performance (provided that you have a system powerful enough that a little processing power won't be missed).

Note:

Sound design is its own art form. If you are interested in being a sound designer, you may want to consider taking a course at your local college. Sound design, like graphic and web design, is one of those artistic areas that combine talent with know-how and technology to create experiences that reach audiences in the way you intend. Good sound design requires a background in music, experience in composition, and instruction in technology—but that's another book.

Finally, the sound you might want to include on your sites—the jingle that plays your company theme; the voice-over from the friendly customer service rep; the background music or sound effects that lead visitors from one place to another on your site—will most likely be interesting additions to your site rather than the main draw. The sections that follow show you some of the foundations of sound development—how to edit, convert, and embed sound files in your web pages.

Sound Formats

Depending on the platform you're using, sound may be packaged in a variety of different file formats. Table 8.1 gives you an overview of the most popular sound formats, and the sections that follow go into a little more depth about the sound file types you are likely to use most often.

The three most common file types you'll use in your web applications are AIFF, MP3, and WAV. The following sections give you more detail about each of these types.

.aiff

AIFF (Audio Interchange File Format) is a common audio file format you'll find used widely on the web. The format, which was original developed for use on Apple Computers, is considered "lossy," which means that the original sound sample will sound better than the compressed sound (in other words, when you compress the sound file, there is a "loss" of quality).

.mp3

MP3 files are everywhere on the web. The format is actually a version of MPEG (Motion Picture Experts Group) 1, Layer 3. MP3 enables developers to compress sound files to approximately one tenth their uncompressed size, with only a slight difference in quality. This means that if you have 20-megabyte sound file, MP3 could compress down to two megabytes—still a large file, but a much more manageable size for an individual song.

.wav

WAV (Waveform Audio File Format) is another common audio format. This was originally developed by Microsoft and was included in early Windows versions as the sound effect files used to announce program events. Like AIFF, WAV files support various Khz ratings and compression scales. Compressed WAV formats also have a distinctive loss of quality of their uncompressed counterparts and are considered "lossy."

Table 8.1   Sound File Types

File Type	Description
AIFF	This file type is an acronym for Audio Interchange File Format, a file type used with the Mac. AIFF is an easy-to-use type that can be easily converted to other formats.
AVI	You're most likely to see AVI files in Windows applications. The name is an acronym for Audio Video interface and, as the name implies, the format includes both audio and video data.
MP3	MP3 files (which are technically part of the MPEG-1 format) are a widely popular format for digital sound.
MPEG-1	MPEG-1 files provide a media format that offers high compression capabilities for file playback and web streaming.
MIDI	This format is a popular sound format that is used for digitizing instrumental music. Samplers and synthesizers, as well as other electronic instruments with digital output, produce MIDI files that can be incorporated in a variety of applications both on and off the web.
WAV	WAV files are found in Windows, in all its incarnations. From the Windows startup sound to the bells and whistles and error signals, WAV files are a standard format that is accessible to most.

> **Note:**
>
> WAV files are often smaller than the same sound file saved in AIFF format.

MIDI and More

MIDI (Musical Instrument Digital Interface) is yet another format that enables you to include sound on your web pages without maxing out space requirements or forcing your visitors to wait for the sound to download or stream to their systems. MIDI files are unlike WAV and AIFF files in that instead of storing the actual audio data, they store instructions that tell the computer how to play the music on the receiving system. The upside is that MIDI files are very small and can be played easily on users' computers; the downside is that the sound quality is limited to whatever capability is resident on the user's system, which gives you as a developer no real control over the way your sound will sound.

Where Do You Get Sound?

Sampled sounds. There are hundreds of companies selling compilation CDs of sounds—everything from crickets chirping to dogs barking to dishwater going down the drain. You can also find samples of office sounds (clicks, whirrs, and beeps), traffic noises, household sounds, and more.

Recorded sounds. Don't underestimate the sound you can record yourself. With a good-quality digital recording device, you can capture your voice (or your own traffic, household, and office sounds). And if you have the sound capability, you can record your own musical tracks for importing into your QuickTime movies or other media creations.

Downloaded music. You name it, they've got it—all the major sites from yahoo.com to msn.com include links to music you can hear and download. You won't have to look far to find music to sample—but make sure before you use a file that it's yours to use. Downloaded music is typically considered fair use only if you use it for your personal listening only; including clips in a project would be illegal without the proper permission.

Sound Editing and Compression

You can use programs like Macromedia's SoundEdit16 v2 to manipulate, compress, or record your own sound files. SoundEdit gives you the power to manipulate and tweak your sound clips and files. This section gives you a look at SoundEdit 16 v2 and provides steps so you can experiment with the program a bit. Here are the steps:

1. Launch SoundEdit16 v2.
2. Open the file ending_gliss.aif. The sound file is shown in Figure 8.23.

figure 8.23

The sampled sound in SoundEdit 16.

> **Tip:**
>
> If you want to follow along with this example, you can find the preceding file by visiting www.htmlartistry.com and clicking the Chapters link.

This file is to be used later in a Flash movie so it is currently optimized for the web at 22kHz/16 bits.

3. In the lower bar on the right, you will see marked lines and a sliding triangle. Move the triangle to the left, and you will get a zoom-in view of the sound file, as you see in Figure 8.24.

4. Save your edited file by going to the File menu and choosing Save As. From there you will get a dialog box where you can choose the final format you want your sound file to be. Here we will choose WAVE (see Figure 8.25).

Sometimes editing is a bit more complex than normal and you will need to edit and cut your sound files. This is especially true when you are working with voice audio. You'll find there may be lots of blank spaces, mistakes, or lulls in the file that need to be cut out so that it can work correctly. Cutting out the excess space also saves on file size as well.

1. Open baby_giggle.aif.
2. Next you can see the highs and the lows of your audio file and "trim" any excess you may see. Figure 8.26 shows the excess white sound (highlighted in pink) at the end of the file, as illustrated with the straight black line.
3. Delete this area by highlighting the area with your mouse and pressing the Delete key. If your sound file is big, it could be tricky. Just know that you don't have to delete it all in one try. In fact, it's best to delete in small chunks and then do a test play to ensure that you aren't cutting out any necessary pauses or voice audio. By deleting this area, you'll not only cut the run time of the audio file but you'll also trim down the file size.

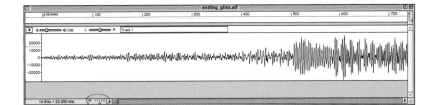

figure 8.24

You can change the view by sliding the triangle.

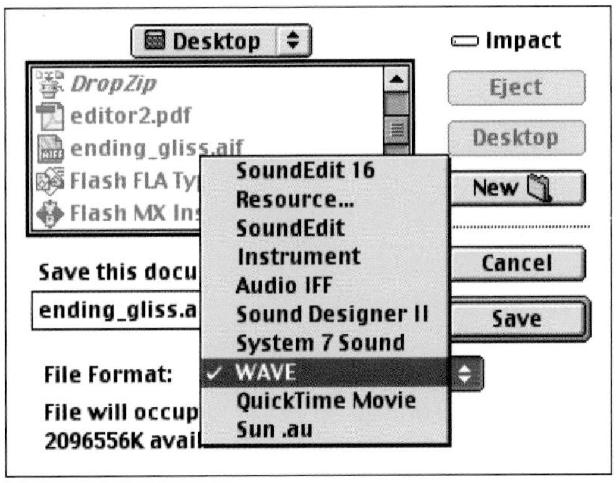

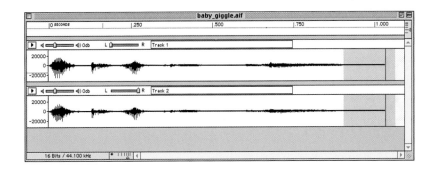

figure 8.25

You can save sound files in WAVE format easily in SoundEdit 16.

figure 8.26

Deleting white sound saves space and gives you a cleaner file.

Other points to remember when you are working with a sound-editing application and converting and optimizing files are as follows:

- When you are converting audio from a CD or other media, always sample audio at the highest sample rate (much like the concept of scanning in movies in high resolution whenever possible).

- Use a sample rate of 44.1kHz/16bit to optimize the file for the web.

- Sample down as necessary—most audio for the web can be sampled down to 22 kHZ/16 bit or 22kHZ/8 bit, depending on whether the audio is a sound clip, narration, or actual music.

- Save the sound files you create directly for the web, in .wav (or WAVE) format whenever possible. You can do this easily with the Save As function in SoundEdit 16.

Sound Loops

Because of file-size constraints on the web, you may have to create music loops that can play continuously either with an animation or as a rollover sound.

Loops can be tricky because you have to make a clip that balances with something that can be long enough to be different, yet not be annoying as it continues to play. This is of course easier with longer music clips—but longer music clips also eat up more space and require longer download times.

For simple loops, you will need to use your keen ear and visually match up the sound waves to make sure they loop at the right point. In order to make the sound loop accurate, you can use the Loop Tuner Xtra in SoundEdit 16.

Here we are going to loop a song, working with the high-quality 44kHz/16 bit (stereo) version. Here are the steps:

1. Load the sound file loop1.aif into SoundEdit by choosing File, Open and find loop1.aif on your hard drive (see Figure 8.27).

2. Select and delete any unnecessary part of your audio file to create your loop. Then select all and from the top menu choose Xtras, Loop Tuner. The Loop Tuner appears, as Figure 8.28 shows.

3. In the Loop Tuner dialog box, use the arrow keys to get both lines to match up and connect together.

4. Once you have the lines connected adequately, click on the Set Loop button (see Figure 8.29).

5. Using your sound Control Panel, click the Loop button to test the loop (see Figure 8.30).
   If the loop didn't connect at the right point, you'll definitely hear slight hiccups in the sound file.

6. Continue to tweak and test the file until the loop is established at the right point. Then save your file by choosing File, Save As.

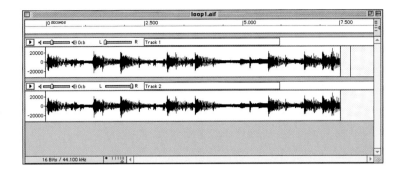

figure 8.27

Preparing to create a sound loop in
SoundEdit 16.

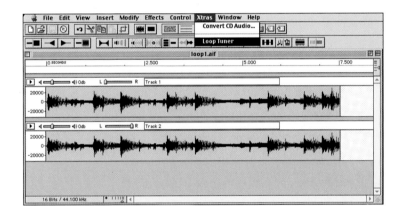

figure 8.28

The Loop Tuner dialog box enables
you to view and connect the loop.

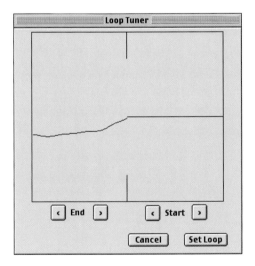

figure 8.29

Connecting the sound loop with the Loop Tuner.

figure 8.30

You can play the new loop using your
sound Control Panel.

> **Tip:**
> You can move the slider in order to zoom in on the sound wave to better clip the front or end of the sound clip so that they can match up better in the Loop Tuner.

Converting to MP3

With Apple's iTunes program, you can convert any AIF or WAV file easily and quickly to MP3 format. Let's try the example with our loop1.aif sound file:

1. Launch iTunes.
2. Open the Advanced menu and choose Convert to MP3 (see Figure 8.31).
3. A dialog box will appear, asking you to choose your sound file (see Figure 8.32). Navigate to the folder containing the sound file you want to convert; click the Choose button to select the file. The application then automatically converts your sound AIF or WAV file to MP3 format. You will find the MP3 sound file in your documents/iTunes/ iTunes Music folder. You can test out the new file by using the iTunes player, as shown in Figure 8.33.

   Now you have two sound files—loop1.aif and loop1.mp3—that are ready for the web (see Figure 8.34). Make sure to keep your AIF sound files in your working files directory in case you will need to go back and edit the sound file at a later time.

figure 8.31

iTunes makes it easy for you to convert sound files to MP3 format.

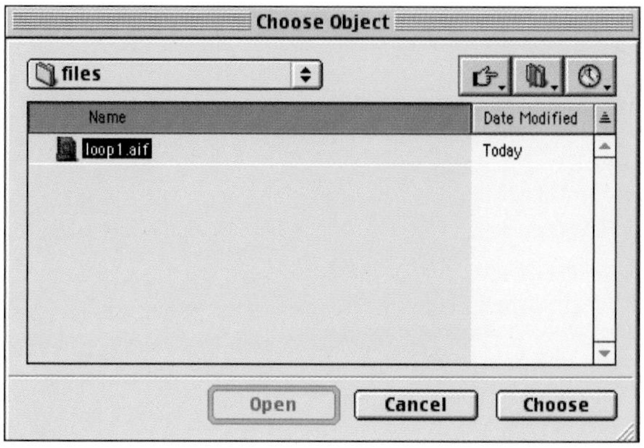

figure 8.32

Select the file you want to convert and then click the Choose button.

figure 8.33

After the file is saved in the iTunes music folder, you can play it using the iTunes player.

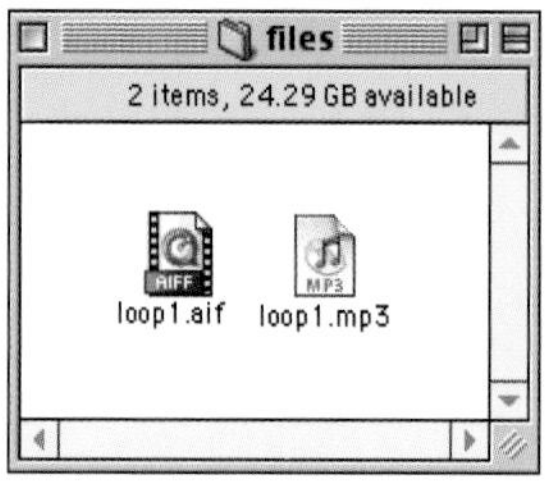

figure 8.34

The AIF and MP3 files are now ready for the web.

> ## Note:
>
> Some people prefer to use the shareware program Audion, which is a great sound app on its own as well (`www.panic.com/audion`).

Embedding Sound into HTML

Now that you know how to find, create, edit, and convert sound files, you need to know how to plug them into your web pages. The process here is slightly different, depending on whether you're using Internet Explorer or Netscape.

If you're using Internet Explorer, you will use the special HTML tag `<BGSOUND>` that will allow your sound files to be played in the background of your web page. Here's the code to do this:

```
<BGSOUND SRC="ending_gliss.wav"
LOOP="false">
```

If you're using Netscape, you'll embed the sound using the following code:

```
<EMBED SRC="ending_gliss.wav"
TYPE="audio/wav" HIDDEN="false"
AUTOSTART="true" LOOP="false"
WIDTH="1" HEIGHT="1"></EMBED>
```

In both Internet Explorer and Netscape, you can create an `<A HREF>` link that will allow a user to click on and then hear the supported audio file. Here's the code for that:

```
<a href="ending_gliss.wav">test</a>
```

Flash Sound

To create a sound-only Flash SWF, we have made a small 20×20 movie that is of a white background so that it can be embedded into the HTML page invisibly.

To start the sound-importing process, first go to the File menu and choose Import. You will get the Import dialog box (see Figure 8.35). It is important to choose the high-end file (loop1.aif) because Flash will compress the sound file and automatically convert it to MP3.

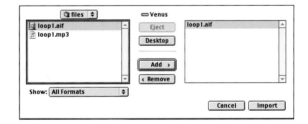

figure 8.35

Flash enables you to import sound files easily.

You will see the sound file added to your library (see Figure 8.36).

Display the sound file's properties by going to the Library, and double-clicking on the audio file. Now you can modify its attributes (see Figure 8.37). For compression format, choose MP3 from the menu and choose your compression settings below it.

Drag the sound file from the symbol library to the timeline and you will see the sound waves appear on the timeline (see Figure 8.38). Here we will have the movie stop after the sound has played by adding an action to stop in the last frame.

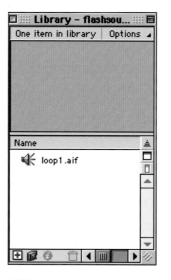

8.36

figure 8.36

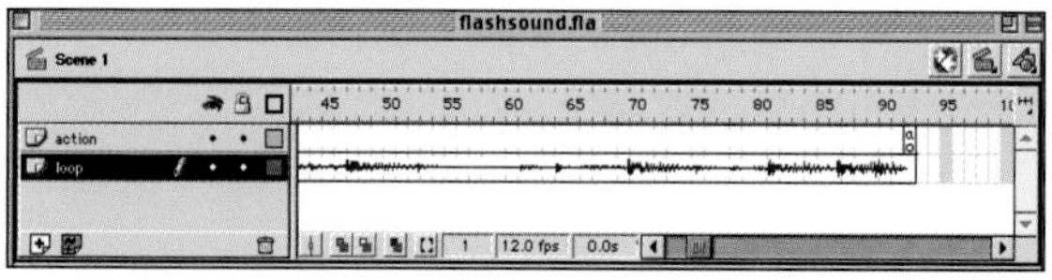

After importing, the sound file is displayed in your library.

figure 8.37

Choose compression settings in the Sound Properties dialog box.

figure 8.38

The sound waves appear on the timeline after you drag the file from the library.

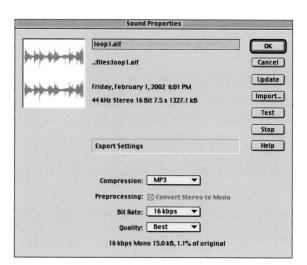

8.37

8.38

Using the controls in the Sound dialog box (see Figure 8.39), you can further control what the sound will do, such as stream or loop through the sound panel. Display the Sound dialog box by choosing Windows>Panels>Sound.

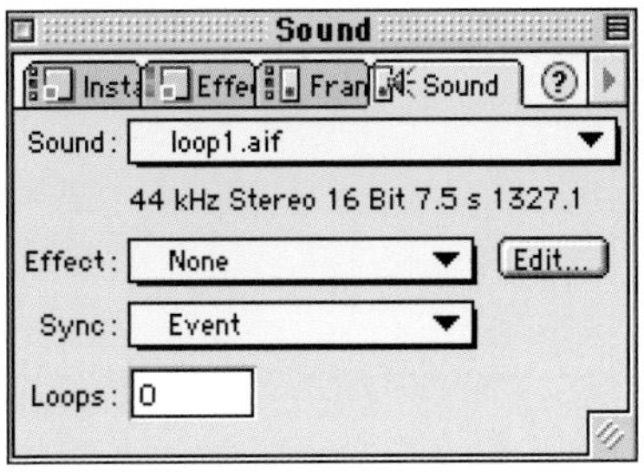

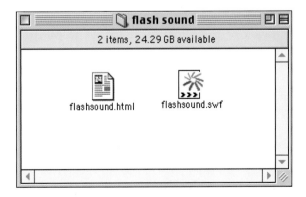

8.39

When you are ready to publish your SWF file, you can double check or modify the sound compression settings by clicking on the audio stream EDIT or audio event EDIT button. The Sound Settings dialog box will appear (see Figure 8.40).

Finally, after you save your file by choosing File, Export Movie, you will have your final Flash sound SWF and the accompanying HTML code, which you can paste into your existing HTML (see Figure 8.41).

8.40

figure 8.39

The Sound dialog box enables you to stream or loop the sound you've added.

figure 8.40

Check your settings in the Sound Settings dialog box.

figure 8.41

The Flash SWF file and the HTML code are ready to be used on the web.

8.41

QuickTime Audio and HTML

A few facts about QuickTime audio:

You can layer QuickTime audio as you would video, adding and moving tracks and editing as needed to get the sound you want.

Audio tracks can store data from CDs, MP3 players, web and television output, and more.

QuickTime supports music tracks, which are tracks that store and play MIDI data. QuickTime includes its own MIDI instruments, enabling you to create quality sound files while keeping the file size small.

QuickTime includes file compression utilities to help reduce the size of audio files.

Beatnik Editor

The folks at Beatnik (www.beatnik.com) have done a great job of bringing sound to the web. If you are still in need of a cool sound application to manipulate or create music and sound effects, the Beatnik Editor is just the software for you. The Beatnik Editor includes a full collection of MIDI instruments, a percussion bank, and instrument groups you can define yourself—up to 400 different instruments. Beatnik Editor works with all kinds of files, from general MIDI to MP3 to most widely supported audio formats.

Tip:

You can download a free trial of the Beatnik Editor to test out for yourself at www. beatnik.com/beatnik_editor.htm.

The Beatnik Editor interface comes pretty slick with its buttons and keyboard setup (see Figure 8.42). You almost can't resist playing, can you?

When you first open up the application, the player appears with an "untitled session" that contains tabs with Songs, Instruments, and Samples (see Figure 8.43). You can also access your sessions through the File menu by Windows, Untitled Session. You can then rename your session to be whatever your project name is. It is this Session panel into which you import audio files so that you can work with them in the Player (see Figure 8.44).

There are some preset audio files already in the Songs panel. By choosing a song or clip from the Songs panel, you can edit and manipulate a file according to your own taste.

Once you have played around with your file and it's to your liking, you can export it in two ways. You can export it to a regular audio file (File, Export to Audio) that will save an AIF or WAV file. Alternatively, you can export it to the Beatnik RMF format (File, Export RMF).

8.42

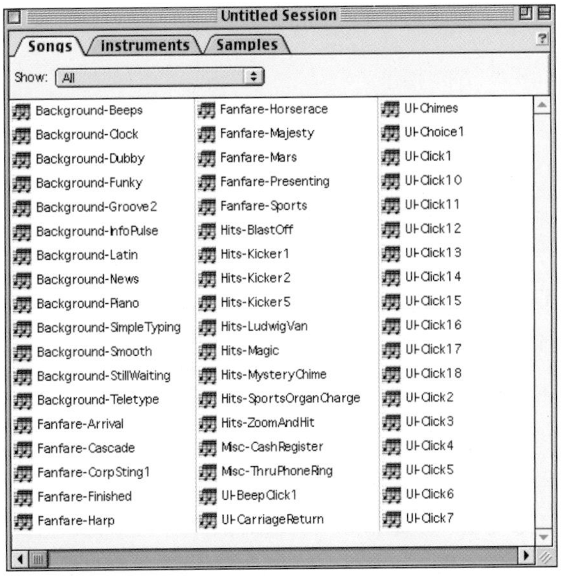

8.43

figure 8.42

You can use Beatnik Editor to play and edit sound files.

figure 8.43

You can choose a song to edit from the Songs panel.

figure 8.44

The Beatnik Editor plays the song on the keyboard display.

8.44

Case Study

Samsung—24-Hour Street Promotional Web Site

Samsung wanted to create a web site to promote its products and speak directly to a young, hip audience. The result was the Samsung 24-Hour Street site designed and developed by SBI and Company in their Portland and San Francisco offices. Since this was to be a slick, all-Flash web site, Flash developer Barry Munsterteiger and sound designer Thomas Greene were able to get creative and show off their sound and Flash expertise. Here, Barry shares some tips on how he and Thomas worked together to optimally control sound in Flash.

The Samsung project was a challenge from the start. "We were faced with the request for dynamic sound that would relate to different areas of the site for both the Products section and the 24-Hour Street section, both of which had similarities and differences," explains Barry. "In the 24-Hour section, the user arrives from four possible different redirection locations, one for each product. Each product is associated with a different time of day; therefore, the sounds that are heard are different during each of the different time slots. At the time we were working on this, we decided it would best if we just created all the sounds from scratch, and fortunately we had an in-house sound designer [Thomas Greene]."

Thomas recorded and created a library of sounds for each of the four different time periods. Each sound file was brought into its own SWF file and was named its own distinct number. Having the sounds in individual SWFs also helped cut down on file size. All of the sounds had a randomly generated number on the main timeline and when the sound's associated number came up it would play. "This created a very natural sound backdrop that seemed to have a more realistic feel to it than anything we would have been able to achieve through a single looping sound clip," describes Barry.

In the products section, there are four different highlighted products, each of which had an associated main music loop. Each product also had supporting sounds to go along with the main loop, either a voice-over or other sound files related to features of the specific product. All of the sounds would look to a variable on the main timeline to set their volume.

Getting all of this to work correctly took some exploration from Barry into the sound object in Flash. The sound object allows much more control over audio in the SWF files than was previously available. The use of setVolume was key to making this all happen seamlessly to the user.

Barry explains, "The best example of the use of setVolume in this was with the Hip Hop Yepp mp3 player sound section of the site. Here we have four different audio tracks that are all playing at the exact same time and, through the setVolume function, we can switch back and forth between audio loops making it look like we are changing the EQ settings for a single track."

How it works in Flash:

> ## Note:
> Please note that all level numbers are for demonstration purposes only and are not exact to the final version.

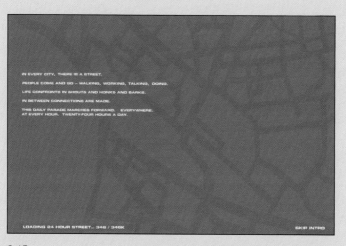

8.45

8.46

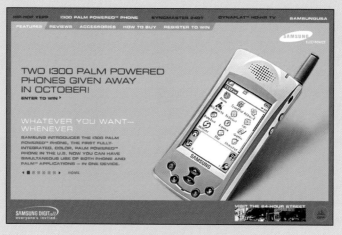

8.47

The yeppSound.swf is loaded to level 10. This then would load the specific soundLoop SWF into level 700. The soundLoop SWF has an internal script that is checking to see what the volume should be from a variable that is on level 1000. Level 1000 is where the value of volume will be stored, as well as the ability to turn this on or off. The potential values for the volume, in this case, were 0 or 100 (on or off).

The yeppSound.swf has four buttons on it that are associated with different EQ settings and different iconic representations of each sound style via an animation. We will call them Buttons 1 through 4. Button 1 is associated with the normal sound EQ setting, Button 2 is for "classic," Button 3 is for "jazz," and Button 4 is for "rock."

As the user rolls over Button 1, it tells the soundLoop on level 700 that the normal sound should be set to the volume from level 1000. This also tells the other three sounds that their volume should be set to 0. This is also duplicated for the other three buttons, changing which sound would be on or off appropriately.

"The reason we had four different sounds loaded in a single movieclip was to ensure that they all started at the exact same time; this also allowed us to have sounds that would approximate the sound settings of the actual device," confirms Barry. "Having all the sounds start at the same time allowed for a somewhat seamless transition from one EQ setting to the next, very similar to that which happens on the real device. The sound object made this possible and kept all sounds in sync with each other."

Although for the most part all this complex scripting is seamless to the end user, Barry Munsterteiger and Thomas Greene show how passionate they are for Flash and sound design. Through their attention to detail and careful planning, they have helped make the 24-Hour Street site pleasing to the ears.

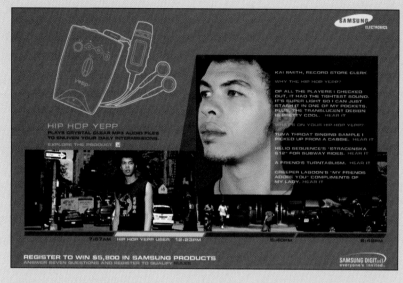

8.48

8.49

Sound Libraries

As web design becomes more Multimedia rich, creating a sound library for your work is a good idea. Organize your sound files into rollover clicks, beeps, audio loops, and so on.

The following sections describe some great resources to get your sound library started.

Ear Shot SFX (Two-CD Set)

`www.dxm.com` (click on Products)

An essential sound effects CD that contains royalty-free clips. Everything from squeaks, whooshes, and hums, to beeps, clicks, and clanks. The CDs contain both high-quality 44kHz samples as well as down-sampled versions (22.050kHz/8bit and 11.025kHz/8 bit) so you can easily grab sound files and use them right away.

Beatnik Sound Database

`ginsberg.beatnik.com/license_music/search.jsp`

If you are on a tight budget and can't seem to carry a tune, much less create original sound clips, the Beatnik site also provides great music and sound clips in a searchable database that allows you to purchase individually so you don't have to buy a whole CD.

The Hollywood Edge

`www.hollywoodedge.com`

For more sophisticated and specific sound effects, you can get great compilation CDs of their best effects or, if you need an entire CD of sports sounds, you can find it here. Prices are a bit higher, but it's well worth it for the professional sound quality.

Summary

As you learned in this chapter, there is much you can do to make your web pages more exciting and inviting for your visitors. Rich media offers you all kinds of flash and sparkle—from streaming QuickTime video to Flash animations and from looping background music to quick-play sound effects.

But on the other side of the excitement is the reality of larger files, longer download times, and the need for compression and smart file handling. This chapter has introduced you to a variety of media possibilities and planted the idea that you need to carefully consider how to get the best-quality audio and video in the smallest possible files. Finally, in this chapter you learned how specifically to edit, convert, and embed sound in your HTML and discovered some popular web sound libraries that may be of help in your own projects.

Inspirational Design Model

Josh Ulm
ioResearch

"I try very hard to keep Remedi as an

establishment that is fundamentally artist

driven...I'm simply the guy that registered the

domain name."

figure 1

ioResearch.com

To say that Josh Ulm is passionate about the Internet as a new medium for storytelling is an understatement. The creation of The Remedi Project (www.theremediproject.com) back in 1997 as a means of exploring the potential of digital art and storytelling has made waves in the digital design community. It has helped this San Francisco-based designer become one of the most sought after interactive thought leaders, because he truly understands the medium and it's potential for the future.

But then there's Josh Ulm, the regular guy. He just wants to ride his motorcycle and go to the movies. If there's anything to be said for having a good sense of perspective and balance, Josh reminds us that inspiration can come from enjoying the simple things in life.

What inspires you?
Different things, though I guess it boils down to elegant execution of simplicity. Simple stories that send chills across your skin. Flocks of birds flying as one. Jellyfish. Yellow. Grey.

What's your creative process when you are working on a project? How do you factor in the technology?
Technology always comes last. I may be intrigued by a technique I've uncovered, or system that allows me to present content in a beautiful fashion, but we fight to uncover the

message first and then find the perfect means to communicate it. I usually get cursed by my team for pulling out "limitation of technology" as an excuse for doing something, and we try to avoid it, but in this day, age, and medium, it happens. We do the best we can.

We still work by intuition and develop for ourselves. Ours is not to meet the needs of the mainstream. There are plenty of developers about attending to that. Rather, we are interested in finding new applications in the medium. Story-telling and interactive are two more fundamental concepts in our work. I present these concepts with slight trepidation that it escalates them as buzzwords, yet we see them very non-traditionally, and perhaps more fundamentally important to our culture that most people recognize. Encouraging the marriage of these forms is the starting point for most of our work.

You have many roles in this industry: designer, teacher, speaker, Flash action scripter, motorcycle lover. How do you balance the client work you do with personal projects, such as The Remedi Project, and also teach?
We have a process that we are quite fond of where our personal work informs our client work. It forms a nice cycle. Typically, a studio moves so quickly from project to project that no time is allowed to reflect on the work. To critique it. When you teach, you are forced to very closely

2

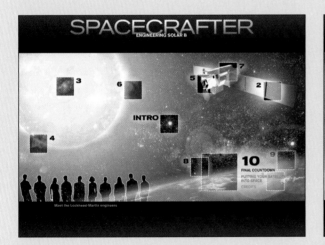

3

4

figure 2
The Remedi Project Launch,
Spring 1998

figure 3 and 4
Spacecrafter, Courtesy the Chabot
Space and Science Center

scrutinize your work, otherwise you will fail in communicating it. By looking at your work with dissemination in mind, you leave with an invaluable study to take into the next client project. And so it goes.

The Ducati just keeps me sane.

The Remedi Project has definitely grown and evolved over the years, making a significant impact on the design world. What inspired you to create it? What have you learned from the project since starting it?
Working on The Remedi Project has reminded me that people respond to the voice of change. One of the most important facts of life, next to the fact that we could all get smacked by a cab tomorrow, is that everything changes. There is an eternal promise that tomorrow holds new questions, and new answers. Remedi will not last forever. It already is very different from what it started as. But its promise is something that each of us will always seek.

What's a project you're working on now?
It's funny how people think our studio, ioResearch, is too busy to take on new work. Of course we are always keeping busy, but the best work is work collaborated on with new clients with new ideas. The client is not the enemy, it is the trophy.

At ioResearch we always like to keep pushing ourselves, and thereby our clients. Our work is constantly evolving, and we are always posting new ideas, new work. Our web site, www.ioresearch.com, is the best place to get a glimpse of what we are up to now. Our studio in Mill Valley is the best place to chat with us about it.

How do you think Broadband or the introduction of wireless technologies will change the way in which the digital medium will be thought of and designed for?
Clarity and distance traveled are two very important qualities of a message. Broadband and wireless promise shifts in both aspects. One of the most fundamental turning points for society was the advent of telecommunications, another was television. The telephone broke down barriers of geography. Its consequences on culture and class are obvious, although taken for granted, and still ripple today. Similarly, television has redefined the place of the individual in society. How will broadband and wireless affect us? The same way the phone and television did—fundamentally.

Who are your design heroes?
My work, and the work of my team at ioResearch, is so interdisciplinary that it would be very unfair to say that my heroes are designers. It is true that many of my peers are

5

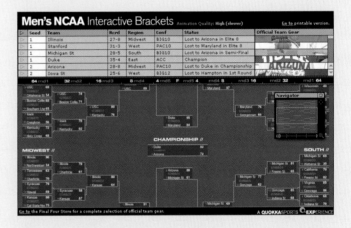

6

7

figure 5

Kind Radio, Courtesy neumu.net

figure 6

NCAA Interactive Brackets,
Courtesy Quokka Sports

figure 7

Cerner Virtual Theater, Courtesy
Cerner Corporation

designers, and yes I hold many of them in great esteem—One9ine, The Chopping Block, Future Farmers—but the most influential people for me have come from disciplines far removed from the Internet. Bar none, my greatest heroes are my parents. Everything I am I owe to them.

Do you have any advice that you would like to share with all the aspiring designers out there?

As the Internet continues to grow in coming years, two kinds of designers will emerge: those that tell great stories, and those who do their production work. My advice? Choose a path now.

If you could be a superhero, who would you be and why?

Well Molecule Man, of course. In fact, anyone who doesn't want to be Molecule Man is going to get beat down. I mean, he can control all matter. Which essentially means he can do anything. It's a little unbalanced in the end, but then again…you'd want to be the "best" superhero.

What are three things in the world you can't live without?

My girlfriend, my dog, and sunshine.

Josh Ulm URLs:

- **ioResearch** `www.ioresearch.com`
- **Remedi Project** `www.theremediproject.com`
- **Neumu** `www.neumu.net/twinklepop/clips/ 0001/0001_video/index.html`

On Remedi:

My work is such a part of who I am that it is hard to talk about work and not talk about who I've become. Perhaps though, one of the biggest misconceptions is that The Remedi Project is about me. I try very hard to keep Remedi as an establishment that is fundamentally artist driven. The artists put their hearts into their projects, and Remedi is created from that. I'm simply the guy that registered the domain name.

8

figures 8 and 9
Dreams

9

Flash Interfaces

Creating Cinematic &

Interactive Experiences

CHAPTER 9

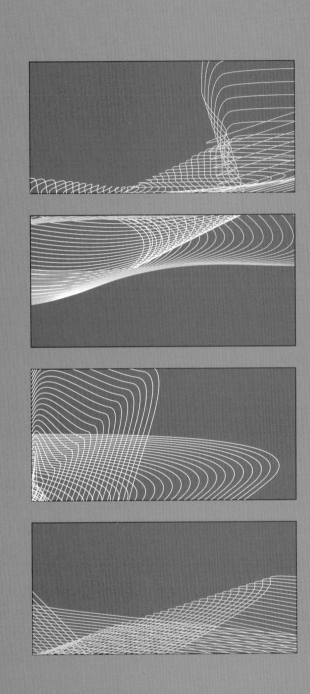

First everyone wanted a web site. Then they wanted a Flash site. They wanted sound, animation—all the bells and whistles. Now they want another Flash site. This time they want graceful transitions, automation and individualization through action scripting—limited bells, no whistles. Hey, we can't complain if the work keeps coming!

Flash has become one of the most powerful and popular Internet tools. It is extremely useful to know Flash because it does so much! There are entire books written about Flash and action scripting alone. We're not going to teach you how to use the program or how to become an action script programmer.

This chapter is for designers. We discuss the problems that come up in Flash design and we offer the best solutions we have found. We will analyze what makes a good movie great, and explain how to add sophistication to your animation. This chapter assumes a basic familiarity with the program.

At the end of the day, the best way to see what you can do with Flash is by looking at and analyzing existing sites on the web. The best way learn Flash is to start playing!

Why Use Flash?

Every day new Flash sites appear on the web. Companies both large and small have quickly accepted the plug-in as mainstream. Everyone wants a Flash site. When Flash first came out, designers immediately embraced it. It solved so many of the problems that HTML web design had presented. The immediate selling points were that it enabled the use of sound and motion, control over typography and graphic scalability…all with an extremely fast download. In addition, the plug-in itself was a small download and comparatively easy to install.

Developers and key decision-makers in the technology community quickly realized the potential of Flash. Before long, the plug-in bundled with the major browsers, automatically enabling use of Flash for thousands and thousands of Internet surfers.

Originally, Flash was a program that anyone could learn. The drawing tools were not nearly as sophisticated as those in Illustrator and FreeHand, and the scripting was extremely simple and limited. The program seems to have developed in two distinct directions: the first for designers and the second for programmers. In many cases, Flash designers and Flash programmers work in teams. It is hard to be an expert at everything, and together action scripters and designers can create complex and exciting sites.

As Flash became more popular, it also, naturally, became more powerful. Flash 3 allowed the use of multiple timelines enabling more complex animation and interactivity. Flash 4 introduced the first generation of action scripting, enabling the programming of movies. In addition, Flash 4 made it easy to compress sound, using the MP3 format for tiny downloads. However, it wasn't until version 5 of the program that programmers truly accepted it as a tool. The Flash 4 scripting language was limited and programmers still preferred Macromedia Director. Flash 5 introduced an almost entirely new version of action scripting thereby multiplying the capabilities of the software. Now Flash has taken it a step further. With new user interface components, designers can easily use prescripted drop-down menus and buttons that talk directly to JavaScript.

Things move fast in the Internet industry. It is no surprise that Macromedia has been able to develop such a powerful tool in such a short time. Like any tool, the more that it can do, the more there is to learn.

Designers and Flash

Designers love Flash because it allows you to design with control and freedom. It allows for beautiful typography that isn't dependent on the users' system typefaces. You can seamlessly transition from page to page and use subtle animation on rollover buttons and page loads. As with any web tool, there are still drawbacks from traditional print design. Photos can be a problem and need to be used properly to look good. What's more, small type can become illegible on certain monitors, and precautions need to be taken.

In addition to Flash being a sophisticated Internet design tool, many designers become fascinated with its programming capabilities. The most powerful programming solutions are enforced with a strong design. A designer who is able to both program and design can create incredibly unique and beautiful solutions.

You don't have to become an "action scripting whiz," although it is a good idea to learn a little about the scripting language. It will expand your mind and enable you to think of more possibilities conceptually and visually within your Flash design.

Designing with Flash

Flash is fun, and it's always tempting to jump right in. Playing and experimenting are the only ways to truly learn the program; however, with client design, beginning in Flash will ultimately waste a lot of your time. It is important to design your site in Illustrator or FreeHand before even opening Flash. All your sketches should be done in one of these vector-based programs. The biggest mistake designers make is trying to use Flash as a preliminary design tool. You should always resolve your designs and layouts before attempting to add any interactivity. Present different layout directions to your clients printed out as screens on boards.

If you need to illustrate animation, storyboard the action that will take place (see Figure 9.1). An Internet company wanted a 30-second animation introducing their services. The designers proposed three individual design directions that illustrated how three distinctly different animations would work. Although no motion was used, it was easy to get a feel for each sequence and the way the final animation would look. The client was able to choose one direction for development. If still frames are grabbed from the final animation, they are almost identical to the frames of the original storyboard.

Putting Design in Motion

Flash makes it very easy to animate vector graphics. In fact, it is so easy that a lot of non-designers end up animating splash screens and Flash animations. Consequentially, there is a lot of cheesy, even gratuitous, use of animation on the web. It is a designer's job to create motion that still remembers that typography and composition are some of the fundamental parts of design.

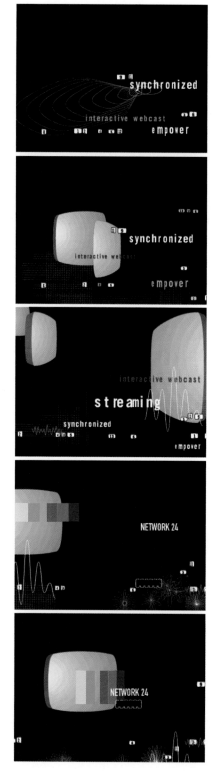

figure 9.1

The storyboard picks keyframes that illustrate how the animation will work.

I taught Flash and interface design at the California College of Arts and Crafts (CCAC) in San Francisco. CCAC has a traditional graphic design program that emphasizes the importance of conceptual design. Classes teach not only how to design, but also the tradition and heritage of design as a profession and passion. From day one, students are taught typography and composition. They learn to kern type by cutting out Xerox letterforms and pushing them together and apart to perfect letter spacing. By the time they reached my class in "level 4" they had portfolios that illustrated their understanding of the importance and nuances of basic, good design.

The first assignment I gave was to use type to animate a phrase. Students were instructed to storyboard their ideas and then animate the sequence in Flash. This was their first experiment with motion and I was amazed at how quickly their design skills disappeared. Suddenly all the "rules" were ignored. I asked everyone to print out a sequence of frames, every three seconds from their animation. Instead of critiquing the motion, we critiqued the still compositions. It quickly became obvious that there was a problem. After this exercise, the work improved. Students started realizing that designing in motion was actually incredibly complex and difficult. Where they previously had to create one composition for a poster of a few spreads for a book, they were now aware of every single frame in a 30-second animation.

As a Flash designer, it is incredibly important to think about why you are using motion. There are many reasons we use motion. Motion can tell a story using time as the means of sequence. Sometimes it is used as a means for loading the different compositional elements on your page, or as a way of transitioning different elements off the screen. No matter how you choose to use it, don't forget everything else you know about design.

Loading Your Pages Gracefully

You can control the way the different elements of the page load by using the timeline. One of the negative things about HTML design is the way that pages appear as they download. There is almost always a clunky, "webby" feeling as images and text are dumped onto one's monitor. One of the best parts of Flash is freedom from that unrefined download feeling.

The US Bridgedale Socks web site loads with a splash animation that then resolves into the home page (see Figures 9.2–9.6). By placing all the elements of the home page on different layers, the designers were able to control the order and motion with which the final home page resolved.

A good way to animate a page resolve is to work backward. Begin by separating each element of the design on to a different layer. We will make this example simple and say there are four layers (background, text, photo, and logo). Name each layer based on what it contains.

1. Create a keyframe on in the first frame of each layer.

2. Move down the timeline and mark another keyframe at frame 30 on each layer. (These keyframes mark how the animation will resolve…. You should have two keyframes on each layer.)

3. Drag the first keyframe in the type layer to frame 5. (Leave a blank keyframe in frame 1.)

4. In frame 5, move the type off the stage and motion tween between two keyframes. (If you preview the animation at this point, the type should move from off the screen on frame 5 and resolve to its proper position at frame 30.)

5. Select the first keyframe on the logo layer and move it to frame 10.

figures 9.2–9.6

This storyboard illustrates how the home page resolved into its final composition.

9.2

9.3

9.4

9.5

9.6

6. In frame 10, increase the size of the logo by 200%.

7. Motion tween between the last two keyframes on the logo layer.

8. Move the first keyframe of the photo layer to frame 15.

9. Move the photo off the stage and motion tween between the last two frames.

10. Put a stop action on frame 30.

11. Preview the animation and notice how the background color remains the same as the type animates in, the logo shrinks into position, and finally the photo animates in and the composition resolves.

Although the animation described above is by no means going to give you award-winning results, you can adapt the idea, timing, and complexity to create a subtle sophistication for each of your page loads.

If you decide not to animate loads, you still have some control over the order in which objects appear on the page. When you export your movie (File, Export Movie), Flash allows you to select the load order. Bottom Up, the default, means your bottom layer will appear first, and items will download from that layer upwards. Top Down is the opposite. For example, if you select Top Down and your top layer is a large photograph, it will have to download entirely first, before any of the graphics on the layers below it begin to show. Only the first frame is included in the load order. After the first frame of each layer loads, the rest of the movie loads horizontally... beginning from frame 1 and ending with the last frame of the movie.

Using Masks with Animation

Fluent Studios was hired to make a splash animation page for a multicultural educational program. The program was an interactive site for teachers and students to learn about the many cultures of the Bay Area. Each month a different heritage or culture is featured. The designers thought it made sense to animate color fields and typography to show all the different heritage months scheduled for the year.

Using a combination of masks and frames to frame animation, they created a sequence that was not only visually interesting, but heightened the concept of the multi-cultural Bay Area. The animation itself is quite simple (see Figures 9.7–9.10). Blocks of color move vertically in four stripes. They create the illusion of painting type on and then pushing it off the screen. The sequence works in a way that groups of words separate as they are broken away from each other and new phrases are created. For example, "Lesbian" and "Gay" separate from the word "Pride." As "Gay" is dropping down the screen, it passes "Black History." The intersection of the two words momentarily creates an entirely new heritage of "Gay Black History." As those words separate, "Black History" passes the word "Women's," which has separated from its group, and the phrase "Women's Black History" is created.

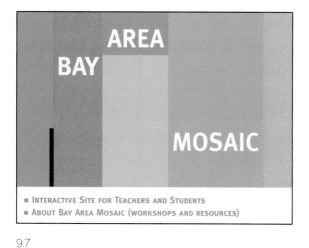

9.7

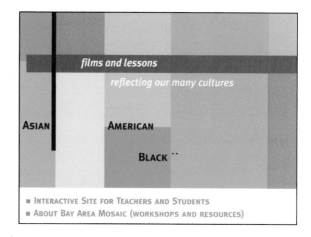

9.8

Using masks, the words appear quite naturally in the composition. The word is placed where it will appear a few frames before it is ready to show. There is a layer above the type that will act as a mask to reveal the word. The designers used two keyframes on the mask layer to create the effect. The first keyframe did not cover the type. The second keyframe was placed and the block was moved down to cover the type. The two keyframes were motion tweened and then the layer was turned into a mask. The last step was to move the masked keyframes around so that they timed perfectly with a passing stripe. The final effect was one of having the stripe paint the word on to the composition. The technique can be best understood by visiting the animation at www.kqed.org/mosaic.

figures 9.7–9.10
The animation uses masks to push words off and on the screen.

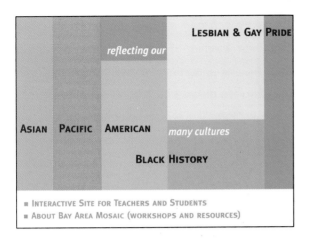

9.9

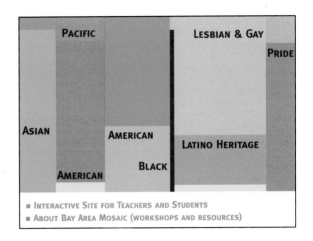

9.10

Working with Tweens

Tween, as in "between," quite literally means the frames between two keyframes. Most likely you have worked with both motion and shape tweens a little already. There are very specific reasons for using each type of tween, and each can be used well or poorly. As a designer there are distinctions you should realize when you are working with either one.

Motion Tweens

Motion tweens are best used for changing scale, position, rotation, opacity, tint, or any other modification to an instance. Motion tweens tend to cause problems when they are animating the position or opacity of large graphic elements. The more elements animating at the same time, and the bigger the scale of the elements, the more potential you have for a clunky animation. If you are animating large pieces of art, limit the motion to one object at a time. One trick to make the animation appear more smoothly is to limit the number of frames within the tween. If your design requires that you animate large objects simultaneously, make sure you embed the movie into your HTML as "actual size." For some reason, PCs seem to handle large complex motion tweening better than Macs.

The reason tweens can appear clunky is mainly because of the processor speed of the computers on which they are playing. As computers become faster, this will be less of a problem. Remember to always test your movies as you are making them. If you test early on, you won't be surprised by the playback quality later.

Shape Tweens

Shape tweens should be used for, well…changing the shape of an object. As you know, shape tweens only work when the object is broken apart. One common mistake novice shape tweeners make is to try to tween between too complex of objects. At first, this warbled mess may look cool, but it is really the indication of a confused animation (see Figure 9.11). You should be careful to avoid this jumbled mathematical mess that occurs when two objects that are not meant to be morphed are tweened. As cool as you think it looks the first time you see it, it gets old fast, not to mention slows down your whole animation.

figure 9.11

Beware of shape tweens that look like this! Unless you have a really special reason, it looks sloppy and unprofessional.

Shape tweens can be beautiful when they are used with intention. For example, we created a web site for Macromedia called Vector Zone. The purpose of the site was to educate visitors about vectors. It's a good resource for designers. If you want to learn about how what vectors are, you should visit the site. The basic concept behind the site is that vectors, when pared down to their most basic level, are no more than a line and a point with some math that can be represented as squiggles. We decided to open the site with a Flash animation in which the characters were those three things…a line, a squiggle, and a point (see Figures 9.12–9.17). As the animation progresses, the line and squiggle react to each other. The squiggle flies away from the line and then it comes back and twists itself around the line, capturing it for a moment. The animation resolves with the line and squiggle both snapping away from each other and flying off the screen.

The line is animated using motion tweens. The squiggle, however, was a little trickier. We began by drawing a very simple squiggle line in Flash. The squiggle was broken apart and placed on its own layer. At each keyframe, the squiggle's position was moved a little further across the screen. Also, at each keyframe the shape of the squiggle was ever so slightly changed (see Figure 9.18). The keyframes were motion tweened and the result was a line that not only changed position, but also wiggled around and had a personality.

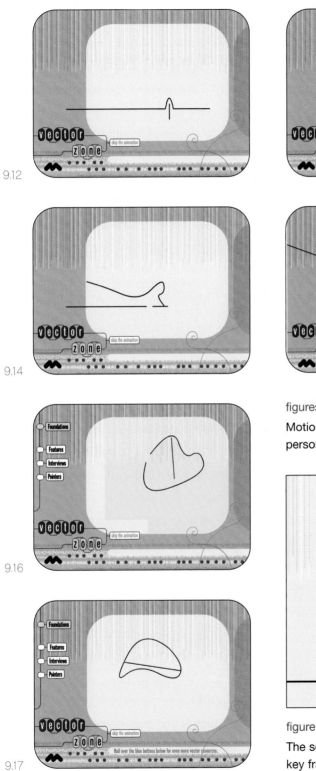

9.12

9.13

9.14

9.15

9.16

9.17

figures 9.12–9.17

Motion tweens give the squiggle
personality.

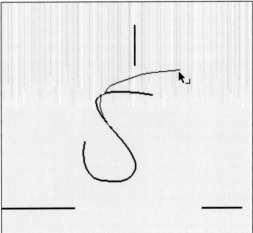

figure 9.18

The squiggle's shape is manipulated a little at each
key frame.

Easing Tweens

Easing tweens can create the illusion of velocity within the motion. Used properly, easing can make motion look quite realistic. A good example is making a circle appear as though it is bouncing. Draw a circle and group it. Place in the middle of your stage for the first keyframe. Make a new keyframe a few frames down in the timeline. Move the circle directly down so it touches the bottom of the stage. Create a motion tween between these two frames and under Easing select "easing type" with "–100" for the value. Notice how the slider moves to the far edge of ease in. Now make a third keyframe a few frames down and move the shape all the way to the top of the page. Motion tween between the frames and this specify the tween to ease out at 100. Test the movie, and you will see that the illusion of a bounce is quite realistic. It would have been impossible without using the ease feature.

You can ease any type of tween you make… opacity, scale, tint—anything. This type of animation can also be scripted using Flash MX. Scripting motion is more complicated than using the ease feature; however, it produces excellent results.

Transitions

A transition, defined by dictionary.com, is a "passage from one form, state, style, or place to another." In Flash design, transitions to and from pages and information can make the difference between a movie that is good and one that is outstanding. Transitions are best when they are barely noticed. When there is no transition between pages you notice immediately that you have left somewhere and gone somewhere new. If you are leaving one web site and going to another, this makes sense. You literally exited one space to go to another. Within one project, though, it is much nicer to have the feeling that you have not left the original space and, rather, the page elements have transitioned into a new composition, or to new information.

Using Levels to Create Seamless Transitions

The Studio eg site uses transitions to enforce the concept of the site, as well as to create a seamless web experience. The site was designed for a company that makes office furniture out of recycled goods (see the case study in Chapter 4, "The Power of Color"). Instead of just switching from one composition to the next, the eg site transitions from screen to screen, using animation. The main background color changes within each section, but the objects are always on the page. You never feel as though you left. When the user selects a new section, all the current page elements exit individually (see Figures 9.19–9.24). Shapes move off-screen, type fades out, and the overall background color quickly

figures 9.19–9.24
The Studio eg site uses smooth transitions to create a sense of flow. This sequence highlights frames from a transition that happens in about three seconds.

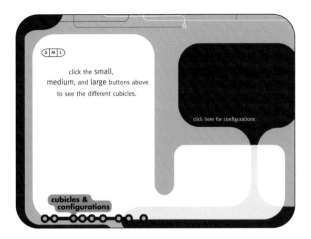

9.19

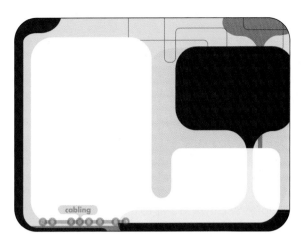

9.20

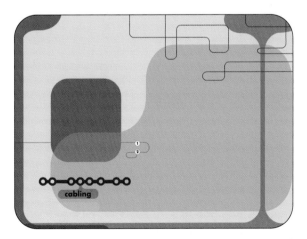

9.21

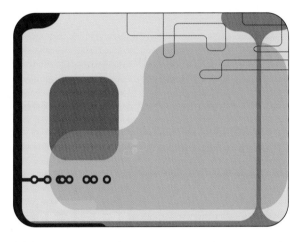

9.22

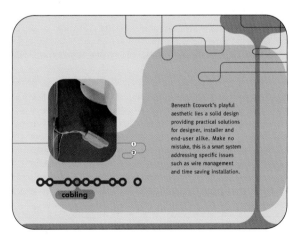

9.23

9.24

Beneath Ecowork's playful
aesthetic lies a solid design
providing practical solutions
for designer, installer and
end-user alike. Make no
mistake, this is a smart system
addressing specific issues
such as wire management
and time saving installation.

changes behind it all. At the same time, all the elements of the new pages animate in. It all happens within a few seconds, and before you know it, you're in a new section of the site. The effect is smooth…so smooth, that you don't even realize what happened, yet you find yourself in a distinctly different place. One of the reasons the transitions are successful is because they happen fast. The secret to a good transition is in its timing—no one, no matter how beautiful the transition is, wants to feel like they are being stalled in getting their information.

The Studio eg site uses the load movie action to create the seamless feeling of never leaving the site. The Flash manual will answer the technical questions you have about load movie. We'll explain how the Studio eg site utilized it to create this effect.

The site is loaded onto four individual levels. Level_0, the bottom level, is simply a series of different keyframes. Each frame has a label that represents one of the site sections with a stop action. The only artwork in each frame is the background color of that section. Level_1 contains the content of the site. The information on this level is constantly swapped out with new info as needed. Level_2 has all the transitions that make the elements of a page disappear (transition out). Level_3 has all the animated transitions that make the sections appear (transition in). Level_4 is simply a big cutout shape that defines the rounded corners.

Level_0 is always the first level to load. Immediately, as level_0 loads, it uses actions to load level_1, level_2, level_3, and level_4. Level_0 stops on the first frame, the background color for the home page. Level_1 has all the content (shapes, text, and navigation) of the home page. Level_2 and level_3 are stopped at a blank keyframe; they are invisible until needed. Level 4 has the corners, and never leaves the first keyframe.

When the user clicks the navigation to go from the cubicles and configurations page to the cabling page (refer to Figures 9.19–9.24), the following actions take place:

1. Level_0 immediately moves to the cabling label (the background color for the cabling section).
2. Level_2 goes to and plays the cubicles and configurations transition out.
3. Level_3 goes to and plays cabling transition in in.
4. As soon as the cabling shapes have transitioned in, the new cabling content loads on to level_1.

The button action told each level to go to a different place on its timeline. All the transition animations were pre-loaded and waiting to be called from the click of the button. The main bulk of the content is on level_1. This is the only new element that needs to download.

The main trick is to pre-load all the transitions on their own levels, and to never have to replace level_0. Because you never leave the timelines, all the changes happen immediately.

Using Movie Clips for Rollover Transitions

Sometimes it is nice to have rollovers do more than a simple color change or swap of images. Morphing rollovers, or transitions within a rollover, can add another level of sophistication to your Flash movies.

The WeMeasureIt site uses movie clips to make rolling over the navigation more interesting (see Figure 9.25). The main navigation of the site is three buttons: services, library, and software. When not active, the buttons are the words with drawings of molecules. When you roll over the word "services," the molecules morph into the

shape of three people (see Figures 9.26–9.34). The effect is quite different than if they had simply switched to the new icon. Everything happens quickly, but the effect powerful. When you roll off the button, the people morph back into the molecules. The site uses this morphing technique throughout and the overall feeling is quite fluid.

To make an animation occur upon rollover and rolloff, you must use movie clips. First, create an image of a button on the stage as it looks in its non-active state. Instead of making it a button, make it a movie clip. Put a stop action on the first frame. Now make a label a few frames down called "over." At this label, create the animation that you want to occur when the user rolls over the button. The quicker the animation happens, the better…again, the subtly of the animation will be appreciated best when the user doesn't feel held back from getting to the information. In the

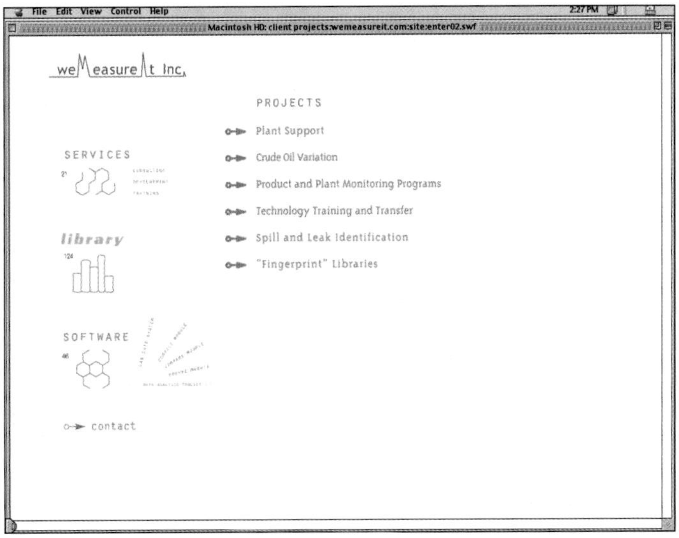

figure 9.25

The WeMeasureIt site uses morphing rollovers.

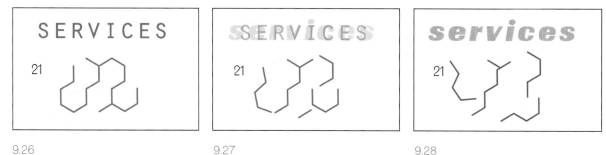

9.26

9.27

9.28

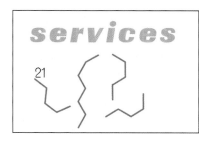

9.29

9.30

9.31

9.32

9.33

9.34

figures 9.26–9.34

Each step of the animation moves closer to the final resolve.

last frame, where the rollover resolves, put a stop action. Now, you need to create the animation for the rolloff. Place another label on the timeline a few frames down. Call this one "off." Make the animation that happens when you roll off the button. Most likely it's the same thing that happened when you rolled over, only backward this time. If this is the case, copy the keyframes from the over animation and paste them in reverse order. On the last frame, put the action "go to and stop frame 1."

To activate the animations, you need to create an invisible button. Add a layer and call it "button." On this layer, draw and fill the shape that will define the hit area for the rollover of the animation. Select the shape and make it a button. Edit the button so that it has only a hit state (the shape you drew). Make sure that the up, over, and down frames are empty. Now go back to the movie clip timeline. You will notice that the invisible button shows up as a bright blue indication of the shape you drew. Don't worry—this won't show up in your final movie. It's just a marker to indicate the shape of the invisible button while you work. On frame 1 in the movie clip timeline, tell the button to go to and play the label over on roll over, and go to and play the label off on roll off. That's it: Your animations should now work. If you want the buttons to perform an action on click, add the action to the invisible buttons.

Photos and Flash

Some of the best features of Flash—fast downloads, scalability, and smooth animation—are eliminated, or at least minimized, when you begin to add photography to your movies. This is not to say don't use photographs. The use of photographs can make your movie look less "flashy." The medium adds a new depth and graphic texture to your movies. However, photos can, when used improperly, make your movies look sloppy and unprofessional. It is important that you understand the limitations photos add to Flash, in order to design around and avoid them.

Vectors and Bitmaps

Flash is a vector-based program and vectors are the reason the animations download fast. A vector is a mathematical representation of a graphic. Where photos are represented through pixels, vectors are defined by points. Photoshop is a bitmap-based application. Applications like Flash and FreeHand are vector-based applications. A vector will enlarge infinitely without losing a resolution (the reason Flash movies scale so well). A bitmap enlarges and becomes pixilated. The basic concepts you need to understand are the following:

- Anything you draw in Flash or another drawing program, including type, is a vector.
- Any photograph or Photoshop file (JPEG, GIF, PICT, and so on) is a bitmap.

Working with Photos

The easiest way to get a photo into Flash is by copy-pasting a 72-dpi image right from Photoshop onto the stage. The photo is immediately added to the library as a bitmap. Don't mistake the library icon of a bitmap as being the same thing as a graphic. It is entirely different. It is a good idea to turn all your photos into graphics. If photos are graphics, you can use them more than once in the movie, and you can also apply graphic modifications like opacity and tint change. Even if you make the photo a graphic, you cannot delete the bitmap icon from the library. Doing so will remove the photo entirely from the movie. If you are importing photos into Flash by selecting File, Import, the best format is PICT. Flash will allow you to import JPEGs and GIFs, but it's better to import uncompressed files. Flash will compress the images when it is time to export. It is best to avoid having any image compressed twice.

Any scaling of the photo should be done before it gets to Flash. Flash will allow you to scale the photograph, but if you make it either bigger or smaller, the resolution degrades.

Avoid animating photography as much as possible. Simple cross or transparency fades are okay if they happen quickly. A large photo fading in over many frames will inevitably look clunky. If photos are fading in and out of the movie, make sure they are removed from the stage after they reach a transparency of 0. Even though you don't see them, they can slow down your movie.

Importing Sequences

It is easy to import pict sequences into your Flash movies to create a video-like effect. Make sure the photos you are importing are all the same size. The first photo of the sequence should be named 01. All subsequent images must be named numerically—02, 03, 04, and so on. Make sure all the photos of the sequence are in the same folder on your computer. From Flash choose: File, Import, and select the first image of the sequence. Select OK. If you named the images correctly, Flash should recognize the sequence. A dialog box will ask if you want to import the rest of the sequence; select Yes. The entire sequence will import directly on to your timeline. If you want the sequence to be inside a movieclip or graphic, make sure you import it into the proper timeline. You can adjust the timing between the frames on the timeline in Flash.

Importing Alpha Channels

You can import photos as they exist in their layers in Photoshop. Some cases for doing this could be if you want to maintain a feathered edge or transparency of a layer. To do this, you must use alpha channels. Make sure your Photoshop document has an alpha channel representing the image on the layer you want to import. Save the file as a 32-bit pict, and import it into Flash. The alpha channel is recognized and maintained.

Turning Bitmaps into Vectors

You can turn your photos into vectors right in Flash. The results are not always what you expect, and you have to experiment a bit to produce an image you like (see Figures 9.35–9.38).

To vectorize a photo, select the photo on the stage in Flash. Select Modify, Trace Bitmap. A dialog box will appear. Experiment with different amounts of Color Threshold, Curve Fit, and Corner Threshold to get varying results.

9.35

9.36

9.37

9.38

figures 9.35–9.38

The first image in the sequence is the original photograph. The rest of the images illustrate varying amounts of color threshold, curve fit, and corner threshold.

Using this technique does not guarantee smaller file sizes. Depending on the level of detail you selected, the new vector images may be even bigger than the original photographs. Traced bitmaps will scale as vectors do, so this may be an option if your photos require scaling within the movie. Trace Bitmap is in no way the same thing as a photo. No matter how detailed, the result will never look like an actual photograph. The technique is fun, though, and you may get some interesting results.

Exporting Options

Bitmaps make your file sizes bigger. In Flash, you have control over the resolution and export quality of photographs. You can also choose whether you want photos to be compressed as a JPEG or GIF. The rules are the same as with image compression for HTML: photographs and images with gradients are better as JPEGs, and graphic images with flat fields of solid color (such as screenshots) are better as GIFs. JPEG is the default compression type. To export the image as a GIF, double-click the bitmap in your library. Under Compression, select Lossless: (PNG/GIF). When you export the final movie, the image will be GIF, even if every other image is a JPEG.

You can select the resolution for JPEGs when you export the Flash movie. Choose File, Export Movie. The dialog box pops up with selection for JPEG Quality. Type a number from 0 to 100. The default is 50. A lower number reduces the file size as well as the quality of the photos.

A recommended amount of compression for manageable file sizes, yet not too much degradation, is quality: 80. Experiment yourself, though; see what happens and what works best for you.

Dealing with the Download

Although the web is getting faster and faster, it is still not at the point where everything happens instantly. Yes, Flash was originally touted as being the fastest graphic-rendering program for the web, yet as it has developed, so have our ideas for how we use it. Naturally, some Flash movies remain small in file size—mainly those that don't use photographs or complex scripting.

Creating a Pre-Load

Depending on the size of your movie and the way it works, you may want to create a pre-load animation. Sometimes, if a Flash movie appears before it has fully loaded, the functionality will get messed up. For example, imagine a movie in which the first frame contains the entry screen and navigation. If the timeline contains the content for each item of navigation, there will be different compositions all along the timeline that need to download before they can be accessed.

The timeline downloads from start to finish, so frame 1, the main screen, will appear immediately. Let's say the navigation has a button called "about us," and the "about us" frame is the last composition on the timeline. If the user clicks "about us" on the navigation and the actual content for that frame has not downloaded, they will jump to a blank screen. The navigation will be gone and there is nothing they can do. Most likely, they'll leave the site, thinking it is broken.

Creating a pre-load will make it impossible to get to any later frame on the site until everything else has loaded. You can make a pre-load without having any sort of animation, but it's better to give your viewers some sort of indication that the site is loading.

A pre-load animation is the animation that loops while the rest of the site loads. It should be small. Don't use photos or very complex animation; after all, you don't want to have to spend a lot of time downloading the pre-load! Keep it under 10k. Create an animation and place it in the first few frames of your timeline. You can have other imagery behind the loading animation, but avoid putting buttons that people may click while the rest of the movie loads. Place the first frame of your actual movie further down the timeline, moving everything after the first frame down too. Label this frame "begin."

A pre-load requires at least two frames. Assign the "if frame is loaded" action to the first frame of your timeline. You can choose how much of the movie you want to load before the beginning starts to play. If it is a long animation, you may only want to pre-load half; the rest can load as the first half is playing. Using the "if frame is loaded" action, select the frame number that you want loaded before the movie plays. Then select go to frame label "begin."

On the next frame, or at the last frame of your loading animation, place the action "go to and play frame 1;" this will loop the animation. Each time the animation passes frame 1, it will check to see if the indicated frame has loaded. If your pre-load animation is long, copy the action you placed on frame 1 and place it every few frames. This way, the check will happen throughout the pre-load animation.

Some designers like to create pre-loads that don't even feel like pre-loads. This way, people don't realize they are waiting for anything. For example, the Praxis Product Design site (see Figures 9.39 and 9.40) loops through a series of quotes while the site loads. The visitor doesn't even know they are waiting, and in fact, they are entertained while the site loads. As soon as the site is ready to go, the quotes exit and the actual site content appears. People on slower modems may have read nine quotes while DSL visitors may only have seen one. The point is that whatever connection speed the user has, they are occupied and maybe even educated during the wait.

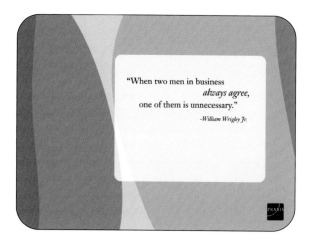

figures 9.39 and 9.40

The Praxis Product Design web site cycles through a series of quotes as the site loads.

Using Levels to Optimize Loading

We talked a little about using and targeting levels to create seamless transitions earlier in this chapter. You can also use levels to load information as it is called or needed.

The Praxis Product Design Site is constantly loading SWF files on top of and in between other flash movies. Using the "load movie" action, the designers were able to load information as it was needed.

Praxis Product Design is an industrial design firm whose main promise is "People Designing Products for People." Praxis came to Fluent Studios wanting a Flash site that not only showed their work and gave information about the company, but also promoted and reiterated their brand promise. Praxis wanted photographs of people all over the site. Right away this presented a small obstacle. A site so rich in photography would take forever to download. The site was designed so that every time a user clicked a button, a new photo or photos of people appeared in the background (see Figures 9.41 and 9.42). Each main section of the site featured a different type of person. For example, the "Who We Are" section showed people from the studio. The "Who You Are" section showed people in a business environment, people who might be clients. The "What We Do" section showed people interacting with products, and so on.

The designers were able to have the photographic images load independently of the rest of

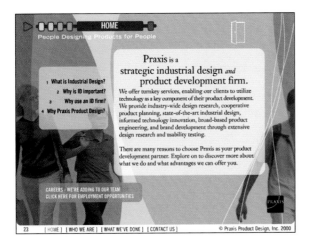
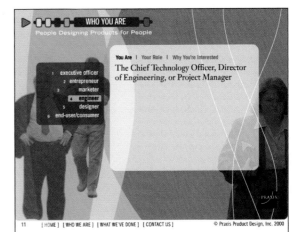

figures 9.41 and 9.42
Photos are constantly loading between levels on the Praxis site.

the graphics. To do this, the site loads all the photographs on the same level (level_2)—above the background (level_0), yet behind the content (level_3). Each time the user clicks a button, the button changes the content on level_3, and says "load movie photosXX.swf" on level_2. Each time a different photos.swf loads, it replaces the previous ones. Using this technique, the photos load constantly as the user navigates through the site, yet the site visitor never needs to download more than one photo at a time.

Type in Flash

One of the best parts about Flash is that it will turn any typeface into True Type. This means you can design with any typeface you want and it will be viewed perfectly on any computer, even if the computer doesn't have the typeface installed. As soon as a Flash movie is turned into an SWF, the rendering is complete. Any computer will universally receive the typeface. Even though the type works on any computer as a SWF, you still need to have the typefaces installed in your computer if you are working with the FLA (source movie).

Type works really well in Flash because it downloads quickly. You only have to download each character used once. For example, if you type a Helvetica capital A, you download the A once. After that, you can use it as many times as you want with no additional download.

The ease of font translation and the quick downloads are some of the best aspects to typography in Flash; however, there are some drawbacks. Unfortunately, if type is too small, it becomes hard to read. Even if you are able to read 9-point type in a rendered Flash movie on your regular monitor, chances are that it will look jaggy on a laptop. This is a big problem for designers who love small type (sound familiar?).

Antialias Text

By default, Flash will antialias text. This means it will smooth the edges, creating nice clean type. The advantage to this is beautiful scaling type that loses no quality as it gets larger.

The disadvantage is that when the type becomes small, it starts to look fuzzy, and becomes hard to read. For sites that require large fields of text, this is a problem. It is not safe to go below 11-point type if the type is antialiased.

Aliased Text

With editable text fields, you have the option to keep text aliased in Flash. The Bay Area Mosaic site uses aliased text to assure legibility for all visitors (see Figure 9.43). The site was designed to fit on a 640×480 monitor. Notice the difference in the text between the body copy and the text on the buttons. The button text, and most of the text in the interface, is antialiased. The anti-aliased text never goes below 12 point. If all the body copy were set in 12 point there would only be enough room for a few sentences on the page. The body copy text needed to be no more than 10 points to fit a logical amount

of information on the page. If the text remained Aliased, it would look fuzzy, it had to be another format.

To create aliased text fields, you must use dynamic text. Select the type tool and type something. With the text box selected, choose Text, Options. A dialog box will appear. The default is static text. Select Dynamic Text. Do not select any of the Embed Fonts items. This is the key to getting aliased type. The text will appear antialiased in the FLA source; however, it will render aliased. You can choose any other modifications you want in this window, (text wrap, disable selection, and so on).

There are a few disadvantages to aliased text. Mainly, you are limited with editing options within the text fields. The text attributes specified for

figure 9.43

The Bay Area Mosaic site uses antialiased text for the interface and aliased text for the main body copy.

the first letter of the text field are carried on to every other letter. For example, if the first letter is a red, bold Helvetica, all the text in the box will render as red, bold Helvetica. Flash will allow you to modify letters within the text box, but when it renders the SWF, none of the edits will show. This makes it impossible to make a single word within a text field bold or italic. As the designer, you need to work around this problem. Either, keep the text antialiased and make it bigger, or do away with your edits.

When you specify "dynamic text," the text font is being pulled from the system of the user's computer. This means two things. First, you should be using typefaces that everyone has (Times, Helvetica, Arial, and so on). Second, you must remember to make the bounding text box bigger than it looks like it needs to be on the stage. If you do not make the box bigger, you may cut type out on some computers. The only way to really understand what is happening is to experiment yourself. You will immediately see the advantages and drawbacks of the different methods for dealing with text.

Making Type Art

Flash, like Illustrator and FreeHand, has the ability to turn type into art. Select your text box and select Modify>Break Apart. The text will no longer be selectable as text, it is now vector artwork, just like an object you bring from Illustrator or draw in Flash. Using the pointer tool, notice how you can adjust the basic form of the letter

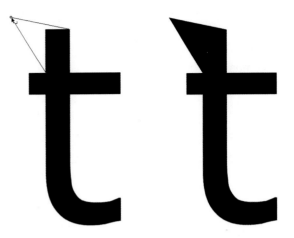

figures 9.44 and 9.45
Text that is broken apart turns into artwork. The shape can be modified with the pointer tool.

(see Figures 9.44 and 9.45). When text is broken apart you can apply shape tweens, and experiment with morphing type. Once type is broken apart, it can never be edited as text again. You should only break text apart if you want to modify the original shape, or perform a shape tween. Keep all words and body copy that may need to be edited later as text. If you break all your text apart, not only do you lose editing capabilities, but also the file size starts getting bigger.

Editable Text Forms

Gone are the days of ugly forms. Flash 4 introduced editable text fields and the ability to actually design the way a form works. The Praxis Product Design site required a form to invite visitors to request a proposal. The entire site was in Flash and it made sense for the form to be in

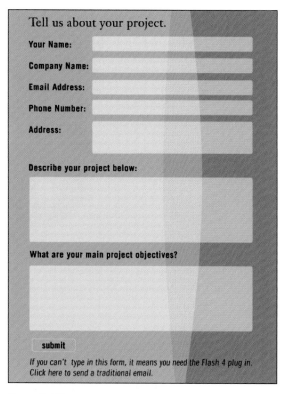

figure 9.46

Flash allows you to really "design" forms.

figure 9.47

The Flash Graphic and navigation are in a table with HTML type.

Flash, too (see Figure 9.46). The designers began by drawing the way the form should look in Illustrator. They wanted the boxes for text entry to have rounded corners like the rest of the site. They were able to make the boxes transparent in Flash. By including all the font outlines in the "dynamic text" field, they were even able to specify the typeface for form entry. With form capabilities in Flash there are no more excuses for ugly pre-formatted forms on the web.

Flash and HTML

Although it is possible to make an entirely Flash site, the Flash component of a site is quite often integrated into the HTML. Even if a site is all Flash, it ultimately needs to be embedded into the HTML to live on the web.

Integrating Flash into Your HTML Pages

The California's Power Play web site combines Flash and HTML to create a simple, text-heavy, yet graphically compelling, site (see Figure 9.47). The California's Power Play home page is laid out in an HTML table. You can learn how to use Dreamweaver to bring Flash into tables in Chapter 7, "Dynamic Web Animation." The top row of the table contains a Flash graphic. The designers use Flash to create the illusion of light sweeping across the word "POWER." Below this graphic, the table is divided into two columns.

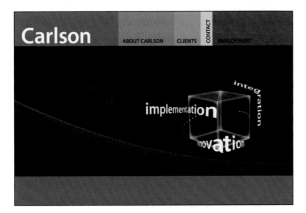

9.48

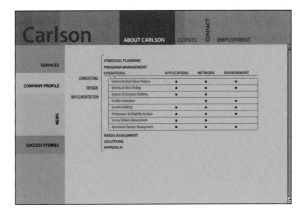

9.49

figures 9.48 and 9.49

The Carlson site has the Flash navigation in the top frame of the frameset. The navigation calls information to the bottom half of the frameset.

One column contains the Flash navigation. The other column contains all the HTML content of the site. Once the main graphics and navigation were created in Flash, the rest of the site was implemented in Dreamweaver. Keeping the main copy of the site as HTML enabled the content to be updated frequently and easily. It also assured cleanly printed text and a rapid download.

Flash and Framesets

The Carlson web site uses a Flash Navigation to target HTML pages to load in a frameset (see Figures 9.48 and 9.49). The main navigation for the site was placed in the top frame. When the user clicks on one of the navigation items, a page loads in the specified frame location. The navigation never leaves the page. In fact, the navigation transitions to a new frame where the current section that has been called is highlighted. The action on the Flash button does two things. First, it tells the Flash timeline to move to a new label, where the active section is highlighted. Next, it loads the HTML page into the specified location of the frameset. This is done with the get URL action. The targeted frame is specified within the get URL action in Flash.

Publishing Flash Movies from Flash

Flash makes it very easy to publish movies directly from the program. This is especially useful for all Flash sites, or sites that don't require the addition of other HTML elements. When you are finished making your movie, select File, Publish Settings. The first place to adjust settings is under the Formats tab. The default selection is Flash (.swf) and HTML (.html). For web publishing these are the only boxes you need selected. Next select the Flash tab. Here you will decide on your preferences for the output of the Flash movie. You will notice they are the same preferences you get when you export a movie. Define your preferences and hit the HTML tab. This is where you make your HTML modifications. The following are the specifications you should be concerned with and what they mean:

- **Template:** Select Flash Only (Default). This defines the file format you wish to export; in this case it is SWF for the web.
- **Dimensions:** Match Movie will embed the Flash movie the exact size of the actual Flash file. Pixels allows you to define exactly what size you want, and Percent will stretch or shrink the movie proportionally with the browser window.
- **Quality:** Select High.
- **HTML Alignment:** Select the alignment you want on the page, (usually default).
- **Scale:** Show All will show everything on your stage, as well as the elements that are pushed off the stage. The best choice for this one is Exact Fit.
- **Flash Alignment:** Select where you want your movie to vertically and horizontally align on the page.

When you have made all your selections click the publish button. The HTML and SWF files will be published into the folder that contains your FLA movie.

Flash Beyond the Web

Flash was originally used for creating fast loading graphics for Internet delivery. As the program has developed, people have begun to use it for much more.

Creating Presentation Projectors

Flash can export movies as Projectors, a file format originally used with Macromedia Director. A projector file can be played on both Macs (as projectors) and on PCs (as executable files) with no need for the Flash plug-in. Executable files work really well for CD-ROM output. You can offer your clients the option to output on CD as well as web, without having to do any extra work! This is a nice selling point and a good reason to push for Flash sites.

To export an executable or projector file, select File, Publish Settings. Select Windows Projector, Macintosh Projector or both. Select Publish. The projector will be rendered to the same folder as the FLA file.

In addition to CD production, projectors can also be used for presentations to clients.

Case Study

Red Advertising, www.redads.com

Fluent Studios was hired to create a web site for Red
Advertising. The advertising firm wanted a site that
would be both an artistic exploration for the visitor, as
well as a place clients could view their work and learn
about the company. They wanted an interactive experience that was unique and fun, and touched on the
human side of advertising. It wasn't important that
it be simple to navigate; rather, it was important that
the visiting experience was unique, engaging,
and beautiful.

Fluent Studios ended up creating site that is a mixture of entertainment and the agency's portfolio. Either can be easily accessed at any time from an always-present interface. The entertainment is in the form of an interactive web show, wherein the viewer navigates connected human scenarios while hearing splices of recorded voices.

The Red site examines how every person is a story, a collection of histories that collide and meld with one another. At times these bonds are obvious; other times they are nonsensical. The connection becomes a doorway, wherein one space is infected by the previous and has the potential to infect the next.

The designers photographed, filmed, and animated multiple human scenarios that connect and overlap. The user is prompted to navigate the image in order to reveal the context of a human situation. As the user navigates along different paths within the space, he or she will happen upon something painted red, which becomes a link to a different situation (see Figures 9.50–9.52). Each scene has multiple links, providing many possible avenues of navigation.

9.50

9.51

9.52

9.50–9.52

The designers painted everyday objects red. The objects were then photographed in various situations.

9.53

9.54

9.57

9.58

Imagery ranges from solid animation to a photo shoot of a man laying in his bed in a hotel room. The man in the hotel room is eventually led to a bottle of pills, painted red (see Figures 9.53–9.60). The medicine is a link to an entirely new scene. When you click on the red link you are suddenly in an animation of a woman taking medicine—next you are in her stomach. And so the experience continues. Through multiple experiences and styles, visitors are carried on a non-linear journey. In the end, the unfolded page becomes a quilt of experience.

9.55

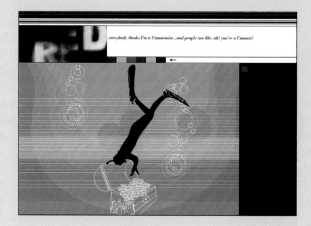

9.56

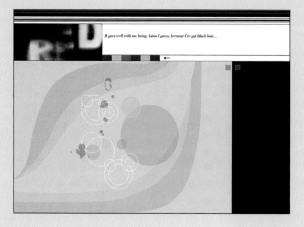

9.59

9.60

9.53–9.60

This sequence beginning in a hotel room links, via the red medicine, to a woman taking medication, travels down into her stomach, and ends up underwater with a diver.

There is no going back through these doorways. For example, the red vacuum cleaner has become real. In other words, once connections are made, they cannot be taken back; however, because there are multiple doorways from each scene, there is a high probability that the user will encounter a scene more than once, enabling new paths of navigation.

The audio sound bites are always in answer the same question: What does "red" make you think of? It is a challenge to realize what the question was. These audio clips do not directly relate to the visual situation in which they are played. They contain their own context; for example, someone may be speaking about red roses while we navigate through a karaoke bar. Another dialog may be in French, while we are viewing an animation.

The user is compelled throughout the show by the process of multiple designers working in multiple styles and mediums for the different scenes. Some use traditional photography (see Figure 9.61). Others use pure animation (see Figure 9.62), 8mm film stills (see Figure 9.63) found photography, and so on.

9.61

9.62

9.61–9.63
Various artistic mediums are used to create interest.

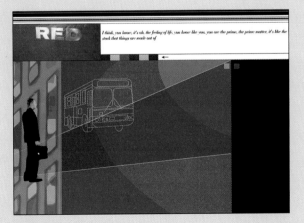

9.63

The other half of the site contains information about the company, straightforward and clean (see Figure 9.64). Visitors can jump back and forth between the two experiences and every time is different.

Design Credits

Fluent Studios: Susan Harris, Sharon Coon, Jennifer Hung, Krista Sweet, Makiko Tatsumi, Regan Beedle; and Interstitch Films: Jim Kenney

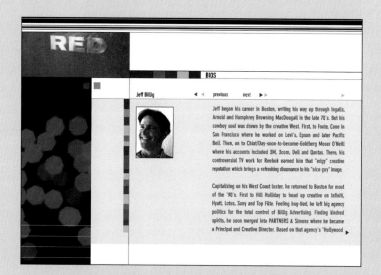

9.64

Company information is cleanly presented on the right side of the interface.

Exporting Flash as QuickTime for Video

Fluent Studios was asked to create a Video and Flash web site to promote Carlson. The designers used a combination of still photography, digital video, and Flash animation in a 5-minute video presentation (see Figure 9.65). Much of the animation was done in Flash and later imported into After Effects as QuickTime for video production. To export Flash animations as QuickTime select File, Export Movie and select Format: QuickTime. A dialog box appears prompting you through the preferences. Select OK and your movie will be turned to QuickTime. You can import the QuickTime movie into After Effects and use it in your video. In the case of the Carlson site the designers were able to use parts of the same Flash animation for the Carlson web site.

Good Flash Site Links

There are hundreds of web sites for Flash designers and developers. These sites are updated frequently and archived well. Any questions you have on Flash can probably be answered with one of these resources. Consider this list a jump-off point. These sites will link you to many more resources:

- **Macromedia's Flash Site:**
  www.macromedia.com/software/flash/
- **Flash Zone:** www.flashzone.com
- **Extreme Flash:** www.extremeflash.com
- **Flash Kit:** www.flashkit.com/
- **Virtual-FX:** www.virtual-fx.net/

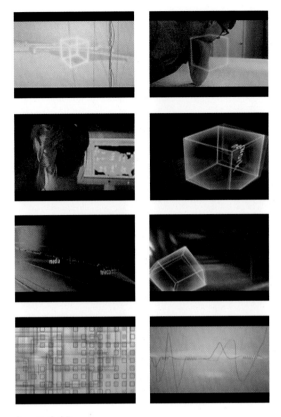

figure 9.65

This is a sequence from the Carlson video. All the line animation was done in Flash.

URLs In This Chapter

- **HTML and Web Artistry**
  htmlartistry.com/urls/bridgedale
  htmlartistry.com/urls/vectorzone
- **KQED**
  www.kqed.org/ednet/mosaic/
  www.kqed.org/tv/productions/
  powerplay/flash/index.html
- **Studio eg** www.studioeg.com
- **weMeasureIt** www.wemeasureit.com
- **Praxis Design** www.praxisdesign.com
- **Carlson Solutions**
  www.carlsonsolutions.com
- **Red Advertising** www.redads.com

Inspirational Design Model

Josh Morenstein
newdealdesign

"I believe that creatives, whether an industrial

designer or a writer or a chef, gain inspiration

by simply going through his or her day...

absorbing what's out there and processing,

refining, and eventually pouring it out into

their chosen medium."

figure 1

HP Pavillion 2000

Among the scattered European design books and magazines, the stacks of pencil sketches, and prototype models, San Francisco based industrial designer, Josh Morenstein surrounds and immerses himself with his latest project. With an eye for detail, Josh knows all facets of design and can bring in elements of a curve or a line that will take a product he's designing to the next level. His level of refinement is a part of his creative process that considers how his work will be part of the progression of design as a whole.

Yet, more importantly, Josh Morenstein possesses an uncanny and infectious sense of humor. With a quick wit that would make Mel Brooks or Jerry Seinfeld proud, Josh's everyday observations in day-to-day work and life can be just as hilarious as a night at the Improv. It's comforting to know that although he takes his work seriously, he doesn't take life so seriously. And that alone is inspiration.

What inspires you?

That's a hard answer to pin down since I'm not sure inspiration is always a conscious reaction. Of course, I'm often inspired by individuals—those who have done things in an interesting and innovative way. Throughout a project, I'll pour through magazines (of all types) to see what's out there, what's been and being designed by others. This always seems to motivate and inspire me.

But I believe that creatives, whether an industrial designer or a writer or a chef, gain inspiration by simply going through his or her day…absorbing what's out there and processing, refining, and eventually pouring it out into their chosen medium. So I guess you could say I'm inspired by everything.

What's your process on a design project?

I can't say I really have a process that is set in stone. As a consultant I organize my work in phases that allow the client to both "check" and understand the progress of the project. I think designers often forget that the actual process of designing is, by nature, somewhat disorganized.

Broadband and wireless technology is said to grow increasingly in the next 5 to 10 years. Handheld devices, cellphones, and smart products will be an increasing part of our everyday lives. How do you see these products evolving in the future?

When a technology or feature is first developed and introduced, there is a tendency to try to integrate it into everything on earth with a battery. We saw this with products like the Apple Newton where it was simply trying to be too much of everything to everyone. Eventually this product failed because, despite nice industrial design and graphics, its functionality was too broad, too diluted.

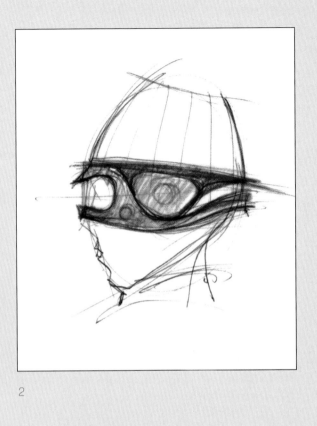

2

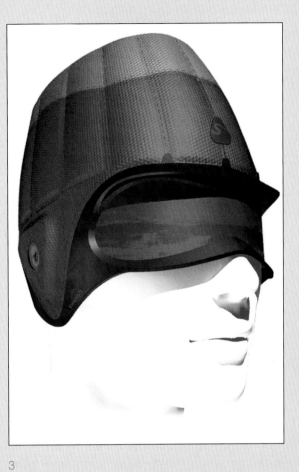

3

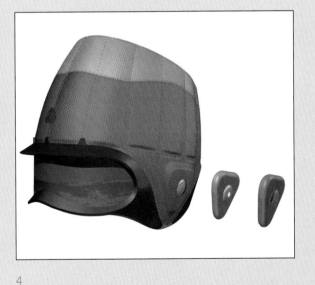

4

figures 2–4

Sketches and final product for Snowsoft *softshell* snowboarding helmet

Currently, the big push is to merge mobile products with the web. The natural tendency has been to try to integrate web browsing into everything from a watchband to a coffee mug. We're already seeing many of these products in stores and we'll see more in the coming months. However, we need to address the way people interact with products in their day-to-day lives. People don't do too much shopping online and they're not going to do any more shopping from a mobile product. What people do want are the existing "killer-apps." Email is the killer-app, looking up the time of a movie is a killer-app, calling up a map when your lost in your car is a killer-app.

Oftentimes, products are overwhelmed with features that betray a product's functionality. It will be our job as designers to help the product "make sense." Generally speaking, mobile products will become "cleaner" and more application specific.

What are some things digital designers can do now to prepare for the future as the design industry becomes more integrated?
I'm not sure how much more integrated the design industry will get. I've worked at studios where "integration" was a big selling point, but at the end of the day there was really very little communication between disciplines. However, this may be an advantage. Sometimes the less one knows about the constraints of a subject,

the better. You end up challenging preconceptions that might otherwise go undisturbed.

Obviously, we all want to make each "product" special—to get the user to engage the design and not just the technology. One way to prepare yourself is to start thinking about how products can better display the digital medium and challenge the hardware. Invent the way people will work.

Can you tell us about a project you're working on now?
I've just finished a series of snowboarding products focusing on headgear and board-top accessories. When we first started exploring this market, the first thing that struck me was the "anti-fashion" mentality that has built up around it. As a designer, I always try to design what I think is cool or what I think others will find cool. When it comes to streetwear, whether it's in the city or on the slopes, the rules for what's cool are totally different than what might be acceptable for an laptop computer or a piece of furniture. When people wear a product on their body, they see it as a very personal statement. It signifies who they are or more importantly who they want to be. As a result, people want these types of fashion-based products to be distinctive and particular to their own lifestyle. When we designed the snowboarding gear, we worked very hard at creating a line of products that are innovative and unique but would also allow the user to "break them in" and customize them to

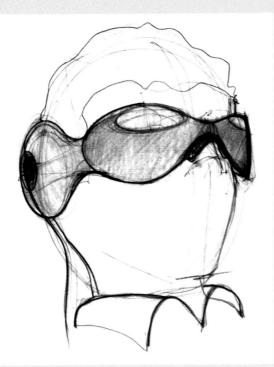

suit their own needs and style. A great deal of this was achieved through the use of quality materials such as rubber and aluminum and, in the case of the soft-shell helmet, fabric and foams that would shape themselves to the user over time. In addition, in the helmets we integrated features like built-in MP3 players and walkie-talkies that would free up the user's hands and pocket space. These types of features seem pretty basic but they're the ones that make a product unique and special to the owner.

What's your dream project?

Designing my own house. My environment has always been very important to me. For as long as I can remember, I've always needed a home base...a place that's familiar and comfortable. Designing your own home is about as familiar as a project can get.

Who are your design heroes?

Tibor Kalman—For looking at things in ways I might have thought to, but am too afraid to admit.

Richard Neutra—His architecture is clean but not overly sterile like the way some of his contemporaries were.

Saul Bass—In particular his opening film credits.

figures 5 and 6
Microvision microdisplay

Do you have any advice that you would like to share with all the aspiring designers out there?

Have fun. I know that this might sound a bit overly simplistic but I think it should be every designer's mantra. Find the things that get you excited about practicing design and latch onto them. If it's seeing your work produced, find a way (whether it's by you or a "manufacturer") to produce it. If you want to be famous, get out there and sell yourself. Oftentimes, the things that initially get us interested in design are different from those that make us stay in design. When I was a kid growing up, I just liked making things with my hands. Design seemed like a good, structured way of doing that. Over the years, as I've matured and changed, so have my reasons for being a designer. The key, for me, is to take the time to check whether I'm enjoying what I'm doing and the way I'm doing it.

If you could be a superhero, who would you be and why?

I'd have to go with marvel comics "Daredevil." He possesses all of the basic boss gymnastic skills (that is, jumping from building to building, hanging out on window ledges of skyscrapers, and so on) and kung fu moves (flying back-kicks, and so on) that today's superheroes require. But most notable was the fact that he was blind but could see with the use of sound waves…as a result he could see in the dark while really playing the sympathy card…strong technique.

A close second would be the Green Lantern.

What are three things in the world you can't live without?

1) beef jerky

2) TV

3) donuts

Please name a bad habit you have.

I tend to let people know what I think of them.

Josh Morenstein URL:

■ **newdealdesign**

  www.newdealdesign.com

On his parents:

My father studied industrial design in the '60s and my mom was an art teacher, so I was exposed to both art and design from a very early age. Eventually he got into architectural metal restoration. This is a very hands-on profession: the antithesis of "silicon valley industrial design." As a result, I've always been strongly influenced by materials, craft, and processes.

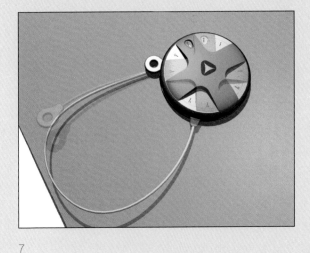

7

8

9

figures 7, 8, and 9
Snowsoft snowboard lock

Conclusion

The web is still such a new medium. Don't forget that inspiration is all around you and can happen at any time. Look around to other sources, such as architecture, photography, and fashion to help fuel your web projects. Quite typically the time we spend away from the computer is when we get ideas for design. Even something as simple as taking a walk around the block could open your eyes to a shape, color, or word that can start the brainstorming process. Keeping yourself open to all ideas is how you can better foster your creativity. Having a sketchbook or notebook handy is another way you can jot down quick ideas when inspiration strikes.

As passionate about design as we are, we also hope that this book has also helped you grasp the ins and outs of technology on the web, as well. Don't get discouraged if you can't seem to program a complex JavaScript or Flash site right away. We hope we have given you the foundation from which you can take your skills and grow.

Finally, we would like to remind you to visit our companion web site, www.htmlartistry.com, for the examples in this book, updates, and reference links. We welcome your feedback and hope that this book has been a helpful resource in your web design pursuits.

HTML Quick
Reference List

APPENDIX A

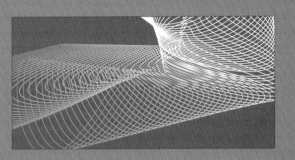

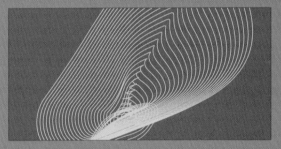

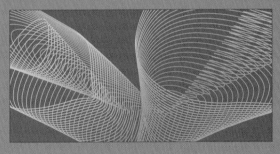

Here is a handy reference chart of the most frequently used HTML tags organized by function
so that you can keep them as a reference next to
your computer.

HTML Tag	Description
Main Tags	
`<HTML></HTML>`	Start/end tags of the HTML document
`<HEAD></HEAD>`	Identifies the document head
`<META>`	Meta-info about document (lives in head)
`<META HTTP-EQUIV="name">`	Binds element to HTTP response header
`<META HTTP=EQUIV="Refresh" CONTENT="n">`	Refresh content every n seconds
`<META HTTP=EQUIV="Refresh" CONTENT="n; URL">`	Refresh content in n seconds by jumping to URL
`<TITLE></TITLE>`	Denotes title of HTML page
`<BODY></BODY>`	Specifies body of document
`<BODY BACKGROUND="URL"></BODY>`	Background texture/image
`<BODY BGCOLOR=="#RRGGBB" or <"colorname"></BODY>`	Background color
`<BODY TEXT="#RRGGBB"> or <"colorname"> </BODY>`	Text color
`<BODY LINK="#RRGGBB"> or <"colorname"></BODY>`	Link color
`<BODY VLINK="#RRGGBB"> or <"colorname"></BODY>`	Visited link color
`<BODY ALINK="#RRGGBB"> or <"colorname"></BODY>`	Active link color

HTML Tag

Description

Type Related Tags

HTML Tag	Description
`<Hn></Hn>  <H1></H1>`	Heading (*n*=1–6, with 1 as the largest heading)
`<Hn ALIGN=LEFT|CENTER|RIGHT|NOWRAP|CLEAR></Hn>`	Align heading 3.0
`<CODE></CODE>`	Text in monospace computer code
`<TT></TT>`	Teletype font
`<PRE></PRE>`	Preformatted text
`<FONT SIZE=n></FONT>`	Font Size (*n* ranges from 1–7; default is 3)
`<FONT COLOR="#RRGGBB">` or `<"colorname"></FONT>`	Font color
`<FONT FACE="fontname"></FONT>`	Specify font (usually common system fonts)
`<BASEFONT SIZE="value">`	Specify Base font (values are 1–6)
`<B></B>`	Bold
`<I></I>`	Italic
`<U></U>`	Underline text
`<STRIKE></STRIKE>`	Strikethrough text
`<SUB></SUB>`	Subscript text
`<SUP></SUP>`	Superscript text

Layout Tags

HTML Tag	Description
`<BLOCKQUOTE></BLOCKQUOTE>`	Block indent
` `	Line break
`<BR CLEAR=LEFT|RIGHT|ALL>`	Clearing line break
`<CENTER></CENTER>`	Center
`<DIV></DIV>`	Division of a document

continues

continued

HTML Tag	Description

Layout Tags

`<HR>`	Horizontal rule
`<HR ALIGN=LEFT|RIGHT|CENTER>`	Aligns horizontal rule
`<HR SIZE=n>`	Thickness of horizontal rule (*n*=number in pixels)
`<HR WIDTH=n>`	Width of horizontal rule (*n*=number in pixels)
`<HR WIDTH=%>`	Width of horizontal rule defined by percentage of page
`<HR NOSHADE>`	Solid black horizontal rule
`<NOBR>`	Prevents line break
`<P></P>`	Paragraph return
`<P ALIGN=LEFT|CENTER|RIGHT>`	Align paragraph
`<PRE></PRE>`	Preformatted (displayed with browser default font, usually Courier)

Image Tags

`<IMG SRC="URL">`	Display image
`<IMG SRC="URL" ALIGN=TOP|BOTTOM|MIDDLE>`	Align image relative to text baseline
`<IMG SRC="URL" ALIGN=LEFT|RIGHT>`	Align image relative to page
`<IMG SRC="URL" ALT="alttext">`	Alternative text displayed when images are turned off; text displayed as tool tips in browsers
`<IMG SRC="URL" ISMAP>`	Image is an imagemap
`<IMG SRC="URL" USEMAP>`	Image is a client-side imagemap
`<IMG SRC="URL" WIDTH="n" HEIGHT="n">`	Image dimensions (in pixels)
`<IMG SRC="URL" BORDER=n>`	Image border (in pixels)

HTML Tag	Description

Image Tags

`<IMG SRC="URL" HSPACE=n VSPACE=n>`	Specifies horizontal or vertical spacing (in pixels)
`<IMG SRC="URL" LOWSRC="URL">`	Specifies low-res version of image

List Tags

`<DL></DL>`	Definition list
`<DD>`	Definition
`<DT>`	Definition term
`<OL></OL>`	Ordered list
`<OL START="n"></OL>`	Start numbering at specific number list
`<OL TYPE=A|a|I|i|1>`	Format of list items (caps, small, numerical, roman, or default)
`<UL></UL>`	Unordered list
`<UL COMPACT></UL>`	Compact version of unordered list
`<UL TYPE=DISC|CIRCLE|SQUARE>`	Specifies bullet style
`<LI TYPE=A|a|I|i|1>`	Controls format of list item
`<LI>`	List item (bullet when used with `<UL>`, numbered list with `<OL>`)

Form Tags

`<FORM ACTION="URL" METHOD=GET|POST></FORM>`	Define form
`<INPUT TYPE="TEXT|PASSWORD|CHECKBOX|RADIO|SUBMIT|RESET">`	Input field for HTML form
`<INPUT NAME="fieldname">`	Field name
`<INPUT CHECKED>`	Checked checkboxes or radio boxes

continues

continued

HTML Tag

Description

Form Tags

`<INPUT SIZE=n>`	Field size (in characters)
`<INPUT MAXLENGTH=n>`	Max length (in characters)
`<SELECT></SELECT>`	Selection list
`<SELECT NAME="listname"></SELECT>`	Name of list
`<SELECT SIZE=n></SELECT>`	n=number of options
`<OPTION>`	Option (items that can be selected)
`<TEXTAREA ROWS=n COLS=n></TEXTAREA>`	Input box size
`<TEXTAREA NAME="boxname"></TEXTAREA>`	Name of box

Table Tags

`<TABLE></TABLE>`	Defines table
`<TABLE BORDER></TABLE>`	Table border (on or off)
`<TABLE BORDER=n></TABLE>`	Table border (width of table border)
`<TABLE CELLSPACING=n>`	Cell spacing
`<TABLE CELLPADDING=n>`	Cell padding
`<TABLE WIDTH=n>`	Desired width (in pixels)
`<TABLE WIDTH=%>`	Width percent (percentage of page)
`<CAPTION ALIGN=TOP|BOTTOM></CAPTION>`	Specifies table
`<TR></TR>`	Table row
`<TR ALIGN=LEFT|RIGHT|CENTER VALIGN=TOP|MIDDLE|BOTTOM>`	Alignment of row

HTML Tag	Description
Caption Tags	
`<TH></TH>`	Table header
`<TH ALIGN=LEFT|RIGHT|CENTER VALIGN=TOP|MIDDLE|BOTTOM>`	Alignment of header
`<TH NOWRAP>`	No line breaks
`<TH COLSPAN=n>`	Columns to span
`<TH ROWSPAN=n>`	Rows to span
`<TH WIDTH=n>`	Desired width (in pixels)
`<TH WIDTH=%>`	Width percent (percentage of table)
`<TD></TD>`	Table cell (must appear within table rows)
`<TD ALIGN=LEFT|RIGHT|CENTER VALIGN=TOP|MIDDLE|BOTTOM>`	Alignment of cell
`<TD NOWRAP>`	No line breaks
`<TD COLSPAN=n>`	Columns to span
`<TD ROWSPAN=n>`	Rows to span
`<TD WIDTH=n>`	Desired width (in pixels)
`<TD WIDTH=%>`	Width percent (percentage of table)
Frame Tags	
`<FRAMESET></FRAMESET>`	Hosts the frame elements
`<FRAMESET COLS=n>`	Column width
`<FRAMESET ROWS=n>`	Row height
`<FRAMESET SPACING=1|0>`	Frame Spacing—adds additional space between frames
`<FRAME SRC="URL">`	Single frame
`<IFRAME SRC="URL">`	Floating frame

continues

continued

HTML Tag	Description

Frame attributes

`ALIGN=left|center|right>`	Frame alignment
`FRAMEBORDER=1|0>`	Frame border (1 is default, 0 is no border)
`NAME="name"`	Frame name
`NORESIZE`	Prevents resizing of frame
`SCROLLING=yes|no`	Scrolling frame
`MARGINHEIGHT="n"`	Frame height (in pixels)
`MARGINWIDTH="n"`	Frame width (in pixels)

Frame Targeting Tags

`TARGET="_top"`	Link will load in full body of window
`TARGET="_self"`	Link will load in frame where link was clicked
`TARGET="_parent"`	Link will load in the immediate FRAMESET parent
`TARGET="framename"`	Link will load in the frame specified by frame name

Style Sheet &
JavaScript
Reference List

APPENDIX B

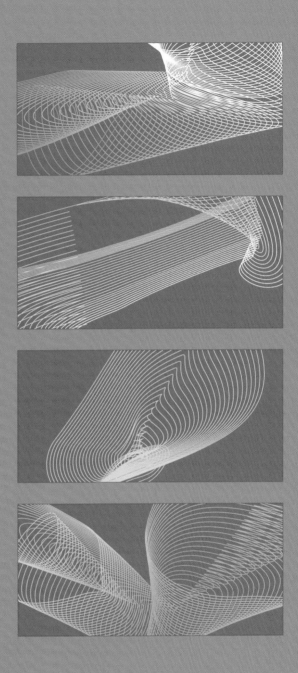

Here are all the Style Sheet properties, as well as a JavaScript reference, as covered in Chapter 5, "Personalization."

Fonts

Property	Values	Description	Example
font-family	font name font family name generic family name	Sets font face	P {font-family: "arial," sans serif }
font-style	normal italic	Sets fit style	P {font-style: italic }
font-variant	normal small caps	Sets font display	P {font-variant: smallcaps }
font-weight	normal bold bolder lighter	Specifies font weight 100-900 (displayed in 100 increments with 100 as lightest and 900 as darkest)	P {font-weight: 700 }
font-size	length percentage absolute-size relative-size	Sets font size	H2 { font-size: 12pt }
absolute-size	xx-small x-small small medium large x-large xx-large	Font-size attribute	H2 { font-size: small }
relative-size	larger smaller	Font-size attribute	H2 { font-size: larger }

Property	Values	Description	Example
font	font-style font-variant font-weight font-size line-height font-family	Shorthand for font properties	P { font: s12pt Times bold }

Colors and Backgrounds

Property	Values	Description	Example
color	color name hexidecimal code RGB value	Determines color of an element	H2 { color: red }
background-color	color name hexidecimal code RGB value transparent	Sets background color	BODY { background-color: white }
background-repeat	repeat repeat-x repeat-y no-repeat scroll fixed	Determines how background image is repeated	BODY { background-image: url(images/image.gif) }

background-attachment	scroll
	fixed
		Determines scrolling or fixed nature of background	BODY {
			background-image:
			url(images/image.gif);
			background-attachment:
			scroll }

background-position	length
	percentage
	{1,2}
	top|center|bottom
	left|center|right
		Gives initial position of background image	BODY {
			background-image:
			url(images/image.gif);
			background-position:
			left,center }

continues

Colors and Backgrounds *continued*

Property	Values	Description	Example
background	background-color background-image background-repeat background-attachment background-position	Shorthand for the background properties (better supported)	P {background url(images/image.gif) blue fixed }

Text and Images

Property	Values	Description	Example
word spacing	length normal	Defines space between words	H2 { word-spacing: 5pt }
letter-spacing	length normal	Defines space between letters	H2 { letter-spacing: 2pt }
text-transform	capitalize uppercase lowercase none	Changes case of text	H2 { text-transform: uppercase }
text-decoration	none underline overline line-through blink	Text enhancements	H2 { text-decoration: underline }
text-align	left right center justify	Align text	H2 { text-align: center }
text-indent	length percentage	Defines indentation	P { text-indent: 1in }
line-height	normal number length percentage	Sets the baseline spacing	P { line-height: 5px }

Property	Values	Description	Example
margin-top	length percentage auto	Sets top margin of element	P { margin-top: 1in }
margin-right	length percentage auto	Sets right margin of element	P { margin-right: 20% }
margin-bottom	length percentage auto	Sets bottom margin of element	P { margin-left: 40% }
margin	length percentage auto {1,4}	Sets all margins of element by specifying 1-4 values	P { margin: 5px }
vertical-align	baseline sub super top text-top middle bottom text-bottom percentage	Controls vertical alignment of text and images	H2 { vertical-align: top }
padding-top	length percentage	Determines space between top border and element	P { padding-top: 30% }
padding-bottom	length percentage	Determines space between bottom border and element	P { padding-bottom: 30% }
padding-right	length percentage	Determines space between right border and element	P { padding-right: 2in }
padding-left	length percentage	Determines space between left border and element	P { padding-left: 2in }
padding	length percentage {1,4}	Shorthand property, set all together at once in order padding-top, right, bottom, and left	P { padding: 10px, 20px, 30px,40px }

continues

Text and Images   *continued*

Property	Values	Description	Example
float	left right none	Float text and images	H2 { float: left }
clear	left right both none	Unwraps text	P { clear: both }
position	absolute relative static	Precision or relative positioning of text and images	P { position: absolute }
left	length percentage auto	An attribute of position, controls horizontal position	P { left: 1in }
top	length percentage auto	An attribute of position, controls vertical position	P { top: 1in }
clip	shape auto	control visible areas of text/images	H2 {clip: rect(20px 25px 30px 35px) }
overflow	clip scroll none	Control visibility of overflowed text/images	H2 { overflow: scroll }
z-index	integer auto	Control layering order of text/images	H2 { z-index: 3 }
visibility	visible hidden inherit	Decides initial display	H2 { visibility: hidden }
display	block inline list-item none	Decides how text/image is displayed	P { display: inline }

Property	Values	Description	Example
white-space	normal pre nowrap	Control browser white space	P { white-space: normal }
border-width	length thin medium thick {1,4}	Specifies the width of elements border between 14 values	H2 { border-width: 1in }
border-color	color name hexideximal code RGB value {1,4}	Sets the border color up to four values for left, right, top, and bottom	H2 { border-color: blue } H2 { border-color: blue, blue, red, red }
border-style	none dotted dashed solid double groove ridge inset outset {1,4}	Sets border style	H2 { border-style: dashed }
border	border-width border-style color	Shorthand for setting border width, style, and color	H2 { border: dashed red }
width	length percentage auto	Sets width of element	IMG.a { width: 20px, height: 40px }
height	length auto	Sets height of element	IMG.a { width: 20px, height, 40px }

continues

Text and Images   *continued*

Property	Values	Description	Example
list-style-type	disc circle square decimal lower-roman upper-roman lower-alpha upper-alpha none	Specifies display of list images	LI.square { list-style-type: square }
list-style-position	inside outside	Determines indentation of item in reference to first item	LI { list-style-position: outside }
list-style-image	URL none	Uses specified image as customized bullet	LI { list-style-image: url(images/button.gif) }
list-style	keyword position URL	Shorthand for list-style-type, list-style-image, and list-style-position	OL {list-style: lower-roman inside }

JavaScript Reference

Common Events

onClick	When the user clicks on and then releases the mouse button
onDblClick	When the user double clicks the mouse button
onKeyDown	When the user presses any key
onKeyUpown	When the user releases any key
onKeyPress	When the user presses and then releases any key
onLoad	When the document finishes loading in the browser
onMouseDown	When the user presses the mouse button
onMouseOut	When the user rolls the mouse off a specific object

Common Events

onMouseOver	When the user rolls the mouse over a specific object
MouseMove	When the user moves the mouse
onMouseUp	When the user releases the click of the mouse
onResize	When the user resizes the browser window
onSubmit	When the user submits a form
onBlur	When the user tabs to a new text box or clicks on another object
onFocus	When the user either tabs into a textbox or clicks on the specified object

Common Window Features

height	Specifies the height of the display area of the window in pixels
width	Specifies the width of the display area of the window in pixels
menubar	Specifies whether or not to show the menu bar in the popped-up window
toolbar	Specifies whether or not to show the toolbar in the popped-up window
location	Specifies whether or not to show the url location area in the popped-up window
scrollbars	Specifies whether or not to show scrollbars in the popped-up window
resizable	Specifies whether a window can be resized by the user
screenX	Specifies the x coordinate (distance from the top of the monitor) for the placement of the window
screenY	Specifies the y coordinate (distance from the left of the monitor) for the placement of the window
dependent	Specifies whether the popped-up window should be a dependent of the parent window that opened it; a dependent window closes when its parent closes
alwaysLowered	Window pops open behind any open windows
alwaysRaised	Window pops open in front of any open windows

Multimedia Reference List

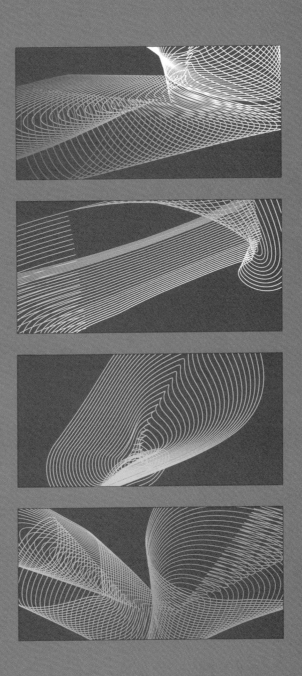

Here are some of the essential HTML tags associated with Multimedia, as covered in Chapter 9, "Flash Interfaces."

QuickTime

QuickTime Developer Resources

```
http://developer.apple.com/quicktime/
```

QuickTime Authoring

```
www.apple.com/quicktime/
authoring/embed.html
```

HTML

```
<EMBED SRC="qt.mov" WIDTH="240" HEIGHT="180"
CONTROLLER="true"></EMBED>
```

Description

Embeds a QuickTime movie

```
<OBJECT CLASSID="clsid:02BF25D5-8C17-4B23-
BC80-D3488ABDDC6B" WIDTH="240"HEIGHT="180"
CODEBASE="http://www.apple.com/qtactivex/
qtplugin.cab">
<PARAM name="SRC" VALUE="qt.mov">
<PARAM name="AUTOPLAY" VALUE="true">
<PARAM name="CONTROLLER" VALUE="false">
<EMBED SRC="qt.mov" WIDTH="240" H
EIGHT="180" AUTOPLAY="true" CONTROLLER="false"
PLUGINSPAGE="http://www.apple.com/quicktime/
download/">
</EMBED>
</OBJECT>
```

`<OBJECT>` code for Internet Explorer 5.5+ for Windows

```
<EMBED SRC="qt.mov" WIDTH="240" HEIGHT="196"
CONTROLLER="true"></EMBED>
```

Show QuickTime controller
true | false
*Add 16 pixels to the height of the movie for controller to appear properly.

HTML

```
<EMBED SRC="qt.mov" WIDTH="240" HEIGHT="180"
PLUGINSPAGE="http://www.apple.com/quicktime/
download"></EMBED>
```

```
<EMBED SRC="qt.mov" WIDTH="240" HEIGHT="180"
TARGET="quicktimeplayer"></EMBED>
```

```
<EMBED SRC="qt.mov" WIDTH="240" HEIGHT="180"
ENABLEJAVASCRIPT="true"></EMBED>
```

```
<EMBED SRC="qt.mov" WIDTH="240" HEIGHT="180"
BGCOLOR="#FFFFFF"></EMBED>
```

```
<EMBED SRC="qt.mov" WIDTH="240" HEIGHT="180"
AUTOPLAY="true"></EMBED>
```

```
<EMBED SRC="qt.mov" WIDTH="240" HEIGHT="180"
KIOSKMODE="true"></EMBED>
```

```
<EMBED SRC="qt.mov" WIDTH="240" HEIGHT="180"
VOLUME="50"></EMBED>
```

```
<EMBED SRC="music.mov" WIDTH="200"
HEIGHT="16"></EMBED>
```

Description

PLUGINSPAGE
If user doesn't have plugin, browser will alert and allow user to go to QuickTime download page.

TARGET
Allows movie to play within QuickTime player rather than browser.

ENABLEJAVASCRIPT
Attributes true | **false**
Allows you to control movie with JavaScript funtions.

BGCOLOR
Hex value | color name
Specifies the background color for areas in which the movie isn't covered.

AUTOPLAY
true | false
QuickTime movie will start to stream play.

KIOSKMODE
true | **false**
More of a security feature, the pop-up menu in the movie controller does not come up and the user can not drag and drop to save the movie.

VOLUME
Sets the volume from 0 (mute) to 100 (max), default is 100.

Sound only movie
Use any width for your movie and have the height at 16 for the sound controller.
*Do not set the height and width to less than 2, even if the movie is hidden.

continues

345

continued

HTML

```
<EMBED SRC="music.mov" WIDTH="200"
HEIGHT="16" HIDDEN AUTOPLAY="true"></EMBED>
```

Description

HIDDEN
Hides the QuickTime movie. Make sure
to have the AUTOPLAY attribute set
to true.

Audio

HTML

```
<EMBED SRC="music.wav" TYPE="audio/wav"
HIDDEN="true" AUTOSTART="true" LOOP="false"
WIDTH="1" HEIGHT="1"> </EMBED>
```

Description

Embed a sound file (WAV)

Index

Symbols

D

declarations (style sheets), 125

Deep Fried Lullabies web site, 28

default fonts versus system fonts, 69-70

deleting
Dreamweaver behaviors, 207
layer markers in Dreamweaver, 200

design, importance when using Flash, 280-281

designers, reasons to use Flash, 279

designing. *See* planning

digital video. *See* video

digitizing video with Adobe Premiere, 239-240

Discovery web site, 228

Dockers web site (sitelets development), 175

download speed (Flash), increasing, 296
levels, 298-299
pre-load animations, 296-298

downloaded music, 251

downloading screensavers, 162

Dreamweaver, 194
behaviors in, 202-203
applying to images, 203-207
applying to layers, 209-212
changing or deleting, 207
Check Browser behavior, 217-218
Check Plugin behavior, 218-219
list of, 204
onLoad behavior, 217
swapping images, 207-209
HTML code in, 194

layers in, 194-195
applying behaviors to, 209-212
background images, 198, 200
creating, 200-202
naming, 196
positioning, 196-197
resizing, 198-199
stacking order, 196-197
visibility, 196, 198-199
Sharon Coon case study, 213-216

drop caps (typography), 71

DV Primer PDF web site, 240

dynamic text in Flash, 300-301

E

Ear Shot SFX sound library, 267

"earthquake" browser windows (JavaScript), creating, 145-146

easing tweens in Flash, 288

editable text forms in Flash, 301

editing sound
with Beatnik Editor, 260-261
with SoundEdit, 252-254

effects. *See* special typography effects

embedding
sound in web pages, 257
style sheets in web pages, 126
video in web pages, 242-243

emotions
color and, 93-94
versus reality in color design, 95, 97

events
in behaviors, 202
JavaScript, 135-136

www.informit.com

Solutions from experts you know and trust.

OPERATING SYSTEMS

WEB DEVELOPMENT

PROGRAMMING

NETWORKING

CERTIFICATION

AND MORE...

**Expert Access.
Free Content.**

New Riders has partnered with InformIT.com to bring technical information to your desktop. Drawing on New Riders authors and reviewers to provide additional information on topics you're interested in, InformIT.com has free, in-depth information you won't find anywhere else.

- **Master the skills you need, when you need them.**

- **Call on resources from some of the best minds in the industry.**

- **Get answers when you need them, using InformIT's comprehensive library or live experts online.**

- **Go above and beyond what you find in New Riders books, extending your knowledge.**

As an **InformIT** partner, **New Riders** has shared the wisdom and knowledge of our authors with you online. Visit **InformIT.com** to see what you're missing.

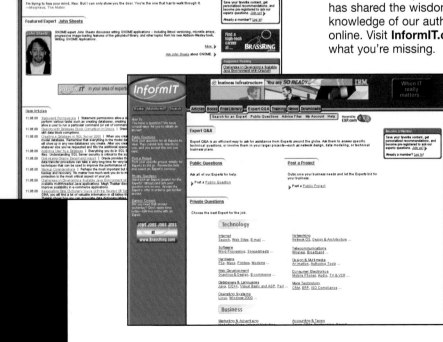

InformIT

www.informit.com ▪ www.newriders.com

New Riders

0735712549
Jody Keating,
Fig Leaf Software
US$49.99

0735709726
Lynda Weinman, William Weinman
US$39.99

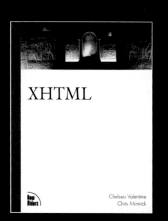

0735710341
Chelsea Valentine,
Chris Minnick
US$39.99

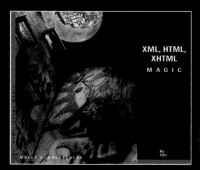

0735711399
Molly Holzschlag
US$34.99

0735712417
Gary Bouton, et al.
US$45.00

0735710201
Steven Holzner
US$49.99

New Riders brings you Web
Design and Development expertise
from the Voices That Matter.

WWW.NEWRIDERS.COM